The World Food Problem and U.S. Food Politics and Policies: 1978

A READINGS BOOK

The World Food Problem and U.S. Food Politics and Policies: 1978

A READINGS BOOK

Ross B. Talbot

THE IOWA STATE UNIVERSITY PRESS / AMES

Ross B. Talbot is Professor of Political Science, Iowa State University

©1979 The Iowa State University Press

Printed by
The Iowa State University Press

First edition, 1979

International Standard Book Number: 0-8138-1155-4

Library of Congress Catalog Card Number: 79-88297

This book was printed by photo-offset from materials assembled by the author.

CONTENTS

viii

PREFACE

I am very beholden to Kay Maas for the fine work she has done in assembling this readings book. She displayed lots of imagination, intelligence, patience, and diligence--and all of this with a fine sense of humor. In the early stages of putting this volume together we were ably assisted by Claudette McMahon, who left us late in February for Costa Rica in order to do the necessary research for her Master's thesis.

Also, I am certainly appreciative of the support of the Iowa Agriculture Experiment Station and the World Food Institute. The responsibility for the contents of this book is wholly mine. But we would have been hard pressed, indeed, to have finished this task without their moral and financial assistance.

Ross B. Talbot

The World Food Problem and U.S. Food Politics and Policies: 1978

A READINGS BOOK

I. *The World Food Situation in 1978*

INTRODUCTORY COMMENTS

When on her deathbed, Gertrude Stein was asked about the final, ultimate answer to the meaning of life; her response, so we are told, was: What is the question? And so it is with the world food problem. If one views the problem as one of increasing the production of grain throughout the world, the latest (November 1978) report from the United States Department of Agriculture (USDA) looks good; it appears that the farmers of the world produced some 170 million tons more of wheat and coarse grains in 1978/79 than they did in 1974/75. If one views the world food problem as one of distribution and consumption, then the situation takes on a much bleaker look. Another USDA report, published at the end of 1978, notes that "total world food production increased close to 3 percent in 1978 ;" . . .nevertheless, because of rapid population growth, per capita food production in the developing countries as a group was essentially unchanged from 1977."

Certainly the world food "crisis," viewed as an international and national (United States) media event, was pushed to a much lower position on the public agenda. Here and there one could even detect a touch of euphoria. Richard Critchfield's articles in The Christian Science Monitor were a case in point:[1] "epic changes" were taking place in "Asia's villages;" the "quiet conquest" of India's agricultural revolution was relentlessly and marvelously at work, or

3

so his observations and interviews at the village level proved to him.

Others were much less optimistic, both in terms of present conditions and estimates of those on the horizon. Bread for the World headlined a story at the year's end: "Abnormal Food Shortages Still Common"; in December, the Interreligious Taskforce on U.S. Food Policy sent a report to all the subscribers to its Food Policy Notes entitled: "An Update on the Food Crisis in Indochina." Two reputable food research organizations emphasized the long-run aspects of the problem. A study by the Food and Agriculture Organization (FAO) showed that the average rate of increase in food production was 2.7 percent annually from 1961-70, but had dropped to 1.3 percent a year in the period from from 1970-77. More ominous, was FAO's translation of that data into per capita terms: the drop, in the same time periods, was from 0.3 percent to a minus 1.4 percent.[2] And a study by the International Food Policy Research Institute (IFPRI), which projected food deficits in the developing nations, estimated that the present (1975) deficit of 36 million tons (food grain equivalent) would grow to 120-145 million tons by 1990, depending on differing assumptions.[3]

Surely there is a food problem today in many of the Asian, African and a few Latin American nations; more basically, there is a "poverty" problem, as the tables and the definitions reproduced in these readings seem to prove beyond any reasonable doubt. In the World Bank's first World Development Report, 1978 there is an estimate that "about 800 million people still live in absolute poverty." Moreover, according to this report, "these people are living at the very margin of existence--with inadequate food, shelter, education health care. For many of them, there has been little improvement in the standard of living in the past 25 years, and for some, there may have been a deterioration."

Obviously there is a very wide range of views relative to the current world food situation. In these readings, two internationally renowned agricultural economists (Kenneth R. Farrell and D. Gale Johnson) explain the reasons for their moderate optimism. Following their discussions are two more "pragmatic" interpretations (David Hopper is now a vice-president in the World Bank), both of which seem to weigh the various factors and then tentatively conclude with a more guarded, somewhat hedged, optimism. But there are also sufficient grounds for some near-Malthusian perspectives, too, and the interview, reports, and book reviews included herein indicate some of the regions of food shortage, the reasons for these conditions, and the fearful consequences that might flow from them. Margaret Mead wonders about the quality of our conscience; David Spurgeon's article points to the very serious problem of post-harvest losses; Jonathan Silverstone's book review--juxtaposed with that of Critchfield--leaves us wondering if they read the same book. And it should be noted that a fair touch of pessimism is evident in Johnson's analysis, too; he believes that we have the "breathing space" (the time and know-how to produce the needed food), but asks" "Will it be used more effectively than it was a decade ago?" His answer is: "I fear it is more likely that the current ease in the world food situation will lead to complacency."

A few tables and a chart are also included in this section in the hope that the reader will kind of "play around" with the data, and then make his/her own tentative interpretations of the trend lines relative to population, per capita income, development assistance, definitional criteria, and grain production, among others. Viewed just in terms of production, utilization and "ending stocks," the world food situation seems to be progressively improving. End stocks, as a percent of use (and including milled rice), have

increased from 11 percent in 1974/75 to 16.5 percent (forecast) for 1978/79.
The experts' rule-of-thumb percentage figure for a "safe" carryover is usually
18-19 percent, so the trend line is progressing nicely toward this pragmatic
figure. However, the other two tables show that one must do a considerable
amount of differentiating: who has sufficient income to buy the food; what is
"absolute," as contrasted to "relative," poverty; how does one go about trying
to estimate "the quality of life"—as that term has been defined by the Overseas Development Council? It is interesting to compare, for example, the
quality of life in Guyana with that of Haiti, or of Sri Lanka with Bangledesh.
The chart ("Total Net Flows to Developing Countries") is positive evidence
that some North to South financial redistribution is taking place. Not necessarily to the extent, nor in the forms, desired by the Group of 77, but the
transfer of funds from the Organization for Economic Co-operation and Development (OECD) and Organization of Petroleum Exporting Countries (OPEC) member-
states to the developing world is impressive, even though it should be noted
that some two-thirds of those funds are non-concessional.

Finally, there is the ever-continuing enigma of weather and climate. Each
week the USDA publishes a document entitled: Weekly Roundup of World Production and Trade. Quite likely it is studied carefully by those who have a particular business or professional interest in the world food situation, but the
information therein must be more than a bit bewildering and perplexing to even
the most careful student of food production trends. Almost without fail there
are reports of droughts, floods, light and medium showers, early frost, freez-
ing, steady and continuing rains, etc. in Brazil, India, Soviet Union, Canada,
the People's Republic of China, France, Egypt—just to note a few of the national actors—not to mention the often mercurial weather conditions in the

main producing regions in the United States. To be sure, drought in one major

region may be a major contributing factor to prosperity in another; a "lovely"

four-inch rain in one region may well contribute to a serious price decline of

wheat or rice in another area. But the vagaries and inconstancies of weather

and climate have been with us for many decades, if not centuries, and so they

will likely continue to be--for at least the rest of this century. At least

that was the best overall judgment of leading meteorologists, when they were

surveyed in a study conducted by the National Defense University.[4] If weather

and climate are determined by the will of God, then God's widsom is still hid-

den from the human mind--and will likely remain so. The world food problem

seems to be man's (and woman's) creation, and so are the solutions thereto.

NOTES

1. July 3, 1978, p. 13, and December 15, 1978, pp. 1,8.
2. FAO, News, 18/78, September 29, 1978, 2 pp.
3. Food Needs to Developing Countries: Projections of Production and
Consumption to 1990 (Washington, D.C.: International Food Policy Research
Institute, December 1977).
4. Climate Change to the Year 2000: A Survey of Expert Opinion (Washington, D.C.: Fort Lesley J. McNair, February 1978). The study was sponsored
by the USDA, Department of Defense, Institute for the Future, and the National
Oceanic and Atmospheric Administration.

THE OPTIMISTS

A BRIGHTER OUTLOOK

by Kenneth R. Farrell

Mankind appears to be slowly pulling ahead in its race against famine, as worldwide per capita food production creeps upward following a period of intense concern in the early 1970's.

From 1974 to 1977, per capita production gained 4 percent, after food prices jumped sharply and supplies dwindled. And the 1978 world grain production outlook makes the picture even brighter.

In other words, the production increases of food outpaced population growth across the globe—even though inequities in distribution continued to result in hunger for millions.

Brighter prospects. While this may be far from ideal, the overall prospects seem considerably brighter than 4 years ago, when many questioned whether worldwide starvation lurked just years away. Responding to such public concern, USDA took a hard look at the issue in the study, "The World Food Situation and Prospects to 1985." The 1974 report concluded that, despite the then-current distress, a long-range worldwide shortage of food was unlikely.

Today's shortrun outlook tends to support that conclusion. Not only did worldwide increases in food production exceed population gains after 1974, but improvements occurred in many nations that needed help the most.

Changes in the developing countries parallel those for the world so that 1978 per capita production in the developing countries will probably exceed the previous high of 1976 and be at least 8 percent above the lows of the early 1970's.

South Asian progress. Most encouraging, South Asian nations, such as India and Pakistan, have greatly improved production and grain stocks. This region is often a problem area, where as many as two-thirds of the world's hungry people may be found—and where two-thirds of U.S. food aid goes in some years.

India, the focus of hunger concern in 1974, may harvest a grain crop so large that, after meeting its considerable domestic needs, enough may be left over for export.

This isn't to say there aren't some bleak exceptions. Bangladesh and some parts of Africa over the years have been losing ground as per capita food production actually declines.

Spotty trend. This trend toward general improvement—spotted with some areas where hunger is getting worse—seems likely even over the long haul. In fact, the good and bad may occur simultaneously within a given region as years pass: Food production may gain regionally, while some areas within that region suffer serious problems in producing and distributing food.

Even with this less-than-apocalyptical outlook, a large portion of the world's poor are not being adequately fed.

And the outlook for years to come is for a continuing struggle, despite a U.S. commitment to fight hunger that is based on a 1976 Congressional resolution on the "Right to Food" that specifically recognizes the human right to a nutritionally adequate diet and makes this a cornerstone of U.S. policy.

This lofty commitment will require much effort and ingenuity, if it is to succeed in eradicating hunger.

Lack of data. Perhaps indicative of the frustrations involved in fighting hunger, there are varying estimates of how many people in the world are malnourished; where they are; and the kind, degree, and specific cause of their affliction.

The Food and Agricultural Organization of the United Nations estimated that in 1970, about 400 million people in developing countries outside of Communist Asia were malnourished, that the number increased to about 455 million during poor crop years in 1972-74, and may have declined some since then. Yet, FAO admitted the figure was, at best, a rough estimate.

For the general world population, the long term outlook for mitigating widespread malnutrition may hinge on food prices and employment. Today, purchasing power—or the lack of it—often governs whether a family in either the poorest nation or richest nation has feast or famine. The food is available, in most cases, but the distribution of the food depends on buying power.

Food price factor. A major factor, then, is the outlook for food prices in the years ahead. If food prices increase faster or slower than the general rate of inflation, then the amount of food that can be purchased with the same amount of buying power would vary accordingly.

The 1974 USDA study focused on the question of whether the real cost of food (farm-produced basic food without expensive processing and packaging) will increase in the future, and concluded that prices will be higher, but not so high as during 1972-74, in part because prices to farmers were so depressed in years preceeding 1972. Also, costs of inputs such as fertilizers will rise.

Farm Index, November 1978, pp. 4-7. (Based on a speech by Mr. Farrell, ESCS Administrator, given at the Festival on Religion and Rural Life, July 31-August 3, 1978.)

Any projection of this future food purchasing power must, however, be very tentative. Much depends on technological developments which could greatly increase production, and on whether there are enough sufficiently productive jobs available to generate adequate purchasing power.

Affluent's consumption. Still another possible factor—albeit a highly debatable one—is consumption patterns among the affluent. Some critics contend that such food forms as meats—much in demand by the affluent in both rich and poor countries—waste grains through inefficient conversion of protein which could be used to feed the world's poor. It is important, however, to recognize that factors such as government policies far outweigh the influence on food prices of the level of consumption by the affluent.

Further, this issue hinges on whether food supplies will keep up with the demand. If the demand unexpectedly overtakes supply, then prices will rapidly—and, to the poor, disastrously—increase. The high consumption rates among the affluent would help push up the prices to the poor.

In examining all the obstacles to improved prospects for food supplies, there's a danger of missing the most optimistic development of all since the 1974 study was issued.

Dropping birth rates. A recent UN study found birth rates dropping rapidly in many developing countries. In fact, since the 1960's, birth rates dropped by about 15 percent in three or four dozen countries that have more than 40-60 percent of the population of all developing nations. Moreover, these are countries where statistical gathering is considered reliable.

A final note of encouragement since the 1974 report is that leading meteorologists, who studied long-range climate trends in a joint effort by USDA, the Department of Defense, and the National Oceanic and Atmospheric Administration, generally agree that world climate patterns aren't likely to change enough by the end of the century to greatly affect agriculture. In other words, speculation that a new ice age, or a climatic warming trend, would soon

dawn to ruin food production has been dampened.

Government policies. Since it appears that nature will cooperate enough to allow continued growth in food production for the next several decades, the next major concern, then, may be government policies. U.S. agricultural and foreign policies have, by far, the greatest impact on the hope of the world's hungry because of America's great food output.

Fortunately for the rest of the world, the U.S. has traditionally exercised great generosity towards people in serious need.

In recent years, however, many Americans were becoming impatient as it appeared that very little of the aid given to developing nations has been "trickling down" to improve the lot of the poor masses. Instead, aid found its way to the coffers of the already rich and privileged.

Aiding the poor majority. So, in 1973, Congress enacted legislation to redirect foreign aid to the poor majority who usually dwell in rural areas of developing nations. At least 75 percent of all food aid was to be sent to nations defined as "poor".

Thus, U.S. policymakers have come to believe that the main obstacles to eradicating hunger are political—not natural or technological.

This doesn't mean that developing nations intentionally force poverty on their masses. Instead, they face the hard political choice between keeping food prices cheap for urban consumers, and thus discouraging agricultural development, or opting for agricultural expansion by allowing higher prices to farmers while angering the urban masses.

Similarly, land reform may be needed, but to break up large landholding blocks and embark on other rural reforms would meet with powerful political opposition.

Creating jobs. So, faced with such political realities, the U.S. is trying to help by providing aid which supports the creation of labor-intensive jobs, and development of appropriate technologies for these nations.

Food aid has also been redirected not only to feed the starving, but to en-

courage creation of new jobs, and to discourage the violation of human rights by governments receiving such aid.

In line with these new policy directions, the Carter Administration is exploring new efforts:

• It is committed to raising development assistance. Bilateral aid other than food rose 23 percent last fiscal year. As for P.L. 480 food aid, the total for fiscal year 1979 is to be 42 percent higher than FY 1977.

• It is forming a Hunger Commission to seek new ways to improve U.S. efforts to eliminate domestic and foreign hunger and malnutrition.

• The U.S. has proposed the establishment of an international system of nationally held grain reserves within the framework of a new International Wheat Agreement.

• A 6-million-ton U.S. wheat reserve has been proposed to meet emergency food needs and to guarantee U.S. food aid commitments.

• Domestic agricultural programs, such as a farmer-held grain reserve, and the set-aside program are designed to stabilize prices. These, together with the proposed international grain reserve system, could cushion the world's poor from the sometimes disastrous price swings of the past.

While no one suggests that these programs are a panacea to the world hunger problem, they offer hope of an improved diet for millions of people, and progress toward realizing the human "right to food" for the poor.

WORLD FOOD OUTLOOK IMPROVES

by D. Gale Johnson

Whatever else history may record as achievements of the 20th Century, it may say that that century saw the elimination of the dread scourge of famine from the face of the earth. Except when caused by war and civil unrest, famine has already been largely eliminated. There remain very few pockets of population that do not have access to the world's food supply to compensate for shortfalls in local production. Much of the world's accomplishment in eliminating famine is due to revolutionary improvements in communications and transportation and increases in the annual stability of food production.

The poor people of the world now have more adequate diets than at any other time in this century.

By the poor people of the world, I refer to the majority of the peoples of Asia, Latin America and Africa who are poor by the standards of North America and Europe. 80% of the world's poor population of 2 billion live in rural areas and villages.

The most compelling evidence that these poor are now better fed is the remarkable increase in life expectancy in the developing countries over the past 30 years. In 1950, life expectancy at birth in the developing world was 35-40 years; today it has reached or surpassed 52 years.

Improvement in food consumption was not solely responsible for the increase in life expectancy, but there can be little question the change would not have been possible without some improvement in the level and security of food supply. Much of the increase in life expectancy occurred through a reduction of infant and child mortality, the period of life where adequate food is an important factor in survival.

The available data on per capita food production in the developing world indicate that there has been a modest improvement over the past quarter century. During that period per capita food production has increased by approximately 0.5% annually. Caloric consumption has increased somewhat more than production due to increased net grain imports by the developing world. While there are those who view the increased level of grain imports by the developing countries as a problem, the increase in net grain imports has increased per capita caloric consumption by more than 100 calories per day (or about 5%) for all developing countries.

The slow growth in per capita food production in the developing countries was not due to a slower growth of total food production. The production growth rates in developing and developed countries were nearly identical. The difference in per capita food production was due solely to growth in population — approximately 2.5% annually in the developing countries and only slightly more than 1% in the developed countries.

It was a major challenge to the agricultures of the developing countries just to keep up with such rapid growth of population. Similar sustained rates of population growth have never been witnessed before, not even during the period of major immigration into the United States.

I do not want to leave the impression that the improvement in nutrition has been uniform. In general, Latin America and East Asia have had the largest increases in per capita food production; South Asia has seen very moderate improvement in the past 15 years. In much of Africa per capita food production has declined since the early 1960's.

A continuation of recent food production trends and population growth rates for the rest of the century will result in little improvement in per capita food production in the developing countries.

I have seen no valid evidence that indicates that the production trend cannot be maintained. There are those who believe that the Green Revolution of the late 1960's has had its full effect and there is nothing to take its place. But the new varieties (primarily rice and wheat) developed during the Green Revolution were suitable for only a minority of the cropland of the developing countries, primarily areas with very good irrigation, and the improvement and adaptation possibilities have by no means come to an end. There is now evidence that population growth rates have begun to decline in the developing countries. In 25 countries the crude birth rate declined by from 15-40% between 1965 and 1975; included were India, China, the Philippines, Costa Rica and Colombia. Due to age composition and further declines in mortality, it will be some years before there are actual declines in population growth rates, but we could well see some rather dramatic reductions before the end of this century in many countries.

Natural and human resources are adequate for a significant increase in the rate of growth of food production.

Crude comparisons of the agriculture of the United States and of the developing countries depict the latter as backward and

<u>Agenda</u>, September 1978, pp. 1-5. Dr. Johnson is Provost and Professor of Economics, University of Chicago.

inefficient. But modern agriculture is a recent phenomenon. Animal power was the major form of power in North America as recently as 50 years ago.

40 years ago grain yields in the industrial countries and in the developing countries were the same —1.15 tons per hectare (a corn yield of 18 bushels per acre). By 1973-75 grain yields in the industrial countries were 3.0 tons per hectare; in the developing countries 1.4 tons. Grain yields in excess of 2 tons per hectare are a recent phenomenon — a consequence of the agricultural revolution of the past four decades. In years of average weather during the first half of this century, grain yields in the United States averaged less than 1.5 tons per hectare compared to 3.5 tons in recent years. Corn yields increased even more — from 1.4 tons per hectare before 1940 to more than 5.5 tons in recent years. Of the industrial countries only Japan achieved significant grain yield increases in the 19th century. Japanese grain yields are now 5 tons per hectare.

Differences in productivity are not due to differences in basic human characteristics. Farmers, even poor and illiterate farmers, are intelligent and interested in a better and fuller life, if not for themselves then for their children. What does distinguish such farmers is that they own little besides their native intelligence and physical capacities.

There is abundant evidence that farmers in developing countries will adopt new ways of doing things if the new ways are superior to the old. Millions of farmers in the developing countries rapidly adopted the new high yielding varieties of grain (often in response to quite modest yield differentials) and an increase in the use of fertilizer, insecticides and herbicides during the past decade.

Are the differences in productivity due to differences in natural endowments, particularly soils and climate? Forty years ago, none of the new high yielding varieties, such as hybrid corn, were then in use to a significant degree. Relatively little fertilizer was applied to grains, and the methods of land preparation and cultivation had changed little since the 19th century. Natural conditions in the country groups resulted in similar yields.

Even if grain yields were similar at one level of knowledge and technology, it may not follow that at other levels the yields would remain similar. There have been different rates of growth of yields in the United States since the 1930s. Yields have increased more in the humid than the dry areas and in the warmer than the cooler areas.

While it is possible that there are fundamental restraints on yields in the tropical and semi-tropical areas of the developing countries, such restraints may not be important. Maximum yields have been obtained under experimental conditions in several tropical areas in recent years. While it may be many years before such yields are obtained on farms, the experimental yields indicate that natural conditions alone are not responsible for relatively low yields in the developing countries.

Corn yields, in experimental trials in 1975 in such widely dispersed areas as Nepal, India, Ivory Coast, Panama, Costa Rica and Turkey, ranged from 4 to almost 9 tons per hectare. This compares to actual farm yields in the United States of 6 to 8 tons. The new varieties of rice grown in South and Southeast Asia have yield potentials of 5 to 8 tons per hectare. These compare favorably to actual yields achieved in Japan and the United States.

The differences in productivity or yields are not entirely due to either human or natural conditions. One important source of difference is the greater investment in research in agriculture in the industrial countries. Agricultural research expenditures have increased tenfold. In 1970 only 15% of the world's publicly supported agricultural research was undertaken in the developing countries.

Modern science applied to agriculture problems made possible the highly productive agricultures of North America and Western Europe. There is no reason why science will not have the same revolutionary impact on agriculture and the food supply in the developing countries.

Science has influenced our agriculture within the lifetimes of many of us. When I grew up on a farm the technology that was used was almost wholly the accumulated experience of generations of farmers.

The rebuilding of world grain stocks and recent increases in per capita food production in developing countries may mean that little effort will be made to realize the potentials for expanded production and availability of food in developing countries.

During the 1970s there has been a great deal of price instability in international markets, usually attributed to instability of production. This is, at best, a half truth. A major factor in the price increases in 1973 and 1974 and the price declines since 1975 was the agricultural policies of numerous governments.

At least half of the world's grain is consumed in countries that stabilize their internal prices to consumers and producers by varying their net trade, insulating their consumers and producers from virtually all variations in world supply and demand variations. When international prices are high, their consumers have no incentive to reduce consumption and their producers no incentive to expand production. When international prices are low, consumers are not encouraged to increase consumption — nor are producers given a signal to reduce production. All of the variability in supply and any random shocks to demand (such as those that result from business cycles) are imposed upon those countries whose domestic prices vary with international prices.

Since the world food situation looks good, is it reasonable to turn our attentions to more pressing matters? In my opinion the answer is an emphatic no. The food problems of the poor people of the world are long-run problems, and only continuous efforts will make any difference in how adequate their diets are in the future.

In 1965 and 1966 there were poor crops in South Asia. Had it not been for food aid, there would have been mass starvation in India and Pakistan. The new high yielding varieties were introduced into the area in 1966, spread quickly and food production reached new peak levels. International grain prices fell and new technology drastically reduced the price of nitrogen fertilizer. At the time, Norman Borlaug, who received the Nobel Peace Price for his contributions to the development of high yielding varieties of grain suitable for the developing countries, told us that the Green Revolution "has won a temporary success in man's war against hunger and deprivation; it has given man a breathing space."

Relatively little was done to take advantage of the opportunities to improve the nutrition of the world's poor people after 1967 and before the food difficulties of 1973.

Once again the world has some "breathing space." Will it be used more effectively than it was a decade ago?

I fear it is more likely that the current ease in the world food situation will lead to complacency.

Developing countries will see no need to significantly change their priorities. There is no evidence that the industrial countries that give a high priority to their domestic price stability have modified their views. Nor have any of the industrial countries taken any significant steps to reduce their barriers to the agricultural and manufactured exports of the developing countries. In fact, in all too many cases, such as textiles, shoes and sugar, protectionism has increased during the past year. In spite of the attention given at the 1975 World Food Conference in Rome to ways and means for increasing food production in the developing countries, I know of no new initiatives that have been taken since then.

There are no quick fixes that will make a difference in the improvement of nutrition for the world's poor people. Continuous concern and action are required. In everything that is undertaken, measurable results come years later. When there is no crisis, it is difficult to mobilize attention and effort for results that will not be apparent until well after the next election.

The nutrition of the world's poor people has improved and will continue to improve in the years ahead. This does not mean that progress will be uninterrupted or that it will be uniform among countries. The outstanding performance of farmers in the developing countries over the past three decades is a basis for optimism for the future. There are indications that developing countries are gradually modifying their policies in the direction of providing more adequate incentives for farmers.

There will be substantial improvements in per capita food supplies and in incomes in the developing countries if there is the political will to give appropriate priority and continuing commitment to efforts to expand food production and agricultural productivity. Approaches must be pragmatic and not ideological. The decision makers must recognize that the most important resources of their rural areas is not their forests, mines, oil, or land but rural people, and the improvement of their welfare is an important objective.

THE PRAGMATISTS

DEVELOPING COUNTRIES SHOULD BE
BIG FOOD PRODUCERS

W. David Hopper interviewed
by Robert Reford

I would like to start by looking at what I think we are all now beginning to realize more and more is a major problem: the problem of food. Are we going to have enough food?

We have a vast potential in the world for increasing food production, but as yet we have not tapped that potential, and it is going to take time to do it.

At the present time the populations of the developing countries represent about two-thirds of mankind, buy they produce less than one-third of man's food. If present population trends continue (and I am not an alarmist on population, I believe we can feed a much much larger population, and I already see signs of a slackening in population growth) we will be in the year 2000 with roughly three-quarters of the world's population in the developing countries. They will still produce, if present projections hold, less than 30 percent of the world's food. On that basis we have a very severe food imbalance. It will either mean that the developed countries are going to have to transport more food to the developing countries, probably on some sort of concessionary terms because these countries do not have the foreign exchange to pay for it, or we are going to have to raise food production in the developing countries.

The drought of 1972, which was a worldwide drought, was what caused the big run on the grain stock supplies of the US and Canada. A similar circumstance today could be met, because again Canada and the US have had bumper harvests, but the difference between today and 1972 is that in 1972 there were 60 million acres of land in the soil bank in the US; that 60 million acres is now under plough. We are now pushing against the capacity of the temperate zone to produce food.

That said, my concern is that the developing countries should be the big food producers, not the residual food producers. They have the sunlight, they have the water, they have the year round growing temperature, they can grow three or four crops in sequence one after the other, which we cannot do. It is the lag in their agricultural development that has been my major concern.

The issue is resources. Just take a drive through our rural areas and take a look at the networks of roads, of service facilities, of machinery depots, of supply facilities, of milk pickup points, of packing plants, and so on, that are all part of our agriculture. Then drive through India, where the roads are 30 or 40 miles apart, where there are none of these facilities, where villages are deep in the interior, where all the paraphenalia of a modern agricultural economy does not exist. That is what has to be built in the developing countries if they are going to pursue their agricultural potential, if they are going to build a modern agriculture and really tap the resources that they have. To do that is going to take colossal amounts of money and they don't have the resources.

The Sahel is a very good example. There are five rivers and a very large lake, the Lake Chad Basin, in this region. Each one of these rivers could be tapped. They could greatly increase the land that they have under irrigation, to produce the kind of crops that they need. The six Sahelian nations among them have about $2 billion of GNP (Gross National Product). It is a ridiculously small GNP. It is less than the profits of the General Motors Corporation. To develop the five rivers and the Lake Chad Basin would cost something like $30 billion. For these countries to say "We are going to embark upon that development" with a GNP that is as small as they have is just ludicrous. It is like Canada, with our GNP of $150 billion, saying that we are going to proceed to develop our north although it is going to cost us, say $1 trillion. It won't be done. Somebody has got to provide the resources if those nations are going to be brought to the point of feeding themselves.

For an investment over the next 10 years of approximately $100-150 billion, and these are very rough estimates, I think we could provide food security for both the populations of the year 2000 and possibly for the populations of the year 2050, when I do see population beginning to level off, mankind having a total population then of about 15 to 16 billion people.

Why isn't it being done?

I think there are three reasons. In the first place the food resources of the world have been sufficient to tide all of mankind through. We have lived in a remarkable period — there has not been a major famine in the world since 1942. Now, there is no other period of almost 35 years of world history where we can identify no really major famine. We haven't had it because the grain reserves of the North American continent, Australia and Argentina have underpinned the periodic recurrence of drought in these large-population countries. With that there has been a lack of urgency.

The second reason is that the developing countries themselves have very limited resources, and the urban industrial complex has attracted the bulk of the investment in the developing countries. They are concerned with building their industries, they are concerned with modernizing the cities, and they have neglected their agriculture.

The third reason simply has to do with the costs involved. No agency, not even the World Bank, has yet been able to muster the resources necessary to mount these very high cost programs, and until the governments of the world are willing to stand up and say "Yes, we are all going to pitch in and cooperate" we are not going to get it done.

The IDRC Reports, March 1978, pp. 25-26. (Dr. Hopper is Vice-President for South Asia at the World Bank.

What happened to the Green Revolution?

For many of the developing countries the Green Revolution varieties, the new high-yielding varieties of wheat, and rice, and sorghum, and maize, would make a terrific difference, but they do not have the infrastructure supporting the decision by the farmer to move to the modern agriculture. And it is that infrastructure that has got to be built.

Can we transfer modern agriculture from our society, as we know it, to the developing world?

What we may not transfer is the high productivity per worker that we have in our agriculture. We may follow what the Japanese have done, and that is a very high productivity per acre. Our productivity per acre in Canada is really very low compared with Japan. We are producing just a little over one metric ton per hectare on our Western grain farms, in Japan they are producing between six and seven metric tons per hectare of rice. They have very small farms in Japan, but they have put the inputs in — the intensive agriculture, the intensive labour that goes to producing a very high yield per hectare, and that's the road the developing countries have to go.

We can help them with the building of the infrastructure, we can help them with the scientific research, and this is where the IDRC is basically operating at the present time, we are financing research in developing countries. The new dwarf wheats that underpinned the so-called Green Revolution cost the Rockefeller Foundation perhaps $10 million to develop over 20 years. When they came into India it was a very cheap transfer, but it cost the government of India $280 million the first year to buy the fertilizer necessary for these crops. So there needs to be, accompanying the technology, a very heavy investment in the infrastructure of supply to the farmer to back him up as he picks up this research.

There must be some things that you have done that you are proud of.

My work in the Indian village in the early fifties convinced me, after visiting all the research stations in India, that the problem was not the Indian farmer, he was not stubborn and unwilling to change. It took seven years to get hybrid corn spread reasonably well in the province of Ontario (Canada). It took only three years to gobble up all the irrigated acreage in India with the dwarf varieties of wheat. India has more than doubled its wheat production from what it was in 1966. India now produces 50 percent more wheat than Canada, and wheat is not their most important crop, rice is. And exactly the same thing occurred in the rice area of agricultural production.

Is India reaching the point of self-sufficiency in food?

India now has a huge surplus in stock; she has over 20 million tons of food grain in a buffer stock at the present time. India can now sustain a very substantial drought and feed herself from her own resources. But if the population continues to grow, agriculture in India will have to grow faster than it has been growing in the past decade.

Let me give you an example. The Mahanadi River delta at the present time produces about three million tons of rice annually. With an expenditure of about $1 billion over the course of the next 10 years, rice production could be increased to ten million tons. That extra seven million tons of rice in one year would be worth about $1.4 billion at the present price of rice on the world market. So India pays off the investment in one year's increase in production. It is a question of how India gets the $1 billion for that purpose.

What about Canada? What has Canada been doing, and what can Canada do?

My own feeling is perhaps that Canada has been too much "me too" in the foreign aid game, when it could have branched out more aggressively to provide world leadership in particular areas. I use agriculture as an example. Canada does have a unique position with regard to the developing countries as being a very neutral country. I think that if we in Canada had said "Look, our concerns are going to be primarily in the problem of feeding hungry nations and hungry people," I think we could have carved ourselves a niche that would have provided far more leadership.

Canada has played an important role. We are in the upper average group of the industrial nations in what we do to assist in developing countries, and for the most part the projects that Canada has supported in the developing countries have been good projects.

What about the individual Canadian? What can I do?

I think that the individual Canadian can become more aware of the issues facing the developing countries. We are going to face in the not-too-distant future the trade-aid question. Many of the developing countries have the skills, the labour force and the industrial base that allows them to compete at the lower end of the consumer goods area — textiles, ready-made shirts, shoes, and so on. These do affect Canadian industry, and Canada has put quotas on developing country products. We in fact may do more harm to the progress of the developing countries when we put these quotas on than we would do good by increasing our aid flows to them.

These are issues that are going to be on the agenda in the future. It is either going to be a very much larger aid transfer, or it is going to be a freer access for the developing countries to Canadian markets.

And do you still remain an optimist?

On the food question, yes. Despite the fact that my feeling is that time is short, that time is quickly running out on us, I see moves by more and more of the developing countries, and even by some of the developed countries, to come to an accommodation. The only new United Nations fund created in the 1970s was the $1 billion which the nations of OPEC and the developed industrial countries put up for the international fund for agricultural development. I think that within 10 years it is likely that, if these trends continue and we do not become complacent again, we will see the foundations laid for an agricultural development movement which is not going to be stopped. □

WORLD DEVELOPMENT REPORT, 1978

The development progress of the past twenty-five years has exceeded early expectations in many respects. Nonetheless about 800 million people, more than one-third of the total population of the developing world, still live in absolute poverty. The central objectives of the international development task must be rapid economic growth and the reduction of poverty.

This report has discussed the policies and prospects for development progress in these main areas:

- *Sustaining rapid economic growth;*
- *Modifying the pattern of economic growth* so as to raise the productivity and incomes of the poor;
- *Improving the access of the poor to essential public services;*
- *Maintaining an international environment supportive of development* by improving the framework for international trade, facilitating an expansion of lending at market terms, and expanding the volume of concessional assistance.

Rapid growth is fundamental to any development strategy. In the Low Income countries, in particular, substantial and sustained progress in reducing poverty will be impossible without accelerating growth rates. But growth alone is not enough. Because the poor tend to share less than proportionately in growth, since they have only limited access to productive assets, education, and employment, deliberate action is necessary in areas that affect the distribution of increases in income. These include the structure of economic incentives, the allocation of investments, and the creation of special institutions and programs to increase the productivity of the poor and their opportunities for employment.

In the Low Income countries, with their large numbers of rural poor and heavy dependence on agriculture, the main emphasis must be placed on raising productivity in the rural economy, particularly the productivity of small farmers. In parts of Asia where a large potential for irrigation can be tapped, output can be increased rapidly by stepping up irrigation investments. Changes will be necessary in the administration and organization of agricultural support services, to assure that information is disseminated broadly and quickly and that the services are responsive to the special needs of small farmers. In rainfed areas, too, there is considerable scope for progress with present knowledge. But in the drought prone areas of Sub-Saharan Africa and Asia, major technological problems remain to be resolved if long-term agricultural growth is to be achieved.

Measures to make crop cultivation more productive should be supplemented by dairy, poultry, and fisheries programs which are particularly important in raising the incomes of small and marginal farmers and the landless. But even on optimistic assumptions about the growth of agriculture, underemployment will be a growing problem in Low Income Asia, calling for greater emphasis on creating non-farm jobs in rural areas and systematic expansion of large-scale public works programs.

Strengthening rural and urban infrastructure to support these development efforts will be highly demanding of investment funds in industry as well as in agriculture. Capital needs to be used more efficiently, but rapid increases in investment rates will still be essential. To achieve the necessary levels of investment will require an increase in domestic savings, both public and private, supplemented by large inflows of concessional capital.

The uncertainty about international trade and capital movements in the next few years poses strategic choices for the Middle Income countries, which are more affected by changes in international economic conditions. In most of them, efforts to sustain the growth of export earnings will have to be supplemented by measures to achieve a more broadly based expansion of domestic demand. This will require a more balanced growth strategy, including the acceleration of agricultural development. Greater priority will need to be given to investments in the physical infrastructure supporting agriculture, the creation of a more satisfactory set of incentives and relative prices, and much improved support services. Measures to preserve the

Annual report from the World Bank, August 1978, pp. 65–69.

growth of foreign exchange earnings include raising export incentives; increasing the domestic value added in manufactured goods exports; and, particularly for the more advanced countries, exporting a more diverse range of manufactured goods. Measures to further the growth of trade among developing countries will also be important.

The poor in both the Middle Income and Low Income countries have very inadequate access to such public services as health facilities, potable water, sanitation, and education. Programs designed specifically to make these services accessible to the poor should be an important part of development. In nearly all countries, there is a good deal of scope for extending such services more widely within the same budgetary allocations, by adapting successful experiments in low cost delivery systems, by using suitable technologies and design standards, and by relying more heavily on the participation and self-help efforts of the communities who are to benefit. Nonetheless, extending the supply of public services to the full population will require substantial additional investments in all types of infrastructure, and large increases in public expenditures to operate and maintain these systems.

Measures to alleviate poverty will run into social, political, and administrative obstacles which must not be underestimated. The strength of deep-seated traditions, weaknesses in administration, and opposition from affected groups can make it formidably difficult for even the most dedicated governments to modify the patterns of economic growth or to alter the distribution of essential public services. These problems are even more severe when economic growth is slow and the resources available for investment and public services remain relatively stagnant.

Serious though these obstacles may be, they are no justification for inaction. Success is far more likely if governments set themselves explicit targets for the growth of incomes of the poorest groups and for the extension of basic public services, and then monitor progress regularly. The paucity of data on incomes, nutritional deficiencies, and access to public services reflects the absence until recently of policy concern with the poor and of anti-poverty programs

with specific objectives. The collection of data on the conditions of the poor is within the capacity of most countries and will be vital to them in evaluating their policies, programs, and investments.

However, progress in the developing countries does not depend solely on domestic efforts. The latter must be reinforced by international action in a number of areas.

The most important of these areas is international trade. The scope for the growth of exports from developing to industrialized countries is likely to be much more limited for the next decade than it was in the last two. The main reasons for this are the faltering pace of economic recovery in the industrialized countries and the rise of protectionist pressures. A coordinated approach to the demand management problems of industrialized countries is essential if they are to avoid a protracted period of slow growth, with its extremely adverse consequences for the growth of trade, including an increase in import barriers. The need for such an approach has been discussed in several forums, including the OECD and the Interim Committee of the International Monetary Fund, but progress has been modest so far.

In considering how to accelerate growth in industrialized countries, the importance of links with the developing countries should be recognized. Twenty-five years ago, these links were imperceptible; today they are significant. Import demand in developing countries has remained buoyant enough in recent years to help maintain production and employment levels in important export-oriented industries of the OECD countries. With more purchasing power, the developing countries can help to stimulate demand further.

The international community faces a long period of shifting comparative advantage, and it is essential that countries be ready to accept and facilitate the changes in industrial structures that this will involve. A few countries have undertaken studies of the direction these changes are likely to take over the longer run. Others should do the same since such information is necessary for framing and implementing appropriate adjustment policies. It would impart a desirable sense of urgency if governments were to commit themselves to formulating such policies and agree to consult on their implementation in an international forum such as the OECD.

The developing countries, too, face problems in adjusting to changing international trade patterns. The more advanced of them need to step up programs to diversify the product composition and markets of their manufactured exports. To promote trade among developing countries will require changes in industrial incentive structures, reduction of trade barriers, and strengthening of the institutional infrastructure in transport, communications, and credit.

In addition, countries must move jointly to strengthen the international framework governing trade relations so as to assure that the barriers to trade, which exist in both industrialized and developing countries, will be gradually dismantled, and that explicit criteria are established for those barriers which must be imposed to deal with temporary difficulties. As international specialization increases, active participation by developing countries in international trade discussions will become more and more important to offset protectionist pressures and progressively reduce the impediments to the growth of trade. For countries that still depend heavily on exports of a few primary commodities, action to reduce fluctuations of prices and to improve the systems which compensate for temporary declines in earnings is of great importance.

Even with a steady expansion of earnings from trade, the resources available to the developing countries must be supplemented by an adequate inflow of external capital. In this area, too, there are uncertainties. They relate to the rate of growth of private lending, the expansion of the lending capacity of the multilateral financing institutions, and the increased availability of Official Development Assistance.

Net disbursements of Official Development Assistance are projected to rise from US$19 billion in 1975 to US$57 billion in 1985 (in current prices), with a gradually rising share of the total going to the Low Income countries. Official Development Assistance from members of the DAC is projected to rise from US$14 billion in 1975 to US$44 billion in 1985. Despite this increase, ODA as a share of their gross national product would rise only slightly—from 0.36 percent in 1975 to 0.39 percent in 1985. This still falls far short of internationally declared objectives. Even the projected availability of ODA is not likely to be realized unless three large contributors—the United States, Germany, and Japan—increase their commitments substantially. Statements have been made in all three countries in support of an enlarged aid effort, but they have yet to be translated into action.

Additional concessional resources would permit both a higher rate of growth and greater progress in dealing with poverty. The large investments necessary to accelerate growth in agriculture and expand public services require an increased flow of concessional capital to the Low Income and to the poorer of the Middle Income countries. Although at particular times, in individual countries, there may be temporary problems of absorptive capacity, there is no doubt that additional resources could be used effectively. Additional external resources cannot guarantee either accelerated growth or success in dealing with poverty, but the absence of adequate resources greatly increases the probability of failure.

The net flow of capital at market terms is of special importance to the Middle Income countries. The projected increase from US$25 billion in 1975 to US$78 billion in 1985 (at current prices) assumes that lending by the private sector and multilateral lending institutions will grow at 12 percent a year. This involves a number of issues.

Much of the recent growth in private lending to developing countries has come from a relatively small number of large banks, mainly in the United States. Future lending from these banks to the developing countries may be limited by the growth of the banks' own capital and by internal considerations of appropriate balance in their portfolios. Other banks, including some in Europe and Japan, and non-bank private investors are increasing their share of developing country financing. If the projected increase in private lending is to materialize, it is important that this trend continues.

The projected growth of net lending from private banks to developing countries involves an even more rapid expansion of gross lending, due to the rather short average maturity of private financing in recent years. The high ratio of gross to net lending has the potential for serious instability. To reduce this will require measures which will extend the average maturity of private lending to the developing countries, including improved access to the long-term bond markets.

Whether the projected net flow of private lending to developing countries will be achieved depends on a fragile mixture of fact and psychology. The concentration of past lending in a relatively few large borrowing countries has made lenders sensitive to developments there. A debt management problem in any one major borrower could easily affect the willingness of private lenders to lend to other developing countries. Present prospects do not suggest a general problem of debt servicing capacity, but individual countries could encounter short-term liquidity problems. Expansion of the resources of the International Monetary Fund would augment the capacity to deal with such problems.

More general difficulties might arise if the trade regime were to deteriorate further, since this would affect countries' export earning capacity and hence their capacity to service debt. The willingness of private institutions to lend might also be affected by the regulatory environment in the capital exporting countries and by their governments' attitudes to lending to developing countries. Some actions designed to assure the stability of the banking system in the capital exporting countries could, by causing abrupt changes in the availability of finance to the developing countries, trigger the sort of debt crises that they are intended to prevent.

International lending institutions are the principal source of long-term capital for the developing countries. Their declining share in the total supply of capital is reflected in the deteriorating maturity profile of the debt of Middle Income countries. The achievement of a better balance between medium-term lending from private sources and long-term lending from the international institutions crucially depends on the capacity of the latter to increase their lending. This requires early agreement to expand the capital of these institutions. Action to do this is now under consideration. Increased lending by the international financial institutions not only helps to improve the maturity structure of debt but also provides assurance to private lenders—either through cofinancing activities or indirectly—about the quality of investment programs and debt management in the developing countries.

One special aspect of the availability of capital is the financing of energy development, particularly for oil and gas resources. Sometimes the known or suspected deposits of petroleum and gas in developing countries are too small to attract the major international companies even if they are of importance to the countries themselves; or the risk of exploration within the limited territory of a small country cannot be offset by exploration in adjoining tracts in neighboring countries; or the investment climate is too risky. To finance the development of energy resources in developing countries will demand substantial amounts of external capital and expertise. Private risk capital, which in the past has been a major source of finance, is now less readily available. The World Bank has begun to provide financing for this purpose, and plans to expand such operations in association with private capital. Other international institutions are considering similar programs. Such programs ought to be expanded rapidly and governments should consider whether expanded insurance and guarantee provisions could augment the flow of private capital.

The above discussion of the areas in which international action is needed has emphasized their importance for the prospects of developing countries. But it should be obvious that the industrialized countries too have a large stake in the rapid growth of the volume of trade—in a liberal, nondiscriminatory trading environment—and in more stable commodity prices. While their rate of economic growth is not as sensitive to short-term changes in international trade, exports play a major role in their economies, and the developing countries are increasingly important markets for export industries. The maintenance of a liberal, non-discriminatory trading system facilitates the continued growth of labor productivity and helps to ease inflationary pressures. Increasing the supply of energy and food to meet growing demand from both industrialized and developing countries is of vital importance to both. The developing countries not only are important customers for the exports of industrialized countries; they are an important element in the world capital markets, and have helped to invest the vastly expanded supply of savings productively.

The interdependence between the developing and the industrialized countries is not a new phenomenon—it has been growing in importance for decades. But it is perhaps not yet fully understood how far the process has come, nor how much further it will go in the next decades. At present, there is concern with the short-term disruptions caused by shifts in trade patterns, rather than recognition of the vital contribution of trade to long-run growth in productivity; concern with the growing indebtedness of some developing countries, rather than emphasis on strengthening institutional capacity for financial intermediation in line with global needs; fear about the implications of shifting economic strengths, rather than acknowledgement of the benefits of accelerated progress in the developing countries. But the current need to adjust is not a transient problem: it reflects a continuing, long-term, structural shift. It is important, therefore, that the implications and benefits of global interdependence be fully recognized. It will be to the advantage of all countries to sustain an international environment that supports the efforts of developing countries to sustain rapid growth and alleviate poverty as rapidly as possible.

THE (ALMOST) PESSIMISTS

BOOK REVIEW

by Jonathan Silverstone

Lester R. Brown, The Twenty-Ninth Day, W. W. Norton & Co., New York, 1978.

Eight years ago, Lester Brown, agricultural economist and head of the USDA's International Agricultural Service during most of the 1960's, saw the Green Revolution as the hope of the future, a "promise to improve the well-being of more people in a shorter time than any other single technological advance in history." All that was needed, he wrote in *Seeds of Change: The Green Revolution and Development in the 1970's*, was greater support for the spread of this technology, improved marketing arrangements, and encouragement for free investment in the Third World by multinational firms.

But he soon came to doubt that vision. *The Twenty Ninth Day* tells us why.

His faith in our technology and our capacity for economic analysis was misplaced. He was caught off guard by convulsive changes in the global economy, including the spectacular rise in the cost of petroleum on whose continued cheap availability the Green Revolution's "new seeds" technology depends. He found that the irrigation canals which are an essential part of the Green Revolution also spread disease. And he discovered that multinational firms' objectives are not always consistent with the general welfare.

"Experts failed to anticipate the energy crisis, food shortages, double-digit inflation, the abrupt alteration of the international political structure, the collapse of major fisheries, the astronomical climb in wheat prices during the early seventies, and a global economic slump unmatched since the Great Depression."

The widely accepted development answers were shown to be wrong; and now, Mr. Brown confesses, we do not even know what the right questions are. "It is not just that the least able are stumbling, but that the finest minds are missing the mark so widely."

Hubris may have been our downfall. We have forgotten the importance of nature and the supremacy of its laws, he warns. We must recognize that all economic activity ultimately depends on the productivity of earth's natural systems and resources. To understand and deal with contemporary economic stresses and dilemmas, we must understand the relationship between the condition of the earth's natural systems and the operation of the economic system. Unfortunately, "communications between economics and ecology are virtually nonexistent, in part because ecological principles and economic theory share so little common ground. Economists tend to think in terms of unlimited exponential growth and to place great faith in 'technological fixes,' while biologists tend to think in terms of closed systems, of natural cycles and of carrying capacities. Economists see specialization as a virtue and as a source of efficiency, while ecologists perceive it as a risk and a threat to the stability of systems."

Mr. Brown urges us to abandon the notion that development and progress will come about through the conquest of nature. The key word for us must be accommodation. We have to find better ways to accommodate ourselves to the earth's natural capacities and resources.

Today's global interdependence goes far beyond the neo-Marxian arguments which have been advanced by supporters of aid in the industrial countries—that our concern with what happens in developing countries (apart from moral considerations) is tied to our need for the resources they have and the markets they might provide for surplus capital and production. Shortages and ecological disasters have widespread international consequences which we cannot avoid, no matter where they occur. The security of nations depends on the healthy survival of biological systems that do not respect national boundaries. In his view, a country does not gain strength by putting scarce resources into the production of more and better weapons systems. That may, in fact, be a good way to undermine national security.

Agenda, June 1978, pp. 19-20. Jonathan Silverstone is Chief of the Civic Participation Division in the Policy Development and Analysis Branch of AID's Bureau for Program and Policy Coordination.

21

"Ecological and economic pressure will force people to cross national boundaries in search of relief. The deterioration of croplands and grassland may transform great numbers of people into international ecological refugees, as they already have in the Sahelian zone. Rising unemployment in densely populated Mexico is already compelling millions of unemployed Mexicans to cross the U.S. border illegally in search of jobs, creating a highly sensitive political issue between the two countries."

The Twenty Ninth Day discusses the current state and possible future of four major biological systems—oceanic fisheries, grasslands, forests, and croplands. It points up the consequences of our attempts to get too much out of each too fast. If we go on as we have, this process will destroy the capacity of the systems and will destroy us.

Development—and survival—depend on our ability to make fundamental changes in the way we do our business, changes which make accommodation rather than conquest our goal. Among other things, the adjustment may require a conscious attempt to reduce, rather than increase, the amount of international trade and investment which create bonds of economic interdependence, Mr. Brown argues.

It may also require a new approach to economics that will bring theory closer to reality than it is today. Unfortunately, there is no great thinker or conceptualizer—"no Keynes in sight" to do this. Although the inadequacy of the current assumptions and techniques of economic analysis are obvious, Mr. Brown indicates resistance to change "by those who have to abandon familiar theories or analytical tools is naturally strong. Galileo advanced a new paradigm and paid dearly for it. When Robert Wegener, German astronomer and meteorologist, first proposed in 1912 the theory of continental drift that was eventually to revolutionize geology in the sixties, he was scorned by fellow professors everywhere. While geology was being revolutionized by an astronomer, genetics was being invaded by chemists, physicists, and microbiologists. Together their work led ultimately to the discovery of the double helix, the seminal concept needed to unravel the genetic code.

"What the source of the new paradigm needed in economics will be remains to be seen. It could come from ecology, systems analysis, or, as some have suggested, from political philosophy. Whatever its origins, it is certain to be resisted by many established economists. But the period following the emergence of a new paradigm could be marked by excitement and intellectual ferment comparable to that in geology and genetics in recent decades."

Perhaps a reader of this book—a layperson without a Ph.D. in economics—will provide the insight or inspiration which is needed before it is too late.

WHERE HOPE FLOATS ON OUR CLOGGED LILY POND

The Twenty-Ninth Day, by Lester R. Brown. New York: W. W. Norton & Co., 363 pp. Cloth, $11.95; paper, $3.95.

By Richard Critchfield

A lily pond has a single leaf. Each day the number of leaves double. When will the pond be half full? Answer: the twenty-ninth day. Hence the title of Lester Brown's latest book on the ecological crisis: our particular pond has a day to go until we are all choking on lilies.

So much has been written about the world's population-food-energy crisis by now that if sheer analysis could rescue us, the world should be well on the way to salvation. The danger is that the authors, forever crying wolf, use so many of the same illustrations, statistics and sources in presenting what is by now the conventional wisdom, we are more impressed by the convention than the wisdom and move on.

In that sense, this is a book written too soon. Brown seems caught between the old — population is exceeding the carrying capacity of the earth's fisheries, forests, grasslands and croplands — and the new — population is starting to stop, completely in much of Western Europe and heading that way in North America and East Asia, with a slower downturn in the rest of southern Asia and Africa. (Latin America is still unaffected.)

Nor does Brown, aside from mentioning that there is "considerable unrealized food-production potential" in the third world, seem up-to-date on the tremendous technological advances being made in China (which hopes to increase grain production from 285 million tons to 400 million tons by 1985) and India (which hopes to increase it from 120 million tons to 240 or 360 million tons by the year 2000).

This agricultural revolution promises to be fully as spectacular as what happened in America in 1890-1950. It is based on the very quick spread of irrigation, multiple cropping of new high-yield grain that matures in half the time, nitrogen-fixing pulses, and the massive application of chemical and organic fertilizer. China is ready to tackle mechanization, and the Indians, behind in the race after over-investing in industry too long, are now worried about a food glut in the year 2000.

If India and China solve their food-population problems, they've more or less solved the world's too. Better contraceptives, more village prosperity and above all, the spread of rural female literacy seem likely to combine to stabilize population early in the 21st century. And in a solar-powered world the 122 poor nations of the poor south may be poor no more; they have the most sun. Far from the apocalyptic vision of mass starvation by the year 2000, we are likely to have food coming out of our ears.

Brown hints of this; but he is too cautious. It is odd to catch him napping this time as he and his crew of bright young researchers, who keep the best tabs of anyone on global trends in their Washington-based Worldwatch Institute, have usually been first to see the shape of the future. Other than the India-China slip (and China does come in for praise), the rest of the book is excellent and probably indispensable to anyone wanting to understand more of today's world than the surface political booms.

The operative word in Brown's analysis is "accommodation" or how global society will have to evolve new lifestyles (Brown seems to avoid the word "culture") in the post-petroleum era (50 years from now but starting in the 1980s). But the bicycling, gardening, solar-heated future he envisages does not sound unpleasant. Chances are, alas, it will not happen, because one of these days a new Thomas Edison now tinkering in his basement will come up with sun-powered batteries to furnish photovoltaic energy electricity and we will all go on getting richer, moving faster, living longer, and becoming more of a threat to nature at an ever more dizzying speed.

And if the day comes when all the tractors and combines stand idle and the fertilizer bags empty because the oil has run out, we can always import grain from India or China. They will have agriculturally caught up with us but will be using biogas, trees, and wind, water, and sun for energy instead.

Man's control over matter and energy has increased at such accelerating speed and his ability to process and distribute his knowledge has grown so global, few forecasts these days, based on statistics of even two, three years ago, turn out to be right. Science is going to prove that that pond can fairly comfortably accommodate a lot more of those lilies than anybody thought. Brown's next book, when some of the changes in India and China and elsewhere have begun to sufficiently sink in will be even more worth waiting for.

SEVERE FOOD SHORTAGES REPORTED
IN 17 AFRICAN COUNTRIES

Washington, May 30 -- Seventeen countries in Africa are facing severe shortages of food resulting from drought, flood and war, according to Edouard Saouma, Director-General of the Food and Agriculture Organization of the United Nations (FAO). Among the 17 countries, conditions are especially critical in Ethiopia, three Sahelian countries and Ghana. FAO warns that urgent action is required for these five countries because they face immediate problems in obtaining enough food and delivering it to areas where shortages exist.

Food production prospects in Ethiopia are poorer than previously estimated. The recently harvested main cereal crop was abnormally small following drought in Wollo, Tigre and Northern Shoa provinces and disruptions by armed conflict. Prospects for the secondary harvest also are poor because of drought. Limited port capacity and internal transportation make import and distribution of emergency food supplies difficult.

Sahelian countries have received only part of the food aid needed to make up for last year's shortfall in production caused by drought. Food aid needs for Sahelian countries have been estimated at 580,000 tons, while food aid pledges through mid-May totaled 417,000 tons and deliveries before the rainy season starts at the end of May are expected to total only 274,000 tons. Rains would make further delivery to the interior difficult. Consequently, rains have already begun, earlier than normal, in Mali and Niger. The food situation appears most serious in Niger, and to a lesser extent in Mali and Chad.

Drought reduced 1977 harvests in Ghana, where the situation is particularly serious in the northern regions on the southern edge of the Sahel. Severe food shortages are likely to occur before the new early millet crop becomes avail- able in July and Auguest, unless food aid which has been requested is received soon.

Food shortages are also reported in Angola and Zaire, mainly on account of the large numbers of refugees. Mozambique's food supply situation has been worsened by recent floods, and more than 200,000 people will have to depend on food assistance until a new crop becomes available in late 1978.

News (Food and Agriculture Organization), May 30, 1978.

MARGARET MEAD:
WE SUFFER WHEN OTHERS STARVE

Margaret Mead interviewed
by Susan Scharfman

Question: Dr. Mead, how do you characterize the importance of the population and food issue?

Mead: As we enter a world where we're dependent on each other, the state of all the different people in the world becomes relevant to each other. Every community has always cared whether there was enough to eat, whether babies that were born could live, and cared for its own people. These used to be tangible groups. Then "the community" became nation states or continents. It's only since World War II that we have had to worry about the whole world. If there are people starving anywhere in the world, this is relevant to us. Especially relevant are those things we do that contribute to that starvation or relieve it.

What we do affects the rest of the world. We grow a great deal of wheat. If we save it instead of feeding it to livestock so we can have marbled steaks, it provides a great buffer against famine in the world.

In terms of population growth, there's a very precarious balance. When you have more food, you run the risk that more people will live. But unless more people live, people aren't willing to cut down on the size of their families. There's a very intimate relationship here. As we feed people better, more children will live and people will be willing to limit their families.

For example, if we feed women who are breast-feeding their children, then the period of infertility that accompanies breast feeding will last longer; the baby will be stronger and less likely to die, and mothers will not insist on having more children.

We have to not only feed people, but feed them what they need to grow, to be healthy, to be able to work. And we have to remember that food doesn't necessarily mean good nutrition. If we feed mothers well, we have a synergistic system where everything works for good. To think about population without thinking about food, or to think about food without population is self-defeating.

Question: How do you regard what is being done by the U.S. and other nations in these areas?

Mead: There was a long period after World War II where everybody believed that the thing to do was to help developing nations industrialize, and if they were industrialized they would then suddenly have a lot of money, they could buy the things they needed, and have a high standard of living. All over the world we neglected agriculture. People streamed into the cities where they thought there was food. The cities became terribly overcrowded. The rural areas were neglected, so people were very hungry there too.

Now this is being reversed. I think that both the United States and other countries are realizing that if we're going to solve the food problems of the world, we have to solve the rural problems and make rural life bearable. We have the means to do it. They have to have education; they have to have health services; they have to have reasons for staying in the country and not crowding into cities.

Although we have some reversal in policy, there's still too much emphasis on growing cash crops that produce money for a country, and too little emphasis on becoming self-sufficient in food.

Question: What impact will the work that is now being done in the area of population have on developing societies?

Mead: Small societies around the world have been able to cope with problems of population growth. In periods of scarcity, fewer children are born. In periods of affluence, more children are born. If we go back in history, we find when population expanded. We find it in our own Southwest where people moved into an area because temporarily the climate was good. Then the climate changed, and there wasn't enough food, and they moved away again.

Today, people can't do this themselves. Newark or Buffalo or Los Angeles are not really capable of regulating their own population growth. It depends on a great number of things: the climate of opinion, whether we have a recession or not, what's done about welfare, and a whole series of things.

These decisions have to be made at a higher level. But the extent that they're made a higher level may distort the life of people at the village level. One of the most important things is to have national policies that devolve as much as possible on the local people so that they can work out, within their own framework of food and opportunity, how many children

Agenda, October 1978, pp. 1-2.

they want to have. In some cases this will mean that they elect to have more, at least temporarily.

Question: How do we motivate the people in the developing countries to improve the quality of their lives? Where does our responsibility end and theirs begin?

Mead: We talk as if it was our business to go out and convert them into having a better way of life. I've never known people anywhere who, if they were given a chance for their babies to live, didn't want them to live. But they may be in such despair, they may be so hopeless, that they have no sense that it's worthwhile doing anything. There are many people in the world who are capable of putting up with terrible deprivation because they believe in reincarnation, for instance. What we're talking about in the United States is completely materialistic. We're talking about the notion that people have only one life and that the most important thing is that they should have enough food and good shelter, good medical care and good education. That is what we talk about when we talk about quality of life.

If people don't have enough to eat and they're given a chance to have enough to eat they will take it. If they don't have comfortable houses that kept them warm or kept the rain out and they're given a chance at a better dwelling, they will take that opportunity. But they will only take them and work for them if they feel it is possible. They will only hope for the future and giving each child a better chance if the children have a chance to live.

If we want to help create conditions in which people can elect a better quality of life then we have to be sure that their babies don't die. We have to educate women because unless women have education and status, they will not be able to make their contribution to change. Matters of population and food are up to women in many parts of the world.

The poorest are the people that have the most children because they have the least hope of any of them living. We have to talk about creating conditions of more equitable division or distribution of income. We have to help the distribution of income, because we've discovered that population has nothing to do with GNP, and a high GNP may simply mean that the elite are very rich and the poor are very poor.

Question: Do you have some predictions about the future?

Mead: The principal hazard of the future is nuclear war. People talk about the population bomb and people worry about what we're doing to the environment, and they *should* worry, because the things that we do now will affect what happens 25, 50 years from now. But the direst predictions we can make are the result of the proliferation of nuclear weapons. We've been living in terrible danger ever since the bomb was invented, and we've been lulled to sleep by the fact that we haven't blown ourselves up yet. This is our greatest danger.

But we also have to address ourselves to the fact that people are starving. We can't let people starve while we're arguing about how we're going to deal with the nuclear situation. Every time we condemn one person to starvation, we lower the quality of life in this country and our capacity to care for ourselves, our children, as well as other people's children.

POST-HARVEST CROP LOSSES:
TRAGIC INEFFICIENCY IN THE THIRD WORLD

by David Spurgeon

Ottawa

For about half the world's population, finding enough to eat remains a problem. Increases in production continue to be outstripped by population growth.

Thus it is that some food experts now are looking beyond means of boosting food production, to try to apply the old adage "waste not, want not" to what they call "the post-harvest system."

They know they can't end hunger simply by curbing waste. Nevertheless, they also know that the magnitude of this waste is enormous, as was pointed out recently at a seminar on third-world agriculture sponsored by the Alberta Institute of Agrologists and Canada's International Development Research Centre.

Some estimates suggest that less-developed countries lose a quarter to a third of their total food crop to post-harvest inefficiencies. In semi-arid parts of Africa, storage losses alone have been estimated from a low of 10 percent in cereal grains to a high of 75 percent in pulses.

Dante D. de Padua, an agricultural engineer from the Philippines, suggested at the seminar that advances in rice production resulting from research now are significant enough to require complementary investments in research to improve the post-harvest system.

By "post-harvest system," experts such as Dr. de Padua mean all the components of the industry that deal with food crops from the time they are harvested to the time they reach the table.

Small margins a problem

One of the problems is that the system operates on small margins, Dr. de Padua explained. Farm prices for rice at the paddy are discounted according to moisture content and purity while the consumer price depends on the yield of milled rice. For a ton of "paddy" that brings the farmer $120, the value at the retailing point might be $187.20, leaving the post-harvest sector only $67.20 to handle, dry, store, process, and distribute a ton of rice.

Yet the price of technological hardware available from developed countries, said de Padua, is "exorbitant."

"An installed three-ton-per-hour drier from Denmark costs $288,000. An installed two-ton-per-hour Japanese rice mill costs about $200,000. Clearly the industry cannot afford these imported components of the post-harvest system to upgrade their efficiencies," he declared.

Cost, however, is not the only factor. Those in the post-harvest industry have invariably tried to copy the wrong model, Dr. de Padua explains.

"The primary mistake," he said, "has been the naïve assumption that the industrial type and scale of hardware used in the developed countries for temperate climates, designed for other grains such as wheat or maize, would work just as well in the developing countries in the hot, humid tropics, and for rice. . . .

"The requirements in the Asian region are unique and complex in a way that makes the introduction of innovations and of the necessary hardware a much more difficult undertaking than it has generally been thought." '

Post-harvest technology requires considerable adaptation for application in Asia, Dr. de Padua maintained. And the hardware must make use of indigenous resources as much as possible.

Attempts to use Western-style facilities, such as bulk silos and industrial continuous-flow dryers in order to increase efficiency, have always failed.

This is because farm sizes are smaller in Asia — typically one-half to three hectares per family (a hectare is about 1.5 acres). Harvesting and threshing are labor-intensive. And with small, independent farmers, a large number of crop varieties are planted in an unsynchronized fashion, so that the harvest comes in small batches of different varieties, moisture, ranges, and grades.

In addition, new high-yielding varieties have made a second crop possible, which is harvested during the rainy months of September to November. The straw is wet and tends to clog harvesting machines. If not dried, it soon ferments, molds, rots, or sprouts.

Dr. de Padua described several simple, inexpensive grain driers that are being developed in Asia to cope with the area's special problems. These include one from the University of the Philippines at Los Baños, made of ¾-inch plywood and a simple fan. Thailand's Royal Ministry of Agriculture has developed its own version, which has been exported to Malaysia and Indonesia under an Australian-ASEAN (Association of Southeast Asian Nations) program for introduction on farms.

Simple as the driers are, a massive extension-type demonstration and training course is being conducted to instruct farmers in the ASEAN countries in their use, Dr. de Padua said. Progress in getting the drier used has been slow, however, because the cost is about $7 a ton compared to $1.37 for sun drying.

Support prices for rice do not recognize the fact that sun drying is not feasible during rainy months. And many rice millers who traditionally have depended on sun-dried crops will simply stop purchasing during bad weather, leaving farmers without a market for their wet rice.

Another option is to develop an efficient system of delivering wet grain direct to central drying stations or millers. But this requires networks of farm roads, methods of receiving, grading, and handling many different grades of wet rice, and a new type of industrial dryer. Finally, entirely new technology, such as wet threshing and cleaning, and partial cooking of rice in its own moisture combined with flash drying, should be considered, Dr. de Padua said.

Dr. de Padua had some reservations about the much-acclaimed high-yielding varieties of rice. It is true that they have succeeded in increasing the yield of "paddy" on a rice field, he said — but that does not necessarily mean more rice on the consumer's table.

Some problems remain

"The high-yielding varieties shatter easily, do not ripen uniformly, have a high percentage of immature kernels, and a much poorer milling and eating quality compared to traditional varieties," he sahs. "Until these deficiencies are corrected by the agronomists, they have to be accommodated in the processing system."

Another factor contributing to lower-than-possible rice yields in Southeast Asia has been the antiquated milling system, Dr. de Padua said. The biggest advance has been the development of rubber roll huskers to take the place of disks coated with emery stone. An IDRC-supported study shows that the rubber rollers have an efficiency of 83 percent compared to only 58 percent for stone disk huskers, and this means 4.5 percent more milled rice from the same paddy stock.

The drawback, however, is that the rollers wear out quickly. Dr. de Padua proposed reducing the cost of replacement by licensing local manufacturers to produce them.

The most significant change in approach to such problems in Southeast Asia in recent years, said Dr. de Padua, has been that countries providing technical assistance are ceasing to try to transfer their own hardware and are leaving the solution of local problems to indigenous people.

FACTS AND DEFINITIONS

WORLD WHEAT AND COARSE GRAINS
JULY/JUNE   1974/75-1978/79

(In Millions of Metric Tons)

	1974/75	1975/76	1976/77	1977/78	1978/79 SEP 27	1978/79 Nov 13
EXPORTS						
SELECTED						
EXPORTERS	43.3	43.9	49.1	51.3	49.1	48.6
WEST EUROPE	12.7	14.5	11.3	13.2	14.9	16.0
USSR	5.0	0.5	3.0	2.0	2.0	3.0
OTHERS	4.4	6.2	5.3	6.7	7.3	6.6
TOTAL NON-US	65.4	65.1	68.7	73.1	73.2	74.2
U.S	62.4	77.9	76.3	82.9	83.0	84.3
WORLD TOTAL	127.8	142.9	145.0	156.1	156.2	158.5
IMPORTS						
WEST EUROPE	32.7	31.2	41.3	33.8	32.1	31.2
USSR	5.2	25.6	10.3	18.6	16.0	15.0
JAPAN	18.5	19.5	21.4	22.7	23.3	23.3
EAST EUROPE	10.6	12.1	14.5	13.7	13.6	13.5
OTHERS	60.8	54.6	57.5	67.3	71.3	75.5
WORLD TOTAL	127.8	142.9	145.0	156.1	156.2	158.5
(+ INTRA EC-9)	139.7	157.7	155.9	170.3	169.5	171.3
PRODUCTION						
SELECTED						
EXPORTERS	95.6	105.2	121.9	106.5	113.8	116.3
WEST EUROPE	141.8	130.0	123.8	135.0	144.1	149.4
USSR	183.7	132.0	211.9	184.7	210.0	218.0
EAST EUROPE	91.3	87.9	94.1	93.6	93.0	91.7
PRC	104.4	109.9	113.4	108.8	114.0	114.0
OTHERS	168.9	186.5	200.0	189.2	199.2	203.3
TOTAL NON-US	785.7	751.7	865.0	817.9	874.2	894.7
U.S.	199.4	242.8	252.2	257.4	257.9	260.2
WORLD TOTAL	985.1	994.5	1117.1	1075.3	1132.0	1154.9
UTILIZATION						
WEST EUROPE	156.3	153.0	153.8	156.4	159.2	160.4
USSR	193.9	171.2	208.2	216.3	223.0	216.0
PRC	110.6	112.0	116.4	117.5	124.7	125.0
OTHERS	394.9	408.9	431.8	437.8	445.1	449.8
TOTAL NON-US	855.6	845.1	910.2	928.1	951.9	951.2
U.S.	140.1	153.4	151.1	158.8	166.1	165.4
WORLD TOTAL	995.8	998.5	1061.3	1086.9	1118.0	1116.6
END STOCKS						
TOTAL						
FOREIGN	94.5	82.0	114.5	91.0	96.5	120.3
USSR: STKS CHG	-9.0	-14.0	11.0	-15.0	1.0	14.0
US	27.3	35.4	60.3	72.2	81.0	81.1
WORLD TOTAL	121.8	117.4	174.7	163.2	177.5	201.4

Foreign Agriculture Circular-Grains USDA-Foreign Agricultural Service, November 13, 1978, p. 2.

COUNTRIES DESIGNATED AS "NEEDY" BY MAJOR INTERNATIONAL AGENCIES

	Country	Population (millions)	LDC	MSA	PFDC	FPC	PQLI
Africa	1 Egypt	38.9		•		✓✓	46
	2 Sudan	16.3	•			✓	33
	3 Mauritania	1.4		•		✓✓	15
	4 Mali	5.9	•	•	•	✓✓✓	15
	5 Niger	4.9	•	•	•	✓✓✓	14
	6 Senegal	5.3		•		✓	22
	7 The Gambia	0.6		•		✓✓	22
	8 Upper Volta	6.4	•	•	•	✓✓✓	17
	9 Cape Verde Rep.	0.3		•		✓✓	46
	10 Guinea-Bissau	0.5		•		✓✓	10
	11 Guinea	4.7	•	•	•	✓✓	20
	12 Sierra Leone	3.2		•		✓	29
	13 Ivory Coast	7.0					28
	14 Ghana	10.4		•			31
	15 Benin	3.3	•	•		✓✓	23
	16 Ethiopia	29.4	•	•	•	✓✓	16
	17 Somalia	3.4	•	•	•	✓✓✓	19
	18 Uganda	12.4	•	•		✓✓	33
	19 Rwanda	4.5	•	•	•	✓✓	27
	20 Kenya	14.4		•	•	✓	40
	21 Burundi	3.9	•	•	•		23
	22 Tanzania	16	•	•	•	✓✓✓	28
	23 Malawi	5.3	•	•		✓✓	29
	24 Mozambique	9.5		•		✓	23
	25 Madagascar	7.9		•		✓	44
	26 Chad	4.2	•	•	•	✓✓	20
	27 Cent. Afr. Emp.	1.9		•		✓✓	18
	28 Cameroon	6.7		•		✓	28
	29 Botswana	0.7	•				38
	30 Lesotho	1.1	•	•		✓✓	50
Asia	31 Yemen AR	5.6	•	•	•	✓✓✓	27
	32 Yemen PR	1.8	•	•	•	✓✓✓	27
	33 Afghanistan	20	•	•	•	✓✓	19
	34 Pakistan	74.5		•	•	✓✓	37
	35 India	622.7		•	•	✓✓	41
	36 Nepal	13.2	•	•	•	✓✓	25
	37 Bhutan	1.2	•				n.a.
	38 Bangladesh	83.3		•	•	✓✓✓	33
	39 Sri Lanka	14.1		•	•	✓✓	83
	40 Maldives	0.1	•				n.a.
	41 Burma	31.8		•		✓	51
	42 Lao PDR	3.5	•	•		✓✓	32
	43 Kampuchea	8		•		✓✓	41
	44 Indonesia	136.9		•		✓✓	50
	45 Philippines	44.3		•		✓	73
Pacific	46 W. Samoa	0.2	•	•			86
Americas	47 El Salvador	4.3		•		✓	67
	48 Honduras	3.3		•		✓	50
	49 Guatemala	6.4		•			53
	50 Guyana	0.8		•		✓	84
Caribbean	51 Haiti	5.3	•	•	•	✓✓	31

LDCs. The list of the 25 Least Developed Countries (LDCs) was established by the Committee for Development Planning during the Fifty-First Session of the Economic and Social Council held in March-April 1971. The classification was based on the following criteria: per caput gross domestic product of US$ 100 or less in 1968, share of manufacturing in gross domestic product of 10 percent or less, and literacy rate in the age group of 15 years or more of 20 percent or less around 1960.

MSAs. At its Sixth Special Session of April-May 1974, the General Assembly of the UN set up the United Nations Emergency Operation to help the countries Most Seriously Affected (MSAs) by the economic crisis. These were countries with a per caput income of less than US$ 400 in 1971 for which projections showed the likelihood of an overall balance-of-payments deficit in 1974 equivalent to 5 percent or more of imports. Forty-five countries are now on this list.

PFDCs. The Consultative Group on Food Production and Investment has designated 18 countries as being Priority Food-Deficit Countries (PFDCs) on the criteria either that:
(i) It is likely to face by 1985 a deficit of more than one million tons of cereals just to maintain present inadequate level of nutrition, or
(ii) Its food deficit, although small in absolute terms, poses a major problem at the national level because per caput dietary energy supplies are not enough now to meet even an average of 95 percent of the country's nutritional requirements.

FPCs. Forty-three countries have been chosen by the World Food Council to be Food Priority Countries (FPCs) as fulfilling at least three of the following five criteria:
(i) Per caput income below US$ 500 (in 1975 prices).
(ii) A projected cereal deficit by 1985 of 500,000 tons or more and/or a cereals deficit of 20 percent or more as a proportion of estimated cereals consumption.
(iii) Degree of under-nutrition in terms of proportion of population which is under-nourished or in terms of the average availability of calories in relation to minimum requirements.
(iv) Inadequate agricultural performance in terms of average historic increase in food production, total and per caput, during the last decade.
(v) Potential for more rapid and efficient increase in food production including the availability of under-utilized resources to produce food.

In 1977, the World Food Council ranked the FPCs according to the severity of their food problem. Rating was based on projected food deficits, calorie consumption, growth of food output per caput in the last decade, and 1975 GDP per caput. Food problems were rated as severe (✓), very severe (✓✓), and extremely severe (✓✓✓).

PQLI Index. In 1977 the Overseas Development Council introduced the Physical Quality of Life Index (PQLI), a preliminary effort to determine how well societies are able to meet the basic human needs of their poor. It is a measure of results, not inputs. ODC selected three indicators—infant mortality, life expectancy, and literacy—to represent the wider range of conditions which development programs seek to improve. Individual countries were ranked on a scale of 1 to 100 for each of the three indicators, then given a single index rating representing an equally weighted average of the three. Sweden received the highest Index rating (100) with a life expectancy averaging 75 years, infant mortality of 9 per 1,000, and a literacy rate of 99 percent.

... reported in the ODC publication *The United States and World Development: Agenda 1977.*

IADS, Report/1977, International Agricultural Development Service, May 1978, pp. 10-11.

LOWER AND MIDDLE INCOME COUNTRIES COMPARED

Analytically, however, it is often useful to consider groups, and this report will focus on two broad categories of developing countries with varying problems and interests. Using income data from the World Bank, the dividing line between these two groups is put at an annual per capita Gross National Product (GNP) of $550 (1976). Countries below this level will be referred to as Lower Income Countries (LICs) and countries above this level, up to a per capita income of about $3,300 will be referred to as Middle Income Countries (MICs).

A. The Lower Income Countries—LICs

There are about 65 countries in the lower income group. They are located primarily in South and Southeast Asia, and in Africa. They rely heavily on concessional economic assistance for their development, and they receive over 80 percent of the official development assistance that goes to the developing countries overall. Their population is about 1.5 billion, about 37 percent of world population and just under 70 percent of the combined LIC-MIC total. In 25 years, if recent population growth trends continue, the LICs will have about 36 percent of the world population.

The LICs have had the slowest per capita income growth of the major country groupings. For the most recent decade for which data are available, 1966-1976,

real per capita income growth for the LICs averaged 1.9% per year, while the MICs are growing more rapidly than both the developed countries and the centrally planned economies, at 4.1 percent per year.

As much as 80 percent of the population of the LICs may be receiving less food than the minimum standard recommended by the FAO, and perhaps 25 percent has a serious food deficiency of over 250 calories per day. Statistics on infant mortality, literacy and percentage of school age children in school are similarly striking. A combination of rapid population growth (over 2.3 percent per year in the first part of 1970s), low income growth and limited food availabilities have combined to make projections of future social conditions equally pessimistic unless fundamental changes occur.

Unlike the MICs, the LICs depend heavily on concessional foreign assistance to finance imports. The poorer LICs are not major commodity exporters. Official development assistance (ODA) per capita to the LDCs in 1975 was about $6.25. For the poorer LICs (those with per capita incomes below $250), ODA has accounted for over three-quarters of capital inflows and for LICs with per capita incomes between $250 and $550, ODA accounts for about two-thirds of capital inflows. Overall ODA inflow to the LICs represents about 25 percent of total investment within these countries.

TABLE 1 Population

	Number (Millions)	World Population	Rate 1971-1976	Projection[1] 2000 Number (Millions)	Share of World Population
Developing	1,821	45.5%	2.2%	3,441	54%
(LIC)[2]	(1,268)	(31.7%)	2.3%	(2,278)	(36%)
(MIC)[3]	(553)	(13.8%)	2.0%	(1,163)	(18%)
Developed	665	16.6%	.8%	805	13%
OPEC	308	7.7%	3.5%	528	8%
Centrally Planned[4]	1,208	30.2%	1.1%	1,570	25%
TOTAL	4,002	100%	1.7%	6,344	100%

[1] Using constant 1971-1976 fertility rate and 1975 per capita country income groupings.
[2] Lower income countries—per capita GNP less than $500 in 1975.
[3] Middle income countries—per capita GNP between $500 and $2,700 in 1975. Includes Spain, Greece, Portugal, South Africa and Yugoslavia. Does not include Israel or Ireland.
[4] USSR, East Europe, P.R.C., North Korea, Mongolia, Albania, Cuba.
SOURCE: IBRD, World Bank Atlas, 1977, 1973

TABLE 2

Number of Developing Countries by Population Size, 1977

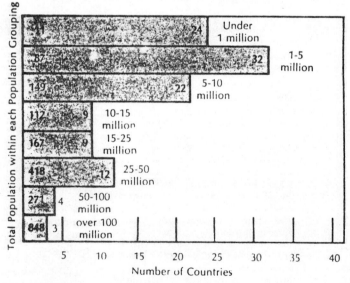

Development Issues, Third Annual Report to the Congress, Development Coordination Committee (Washington, D.C.: April 1978), pp. 6-10.

On the import side the situation is equally severe. Many of the LICs are net importers of commodities, especially food. In many cases, they have not yet fully exploited their commodity export possibilities, and many suffer from the effects of international commodity arrangements which restrict their access to world markets. While the LICs have suffered from the increases in energy prices and the world recession in the last several years, the impact has been somewhat less than the impact on the MICs, since the LICs' less modern economies generally depend less on imported energy and have not achieved as important a place in international trade.

B. The Middle Income Countries—MICs

The MICs have per capita incomes ranging from $500 up to about $3,300. The 50 MICs, which are located primarily in Latin America, the Mediterranean, the Middle East and the Far East, had a population of 553 million in 1976. Population growth in these countries has been less rapid than in the lower income countries—approximately 2 percent per year in the early 1970s—and has been dropping rapidly in several countries where vigorous family planning programs have been instituted and where social and economic conditions have been improving rapidly.

TABLE 3
Per Capita GNP ($/1975)
1966-1976

	1966	1976	Annual Growth Rate 1966-1976
Lower Income Countries (1976 Per Capita GNP Below $500)	147	179	1.9%
Middle Income Countries (1976 Per Capita GNP $500-$3,300)	780	1,170	4.1%
All Developing Countries	341	479	3.4%
Industrialized Countries	4,546	5,981	2.8%
OPEC	486	873	8.0%
Centrally Planned Economies	770	1,056	3.2%

SOURCE: IBRD

Unlike the LICs, the MICs as a group have enjoyed rapid growth in per capita income in the last decade. A number of MICs have only recently moved into this category following periods of rapid growth, and have ceased to be major recipients of concessional assistance. While living conditions are still poor in many of the middle income countries, their overall economic strength has increased rapidly in the past decade; if the trends of that period can be continued, their poverty programs will become increasingly manageable with internal resources.

It is estimated that 34 percent of the population in the MICs receives less than the required minimum daily calorie level, but only 8 percent had a deficiency of over 250 calories per day. If projections are made using per capita income growth rates for the last decade and population growth rates for the early 1970s, and if relative food prices remain constant, by 1990 less than 16 percent of the MIC population will have less than adequate calories and less than 5 percent will have severe deficiencies. Further, the absolute number of people in these categories in the MICs would fall by 1990. Similar projections for the LICs show over 60 percent of the population with inadequate food intake in 1990, with the absolute number of people substantially higher, particularly those with deficits over 250 calories per day. Relative improvement of these and other social indicators will be even greater in the MICs if population growth rates decrease from the levels of the recent past as many demographers expect.

Total GNP in the MICs is more than 2½ times larger than that of the LICs, while the MIC population is only 40 percent of that of the LICs. The MICs received less concessional development assistance per capita than the LICs in 1977, and this trend will continue in the future, as disbursements for commitments to the MICs that were made several years ago are being completed. Concessional assistance now constitutes less than 10 percent of the total resource flows to the MICs, and only 1 percent of total investment. Even for MICs with per capita incomes under $1,000, ODA was approximately one-third of total external capital inflows in 1977.

The MICs are much more important in international trade than the LICs. The former received nearly 25 percent of U.S. exports in 1977, and even the less affluent MICs have annual exports of almost $150 per capita.

Two broad generalizations can be drawn from these comparisons of LICs and MICs. For the LICs, the problem is to break with past trends and move rapidly to improve the conditions of the majority of their populations and rapidly increase income and production. Concessional assistance is and will remain of great importance, although trade opportunities are also important and domestic development programs and policies are crucial. For the MICs, the problem is to maintain and increase the rapid rate of gains in the last decade and to distribute the benefits of this increase to all their populations. Trade and capital market access—together with improved domestic programs—are of the greatest importance. Concessional economic assistance is rapidly declining in importance, although specialized assistance in key areas will remain critical.

TOTAL RECEIPTS OF DEVELOPING COUNTRIES

**TOTAL NET FLOWS
TO DEVELOPING COUNTRIES**
$ billion

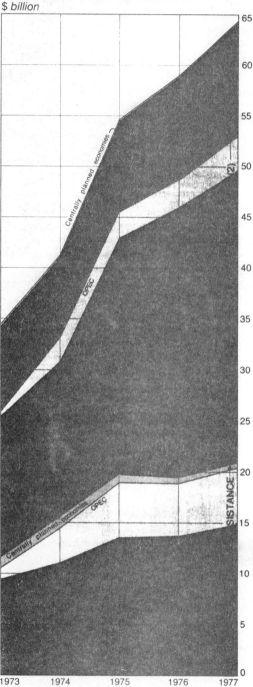

(1) Including multilateral pipeline, i.e. difference between inflow and outflow from multilateral agencies.
(2) Other official and private flows.

In 1973, the year before the oil crisis, the total net resource inflow into developing countries from all sources was $35 billion. It increased to $58 billion in 1975, $59 billion in 1976, and $64 billion in 1977, reflecting to a large extent developing countries' needs of finance as expressed in their current balance deficits, which for non-oil developing countries, amounted to $59 billion in 1975, to $46 billion in 1976, and to $42 billion in 1977.

The additional resources were used in 1976 and 1977 by a number of developing countries to increase their depleted reserves; the total reserves of non-oil developing countries increased by some $11 billion in 1976 and by some $12 billion in 1977. However, as real imports rose, reserves for most non-oil developing countries represent a lower number of months of imports than in the early 1970's

The Chart at left shows total resource flows by major type and origin. Three major sources can be distinguished.

● *DAC Countries*

As already noted, DAC countries provided in 1977 $43.7 billion of net financial resources to developing countries. About one third of this was provided at concessional terms. These flows from DAC countries represent over two-thirds of the developing countries' total receipts; if international bank lending is added, well above four-fifths.

● *International Bank Lending*

International bank lending (sometimes referred to as Euro-lending), is estimated to have amounted to some $11 billion net in 1977 compared to $10 billion in 1976

● *Non-DAC Donors*

The flow of financial resources from OPEC countries is estimated to have amounted in 1977 to some $9 billion, over 60 per cent of it at concessional terms, compared to $8.1 billion in 1976. Total OPEC flows represented over 3 per cent in terms of these countries' GNP in 1977 and concessional flows some 2 per cent of GNP. The major donors were Saudi Arabia, Kuwait, the United Arab Emirates and Iran. There are no data available for 1977 for aid from the centrally-planned-economy countries, which in 1976 amounted to $0.6 billion.

Reprinted from the OECD Observer, July 1978, p. 22.

II. *World Food Institutions and Policy Developments: Progress and Delays*

INTRODUCTORY COMMENTS

The decade of the 1970s has been one of intellectual and political ferment in the area of world food institution-building policies and programs. New institutions have been created; new funding policies have been devised and implemented; new trade negotiations, both in the General Agreement on Trade and Tariff (GATT) and the United Nations Conference on Trade and Development (UNCTAD), have been initiated, and are continuing; and, perhaps most importantly, the developing nations have organized themselves into the Group of 77, have formulated an extensive set of demands (the New International Economic Order-- NIEO), and are endeavoring through UNCTAD to have these NIEO demands translated into operational programs. World food policies and programs, of course, are only one, but an essential, aspect of all this international activity. The readings in this chapter were selected for the purpose of indicating the progress that has been made, and explaining why some of the delays have been politically unavoidable.

The World Food Council (WFC) was established by the UN General Assembly in late 1974 at the behest of the delegates to the World Food Conference. As stated in Resolution XXII, the duties and responsibilities of the World Food Council were designed to be, at least potentially, of major import. The resolution states: ". . .to serve as a co-ordinating mechanism to provide overall, integrated and continuing attention for the successful co-ordination and follow-up of policies concerning food production, nutrition, food security, food trade and food aid, as well as other related matters, by all the agencies of the United Nations system."

However, the Council has not been able to live up to the duties and obligations placed upon it. Nor should this have been expected; a "co-ordinating mechanism" is not designed to become a major instrument of power. The first session of the WFC, held in Rome in June 1975, was a "disaster" according to most U.S. delegates and observers, although to others the aggressive demands and disruptive tactics of the Group of 77 were only justly contentious and ideologically constructive. In any respect, the proposals and decisions of the Council at its subsequent meetings have, at best, brought about "some modest breakthroughs," to use Larry Minear's phrase. By and large, the Council meetings have provided a mechanism whereby the participating nations could reaffirm their acceptance of the resolutions accepted at the 1974 World Food Conference, and then re-assert their desire to fulfill them at some later date. Minear's review is more positive in its evaluation, but it seems fair to conclude that the WFC's Manila Declaration (1977) and its Mexico Declaration (1978) are, by and large, restatements of the resolutions adopted at the World Food Conference.

The World Bank has clearly established itself, in tandem with the regional development banks, as the international prime mover for agricultural and rural development funds to the poverty nations. Montague Yudelman's review of the World Bank's role is a useful description of that very important policy development.

The World Food Program (WFP), administered through the 30-nation Committee on Food Aid Policies and Programs, and responsible to the FAO and the UN's Economic and Social Council, has established itself as an influential international agency. Many nations are channeling all of their food contributions, in kind or money, through this organization. WFP programs are directed toward: (1) food for resource development; (2) food for infrastructure improvement projects; and (3) emergency situations. However, bilateral food aid from OECD countries to the developing nations still clearly dominates in this program area. Out of a total (estimated) food aid of just over $1.8 billion in 1977, slightly more than $1.3 billion was bilateral food aid, primarily through the P.L. 480 program of the United States; WFP accounted for the remainder-- $382 million.

Also, a new world agency--the International Fund for Agricultural Development (IFAD)--was finally established in 1978, with guaranteed funding of slightly more than $1 billion. Somewhat over half of that amount was pledged by OECD member-states, and most of the remainder by those within OPEC. How important IFAD will prove to be as a (concessional) lending agency cannot be determined at this point in time, but--assuming the continuing financial support of OECD and OPEC nations--its contributions could be significant.

The FAO, under new and aggressive leadership, is striving to reassert itself as the principal international food agency. Every two years (on the odd numbers) the FAO Conference, composed of all the member-nations, meets in Rome to review and direct, and budget for, the operations of FAO. Martin Kriesberg's account of that meeting indicates that there was a consensus on goals and objectives, with a fair amount of doubt and uncertainty over matters pertaining to strategies and funding.

The Multilateral Trade Negotiations (MTN) and the UNCTAD negotiations have been underway for several years now--since 1973 and 1975, respectively.

The MTN negotiating sessions, which take place in the GATT, are now coming to

an end; the UNCTAD meetings are continuing. In the former (i.e., MTN), agri-

culture has always been a kind of thistle in a bed of thorny roses, primarily

because all (there may be an exception or two) nation-states have protection-

ist attitudes and policies in the area of agricultural policies, differing in

degree but not so much in kind. Food grains, notably wheat and rice, are ex-

tremely difficult to negotiate in an international arena because of the con-

tinuing, uncompromising, populist political stands of domestic farm organiza-

tions, in particular. And the most persistent and well-nigh irreconcilable

controversy has been that between the United States and the European Economic

Community. By the end of 1978, it had become fairly clear to the interested

observer that some progress had been made in negotiations aimed at breaking

down the so-called NTBs (non-tariff trade barriers) and in consummating some

minor (yet undisclosed) tariff concessions, especially involving the United

States, European Economic Community, and Japan (a decrease in the U.S. protec-

tive tariffs on dairy products, for example). Nevertheless, the renewal of

the International Wheat Agreement was still unresolved at the year's end--

pricing decisions, release mechanisms, reserve stocks, and food aid allocations

were among the important matters yet to be successfully negotiated. And

success in the international fora (including the International Wheat Council)

would not necessarily, by any means, assure success in terms of their accep-

tance by the U.S. Congress.

The fifth reading in the MTN section is a bit of frosting, an interesting

example of how a seminal idea (one of Gale Johnson's) can be adopted by intel-

ligent and imaginative specialists (some staff members in IFPRI) and transformed into a policy proposal which could be useful to the developing nations, but which for several political reasons will not be negotiable. Its policy time is yet to come, perhaps.

Finally, it should be noted that the MTN negotiations in GATT have never provided a favorable forum for decision-making, in the view of Third World nations. Their weak power position in GATT was one of the principal reasons for the establishment of UNCTAD, and for the demands made for a New International Economic Order. Julius Katz's review of that controversy, and of the U.S. position in regard to it, is worth a careful reading, although it is clear that the policy positions of Third World nations would often be at serious odds with those of Katz. And the excerpt from Guy Erb's essay (a "development paper," to use the classification of the Overseas Development Council) is a pointed reminder that the interests, wishes, and concerns of human beings are at stake in these negotiations. This is an obvious deduction, to be sure, but there is a strong tendency for participants and observers to view such negotiations as an international chess game, more concerned with strategy and tactics than with moral compassion and human dignity.

WORLD FOOD COUNCIL

ISSUES BEFORE THE WORLD FOOD COUNCIL'S
FOURTH SESSION

prepared by the World Food Council, Rome

The World Food Council's fourth session will be held to review and spur further action on the decisions it took at its third session held in Manila in June 1977. The "Manila Communiqué: A Programme of Action for Eradicating Hunger and Malnutrition", adopted by the third session, is one of the most significant documents to appear in man's struggle with the problem of hunger. The Communiqué:

*identified major food issues;
*offered a comprehensive set of measures for the world community to act on;
*showed precisely where the stumbling-blocks are.

A year after the Manila Communiqué, many of the stumbling-blocks are still there, but the way to surmount them is becoming clearer. The fourth session will meet, stimulated by the hope engendered by the Programme of Action, but painfully conscious of the distance yet to be covered.

Focal Points of Debate

The focal point of the fourth session will be the implementation of the "Manila Communiqué" A Programme of Action to Eradicate Hunger and Malnutrition" with special consideration of specific measures to promote the implementation of the recommendations on food production, including the flow of resources and agricultural inputs, improving human nutrition, food security, food aid and food trade (Item 6). The specific points enumerated are those which the Manila Communiqué identified as the key aspects of the food problem requiring top priority consideration by the world community. The essential objectives of a strategy to solve the food problem and eradicate hunger and malnutrition were established by the World Food Conference held in Rome in 1974. What the Manila Communiqué did was:

*sharpen the focus of these objectives by outlining a medium and long-term programme of action to progressively eradicate hunger and malnutrition;
*identify certain areas in which action must be taken by governments and international agencies to achieve specific objectives.

Increasing Food Production and External Assistance

The basic solution to the world's food problems is to increase food productions, particularly in the food deficit developing countries. The Council called on governments and international agencies to accord special treatment to food priority countries (FPCs), those countries that have the worst food deficits, the greatest degree of malnutrition and the slowest rates of growth of food production, and to develop specific proposals for accelerating food production in these countries to at least 4 per cent per year. The Manila Communiqué also called on the international community to

Centre for Economic and Social Information, OPI/CESI Note Food/27, May 1978.

increase assistance to developing countries particularly FPCs, to $8.3 billion, of which $6.5 billion should be in concessional terms, in order to help them attain the 4 per cent growth rate. This amount is about double the present level of external assistance and it would have to be matched by a "substantial increase" in investments in food production in the FPCs themselves.

The Manila Communiqué recommended that the FPCs themselves determine:
a) the internal and external investment requirements to achieve the minimum 4 per cent rate of growth of food production; and
b) the internal policy and other constraints to be overcome to attain this growth.

The past year has recorded little positive progress toward these objectives. Fundamentally, food production is still not given the priority that the international community recognizes as necessary. The flow of external resources to agriculture, although it doubled in current prices between 1973 and 1977, has increased little in real terms since 1975. One notable achievement has been the creation of the International Fund for Agricultural Development (IFAD) as a new United Nations agency to marshall resources for food production. Its funds of $1 billion, however, are not adequate to meet the total requirements. IFAD's funds will need to be replenished promptly and major increases in other multilateral and bilateral development assistance funds are needed.

World Food Security
One intermediate objective of the Manila Communique is the establishment of an adequate world grain reserve system, which is essential in achieving world food security. Without food security, particularly in grain reserves, efforts to increase food supplies to the poorest populations will continue to be disrupted by shortages leading to high prices. Excessively low prices also threaten food security. They discourage farmers and production falls to dangerously low levels. The Manila Communiqué recommended that all countries with accumulated food grain stocks as a result of good harvests should convert these stocks into nationally held reserves.
The question of world food security is now dominated by the negotiation of a new Agreement to replace the International Wheat Agreement of 1978. An important feature of the new Agreement should be an international system of nationally held reserves. The Geneva Conference, held in March 1978 under the sponsorship of the United Nations Conference on Trade and Development (UNCTAD), ended without reaching an agreement and is to reconvene in September.

Nutrition
The Manila Communiqué called for nutrition improvement as a major objective of development efforts. In the past the problem of nutrition has largely been considered a part of the welfare sector, widely associated in the public mind with such fields as feeding programmes, nutrition education and the promotion of better balanced diets. The thrust of the Manila Communique's recommendations was to point to the need for a hunger-oriented nutrition effort to make more food available for the hungry through both fundamental development and welfare efforts.
The Council's eyes are now on the question of how major development actions are affecting food production and consumption directly or indirectly. Some development efforts are creating negative effects on the hungry.

Improving human nutrition through better development efforts combined with effective welfare actions is a formidable task, particularly in view of the general lack of understanding of the issue. The Manila Communique, in calling for new thinking by governments on the relationship between nutrition and development plans, recognized the need for increasingly forceful support by the United Nations system. The majority of the Communique's recommendations are directed at the agencies concerned, requesting them to take the first essential steps towards resolving obstacles to progress. The fourth session of the Council will consider a report by a committee of the agencies and consider what additional actions by governments and agencies are needed.

Food Aid

The World Food Conference of 1974 set a target for the minimum annual level of food aid to 10 million tons of cereals and called for "forward planning" by donor countries to maintain a stable supply of food aid. As the Council's fourth session meets, the 10 million ton target is still short by 400,000 tons. Moreover the certainty of these supplies is still not assured through forward planning and firm commitments.

The objectives of food aid, as indicated at the World Food Conference and the subsequent Council sessions, are to:
    *facilitate implementation of development programmes;
    *help developing countries build and maintain minimum food stocks;
    *help meet the requirements of nutrition programmes.

For this to happen, there should be an effective policy framework set by the international community and, at the same time, a formal international agreement which would assure continuity of a minimum level of 10 million tons of food aid irrespective of fluctuations in production and prices. The Manila Communique recommended the negotiation of a new Food Aid Convention (FAC) as part of a new International Wheat Agreement. At the negotiations at Geneva in March 1978 it was agreed that the new FAC should provide for 10 million tons a year. But the Conference ended inconclusively, to be reconvened in September 1978.

The General Assembly at its Seventh Special Session called for the establishment of an International Emergency Reserve to assist in meeting local food crises. Contributions to this Reserve, which is managed by the World Food Programme (WFP) reached 436,000 tons by February 1978 against the target of 500,000.

Food Trade

The Council's interest in trade lies in its potential contribution to stimulating food production in developing countries and overcoming the problem of hunger and malnutrition. Agricultural protection in developed countries has had an adverse impact on the food production prospects of developing countries. The Manila Communique called on governments to reduce the adverse effects on their domestic and foreign trade policies on the developing countries, particularly in the areas affecting food. The problem is on a negotiating table at UNCTAD and GATT, but little progress has been reported.

REPORT ON THE 4TH ANNUAL MEETING
OF THE WORLD FOOD COUNCIL

The United Nations World Food Council held its fourth annual meeting in Mexico City from June 12-14, following a preparatory session the previous week. In attendance were Cabinet-level representatives of most of the Council's 36-member governments as well as observers from non-member governments, international agencies, and non-governmental organizations.

The Council was set up following the 1974 U.N. World Food Conference to monitor the changing world hunger picture and to keep before governments and international agencies the needs of the world's chronically hungry and malnourished people. This year's session took a limited number of specific actions which should prove useful to the international community in the coming years. Contained in the Mexico Declaration approved by consensus, they include the following:

(1) The adoption of a world food situation assessment which accentuates the persistence of the world food problem.

The Council noted progress in a number of areas in the past year. Food production has increased worldwide, with "global food and fertilizer supplies (now) relatively plentiful." The International Fund for Agricultural Development (IFAD) has been established and has funded its first projects. Pledges of almost 450,000 tons of food have been received for the 500,000 ton international emergency reserve, and food aid pledges toward the annual 10 million ton target are up. Several individual countries have now developed national food and nutrition strategies. India has made considerable progress in improving its production and stock performance.

At the same time, the Council expressed concern about such developments as these:

● Many of the above gains have resulted from more favorable weather rather than from revamped policies of governments and "could have been expected to materialize in the normal course of events." Most such gains were not experienced by the Food Priority (or poorest) Countries, wherein per capita food production has actually declined in the 1970s. Particular concern was expressed for emergency situations and abnormal shortages in the Sahel, Afghanistan, Indonesia, Laos, Lebanon, Nepal, and Vietnam.

● The world's undernourished people increased in number from about 400 million at the beginning of this decade to about 455 million at mid-decade. Almost all of the new hunger

Larry Minear is with Church World Service/Lutheran World Relief and served as an advisor to the U.S. delegation to the World Food Council meeting in Mexico City, June 1978.

localized in the Food Priority Countries, where "the level
of human nutrition...has deteriorated." The general picture
is "pessimistic," with the most vulnerable groups continuing
to be pre-school and school-age children and younger women.

- Up to one third of the world's children die from malnutrition
  and disease before age five; 25-50% of those who survive
  experience severe or moderate protein-energy malnutrition.
  Each year there are at least 100,000 new cases of blindness
  in children caused by vitamin A deficiency. About 200 million
  persons suffer from endemic goitre related to iodine deficiency, millions from nutritional anemia related to iron
  deficiency.

- Resources available for development have not grown significantly, either external aid from donors or internal resources
  from developing countries themselves. After gains in real
  terms of 59% in 1974 and 14% in 1975, official commitments
  of external assistance to agriculture (broadly defined) showed
  a net loss of 15% in 1976.

- An international network of national food reserves has yet to
  be established, although negotiations are continuing to
  replace the expiring International Wheat Agreement with new
  arrangements. The world's annual food aid target of 10 million tons
  has not been reached, although commitments of 9.2 million tons
  for 1977/78 represent the largest amount made available since
  1972/73.

- Changes in international trade arrangements have not been
  negotiated which would provide economic stimulus and stability
  to developing countries. Rising protectionism is felt to be
  handicapping the food production, development, and trade
  efforts of such countries. Export earnings in 1977 of the
  non-OPEC developing countries increased by about 20% over
  1976, the cost of their imports by about 13%. Their 1977
  trade deficit of $20 billion was down from $27 billion the
  previous year.

In short, the Council's consensus about the food situation was a sober-
ing if not lugubrious one. "The rate of progress toward solving fundamental food problems is too slow....The world community seems unwilling
to go beyond a certain minimum point in solving food problems, and (a)
tendency is emerging to return to traditional methods within traditional priorities."

(2) A reaffirmation of political will.

Ministers at the Council meetings recognized, as had the World Food
Conference itself, that "a higher political priority for food" is
urgently needed. They reiterated pledges made by governments in 1974
and at Council meetings each year since. They reaffirmed the basic

compact between developed and developing countries, the former agreeing to increase the flow of resources for food production and integrated rural development, the latter to revise their own policies toward faster progress on the hunger agenda.

Many of the Council's policy recommendations simply reiterated earlier commitments, now with somewhat more country-specificity and urgency than previously. Developed countries would "take urgent steps to reach the official development assistance target of 0.7% of GNP." Developing countries would "ensure a more effective use of available resources," also fashioning national food and nutrition plans which would then receive priority consideration by the international community.

In the key policy areas of food production, nutrition, food security, food aid, and food trade, the language of the Council's discussions and of the resulting Mexico Declaration was framed largely in terms of "reaffirming," "continuing to address," "accelerating" and "intensifying" current efforts. The basic course of action has long since been agreed upon. What the Council felt to be needed is not a rethinking of solutions but an acceleration of their application to existing problems.

For the most part, the Council's role is primarily one of monitoring and urging governments and international agencies. The principal responsibility for action lies elsewhere:

- For carrying out projects, with governments and U.N.-related agencies such as the FAO, the U.N. Development Program, and the World Bank.

- For improving the effectiveness of nutrition efforts within the U.N. system, with the Subcommittee on Nutrition of the U.N.'s Administrative Committee on Coordination and individual agencies such as the FAO, UNICEF and the World Health Organization.

- For negotiating improved food security, with the International Wheat Council, the U.N. Conference on Trade and Development (UNCTAD) and, more generally, with the Committee on World Food Security.

- For negotiating better policies for food aid programs, with the World Food Program'_ Committee on Food Aid Policies and Programs, and for negotiating more responsive trade arrangements, with the Multilateral Trade Negotiations (MTN) of the General Agreement on Tariffs and Trade (GATT), UNCTAD, and the Negotiating Conference on a Common Fund.

The Council took note of the need for more decisive action on all of these various fronts and sought to rekindle the necessary commitments at the highest political levels to get on with the job.

(3) <u>Some modest breakthroughs</u>.

For all of its reaffirmations, the Council did break new ground in several areas. These included the following:

- Agreement to request the U.N. General Assembly to make the 500,000 ton <u>international emergency reserve</u> a "continuing reserve with yearly replenishment." Previous discussions had viewed the reserve as an interim device pending the establishment of a world food grain reserve. Soon the reserve is likely to become more permanent, existing side by side with whatever broader world food reserve is agreed upon. A pledge announced at the Council meeting by the Netherlands brought aggregate contributions to 445,000 tons.

  (Other food aid pledges were also announced: West Germany, 47,000 tons to the Sahel emergency; Australia, a substantial increase for each of three years in its ongoing food aid program; and Canada, a moderate increase as well.)

- The adoption of specific steps to improve <u>human nutrition</u>. In this area, which proved the least contentious of any, the Council agreed on the goal of eradicating vitamin A-deficiency and endemic goitre within a decade and of combatting iron-deficiency anemia. The World Health Organization, which had urged the vitamin A and goitre targets, will be asked to develop an action plan to accomplish these objectives.

  The Council also urged that steps be taken to assess better the extent of malnutrition from year to year, to improve income distribution, to factor nutrition objectives into other development activities, to establish food and nutrition surveillance systems, and to make the eradication of hunger and malnutrition a major objective of the U.N. system and of governments.

- Action to encourage <u>pairing developing country needs with existing and potential international resources</u>. Matching external resources with internal food production needs and strategies constituted the major mission of the now disbanded Consultative Group on Food Production and Investment in Developing Countries (CGFPI). Consortia of bilateral donors and multilateral agencies also perform this function to a certain extent with reference to specific countries such as Bangladesh and Indonesia. However, the Council felt that better and wider coordination is a necessary and useful means of encouraging developing countries to do long-term planning and bilateral donors and international agencies with external resources to target them accordingly.

These reaffirmations and steps forward represent, it must be said, fairly modest achievements for the World Food Council at its 4th Session. Many had hoped for more. Many delegations came, like the U.S., prepared to participate constructively, and did so. But the results provide little to write home about. There was a general feeling that optimum use was not made of the time of Cabinet-level government officials, that too much was reaffirmed and too little forward movement generated. Some of these problems have resulted in changes agreed upon for the 5th Council meeting, to be held in Canada probably in the fall of next year.

It is true that the Mexico City meeting did not generate a new burst of international political energy on food issues. Though many of the major players were present, their interaction did not crystallize into any new initiatives or produce any noteworthy new momentum. Before writing off the meeting or the Council, however, it would be well to keep several factors in mind.

While the Council is the U.N.'s highest political body dealing with food issues, its political task extends beyond the Council itself. Its report goes to the Economic and Social Council of the United Nations for discussion and action this summer and then on to the General Assembly for adoption in the fall. Its findings and recommendations therefore may generate additional attention and support in the process.

The Council's role, while a high-level one, is at the same time rather limited. "We recognize our responsibility as the guiding force within the United Nations system on all food matters," declared the ministers. "We also recognize that operational decisions are made by governments, international organizations and fora whose activities bear on the world food situation and we seek their full cooperation." The makers of operational decisions have their own parliaments, cabinets, juntas and governing councils--some more cooperative and effective than others, but none responsible to the World Food Council as such.

In the matter of world food security, for example, the governments which make up the Council, many of them themselves deadlocked in discussions in Europe to negotiate a new International Wheat Agreement, called on each other "to re-examine their commitment to world food security" and to "seek out new initiatives with a view to achieving an early agreement" which will safeguard the interests of developing countries. In the matter of linking increased funds for development with decreased expenditures on armaments, the Council simply noted the connection and challenged governments at the U.N. Special Session on Disarmament to act on this crucial issue. In neither case were there any "breakthroughs." Governments were not willing to be more forthcoming in Mexico City than in other forums--nor was pressure generated at the Council meeting sufficient to facilitate progress elsewhere.

The Council is, in the final analysis, only as good a vehicle for progress in international food matters as governments are willing to make it. Certainly after four years of existence, it is now taken seriously by most governments and international agencies as a monitor of the world food scene, an advocate of the world's malnourished people, a goader of governments and international organizations, an orchestrator of resources, and, to a limited extent, a focal point for the concerned international public. It has also played a role in the progress made since 1974, such as it has been, on hunger and malnutrition issues.

What continues to elude the Council, and for that matter the international community, is how to turn the Council's somber message--that the World Food Conference goal of a hunger-free world will never be realized at the current rate of progress--from an annual lament into a springboard for action. The Council's "fears for the future" have yet to become an engine to head that future off. Its elaborate documentation, based on comprehensive data-gathering and analysis primarily by FAO, need to become energizing rather than paralyzing.

There are some encouraging straws in the wind. Governments in Mexico City expressed the desire for the Council to become a more activist body, more visible in the months between its annual meetings, more hard-hitting in its monitoring and more persistent in its badgering. There are indications that the Council's dynamic President, Philippines Minister of Agriculture Arturo R. Tanco, will be able to give even more time to Council responsibilities during the coming year. The appointment announced this week by Secretary General Kurt Waldheim of Maurice Williams (formerly of AID and the Development Assistance Committee of the OECD) as the Council's new Executive Director, replacing Dr. John A. Hannah, should provide an occasion for re-examining the Council's style and approach.

However, whether the Council will become more successful in helping the international community accelerate its hunger action remains to be seen. Indications are that few governments take seriously enough the magnitude of the task, either in terms of internal policy changes or of substantially expanded external resources, to abandon the current "business as usual" approach. Few seem willing to address, singly or in concert, the structural changes which continue to prevent the world's food system from working for everyone. The international community has been slow to act during this sheltered time between excruciating world food shortages to build a more food secure future. While governments are accepting the Council's message that the world's emperors and institutions are down to their socks, they hardly seem to be queuing up at the tailor's.

Meanwhile, however, the Council remains an agency whose future needs to be assured and whose multi-faceted work deserves the active support of all who are concerned about the intractable problems of hunger and malnutrition.

THE WORLD BANK

BACKGROUND PAPER ON THE
WORLD FOOD SITUATION (EXCERPTS)

by Montague Yudelman

III. WORLD BANK ASSISTANCE TO AGRICULTURE AND RURAL DEVELOPMENT

22. The World Bank and its affiliate, the International Development
Association (IDA), will be lending almost $3,300 million for agriculture and
rural development during the fiscal year ending June 30, 1978. The year's
record lending brings the cumulative total of Bank and IDA commitments for
agriculture and rural development in the last five fiscal years to some
$10,000 million (in current dollars) -- making the Bank and IDA the largest
source of multilateral assistance for this purpose.

23. Increased Bank and IDA lending for agriculture and rural development
is part of a strategy first enunciated by the World Bank President McNamara
in 1973. The objectives of the Bank's rural development policy include
sustained increases in per capita output and incomes, expansion of productive
employment and greater equity in the distribution of benefits of growth.

24. The Bank also tries to alleviate the world's food problems by
increasing food production in the developing countries where the malnourished
people are. This in turn means increasing the productivity of the small
farmer. Recent studies in developing countries demonstrate that, given proper
conditions and incentives, the small farms can be as productive as big farms.

25. The Bank's lending for agriculture and rural development during
the past five years has been as follows:

World Bank/IDA Lending for Agriculture and Rural Development

Fiscal Years	Amount in $ Millions
1974	956
1975	1,858
1976	1,628
1977	2,303
1978	3,300 (Estimate)

Printed by the World Bank June 6, 1978. Montague Yudelman is Director,
Agriculture and Rural Development Department, The World Bank.

26. Estimates are that at full development the agriculture and rural development projects financed by the Bank and IDA during the five years would result in additional production of 13 million tons of cereals annually in the late 1980s.

27. Figures available for 359 agriculture and rural development projects approved during the past five fiscal years indicate that the number of direct beneficiaries may exceed 18 million farm families. Most of the beneficiaries are small farmers with low per capita incomes. Thus, over the period FY 1974 to 1978, some 100 million people stand to benefit directly from Bank and IDA assisted projects in this sector. Moreover, within the total for agriculture and rural development, there has been a sharp rise in the share of lending for rural development -- that is, for projects in which more than half the direct benefits are expected to accrue to the rural poor. In FY 1978, the share of rural development is estimated to be 55%, compared with 61% in 1977, 50% in 1976 and 53% in 1975.

Evolution of the Bank's Strategy

28. It is important to emphasize the evolving nature of the Bank's approach to agriculture. At first it made no loans for agriculture, because agriculture was not seen to be a major problem. Development thinking concentrated on industrialization, transport, power, etc. It was assumed that there was enough land and local labor to produce all the subsistence needed by local populations. However, the Bank soon recognized that agricultural growth and increased production was necessary for development, and that agricultural development required involvement in a wide range of rural investments. The Bank embarked on a very wide spectrum of activities -- irrigation, credit mechanisms, agricultural research, extension services; all the panoply needed to make farmers more productive.

29. By widening its lending, the Bank was increasing production, but the benefits of this increase were not necessarily widespread. A classic illustration of this has been the Bank's lending for livestock in Latin America. Its first efforts were made largely through commercial banks. Funds were made available to governments which passed these through commercial banks to large livestock producers. The large cattle ranchers increased production, and both exports and growth increased. The Bank's analysis showed, however, that these loans had little direct impact on the creation of jobs, and that the income that was generated from these investments was not being widely distributed. It appeared to us that very large numbers of small farmers were getting no benefit whatsoever from loans of this kind. The Bank moved, therefore, to the next phase of lending: that of rural development. This is the phase in which the Bank is at the moment, and involves trying to raise the productivity and incomes of many who seldom benefit from traditional investments.

30. Rural development, in our terminology, means addressing poverty head on. To do so, the Bank has shifted its emphasis from financing large-scale producers to financing small-scale producers, although large farmers

are assisted in many projects. The importance of this small-farm thrust is
nowhere more evident than in dealing with the rice producers of Asia, especially in, say, West Bengal in India, where there are extremely large numbers
of very small producers and where rice production has tended to be stagnant.

31.   Part of the purpose of this new emphasis is to deal with the
problem of poor people and low consumption. We strongly believe that if the
small producers of, say, West Bengal increase their production of rice -- and
our projects indicate that this can be done -- they will then consume more
of this rice and will have a larger market surplus. This in turn will help
the country in two ways: by increasing production and reducing the need
for imports; and by raising the levels of consumption and nutrition of low-
income groups.

Capital Requirements of Agricultural Development

32.   A number of excercises have been attempted to evaluate the capital
requirements for agricultural development and food production. The major
lesson which the Bank has learned is that we have to reject many previous
assumptions about agricultural development in developing countries which were
a carryover from "colonial" thinking. We thought that there was enough land
and enough labor; that the indigenous population could produce enough food
for themselves; and that the main constraint on food production was a demand
constraint, i.e., one could easily produce food but there was no market for
it. We are finding out in reality that food production requires more and
more capital and that low-cost means of agricultural production are very
difficult to find. In some parts of the world, the World Bank has certainly
evolved low-cost improvements. It has worked to help governments to improve
their research and extension services, their credit facilities and so forth.
This has been effective -- but, in terms of infrastructure, we have found
that there is simply no cheap means of developing agriculture. The amount
of this capital requirement varies enormously and it is almost impossible
to give a figure. But we do know that requirements for development of
irrigation alone are well in excess of $100 billion. Total flow of funds
from all sources to developing country agriculture was just over $5 billion
in 1976.

33.   The problem is becoming more serious and the capital requirements
greater. This worsening is due in great part to the population side of the
equation, especially when one wants to deal with nutritional issues instead
of concentrating merely on the issue of market demand. Recent progress
has been heartening, especially in South Asia, but this should not blind us
to the tremendous task of meeting both market requirements and nutritional
needs of the poor.

INTERNATIONAL FUND FOR AGRICULTURAL DEVELOPMENT

NEW AGRICULTURAL FUND APPROVES
FIRST CONCESSIONAL LOANS TO
SRI LANKA AND UNITED REPUBLIC OF TANZANIA

prepared by IFAD, Rome

Four months after its establishment, the International Fund for Agricultural Development (IFAD), the $1 billion fund for agricultural development and the newest United Nations specialized agency, has approved its first loans on highly concessional terms to two food deficit developing countries, Sri Lanka and the United Republic of Tanzania. The two IFAD loans are $12 million each, with a 50-year amortization including a 10-year grace period, and a 1 per cent service charge a year.

The announcement was made in Rome on 14 April by the IFAD President, Abdelmuhsin Al-Sudeary, at the end of a meeting of the Fund's Executive Board (10 to 13 April). The Fund was established last December when the 114 Member States met in Rome to start activities. The 18 Executive Directors and the alternates who make up the Board were elected by the Fund's Governing Council, with six of them representing each of the three categories of membership-- Organization for Economic Co-operation and Development (OECD) developed countries, the Organization of Petroleum Exporting Countries (OPEC) developing countries and the developing recipient nations.

In his announcement, Mr. Al-Sudeary said in the four months since the beginning of operations, the Fund had already shown that it was "an action-oriented organization." A major increase in food crop production with direct benefits to some 8,320 farm families, mostly small farmers and landless cultivators, was expected to result from the project IFAD will help finance a co-financing arrangement with the Asian Development Bank in Sri Lanka, he added.

On the other hand, a major integrated rural development project in the United Republic of Tanzania will yeild substantial economic and social results. It will use the recently constituted villages as the main vehicle for development. This project is expected to be co-financed with the International Development Association (IDA) of the World Bank Group. The IFAD loan will become effective as soon as the IDA credit is approved.

The President said he would submit a number of other projects to the next meeting of the Board in July, for possible co-financing with international financial institutions. Meanwhile, IFAD would organize several project identification and preparation missions to build up its own pipeline of projects for exclusive financing by the Fund. He added that requests for such missions had been received from some 17 countries so far. The investment centre of the Food and Agriculture Organization (FAO), in particular, was co-operating fully with the Fund to accelerate the manning and expeditious field work of these missions. "Subject to the availability of good projects, our aim is to commit about $150 million during 1978 and possible $300 to $350 during 1979,"

Centre for Economic and Social Information, OPI/CESI Note Food/35, 17 April 1978.

the President pointed out.

IFAD has laready concluded co-operation agreements with FAO, the United Nations Development Programme (UNDP), the World Bank and the three regional development banks--the African Development Bank, the Asian Development Bank and the Inter-American Development Bank. In addition, it will be discussing soon other possible agreements with the International Labour Organisation (ILO), the United Nations Industrial Development Organization (UNIDO), and the Islamic Development Bank. Thus, the Fund will expand its co-operation with the United Nations system as well as with regional and also national institutions.

Mr. Al-Sudear said an intensive staffing and organizational work had been carried out during the first months of activities. He had appointed Philip Birnbaum (United States) as Vice-President and Sartzj Aziz (Pakistan), Abbas Ordoobadi (Iran) and Moise Mensah (Benin) as Assistant Presidents in charge of three departments--economic and planning, general affairs and project management, respectively. Meantime M. P. Benjamin is acting head of the project management department. Other appointments had been made at all levels and with a small staff of less than 50 professionals and an equal number of support staff during the first year of operation the Fund would in no way duplicate the work of existing international institutions.

Focus on the Poor

The first loans approved by IFAD meet the three main objectives of its lending policies and criteria: (1) increasing food production; (2) reducing rural poverty through larger incomes and new employment opportunities for rural populations; and (3) improving nutritional standards.

The main reason for the establishment of the Fund as a new aid-giving agency was to provide additional resources for a large but specific goal: To help launch a direct attack on malnutrition in developing countries. It is essential, IFAD holds, to substantially increase food production in many developing countries as soon as possible, particularly those food deficit countries in which food production is not keeping pace with the growth of population. IFAD believes that if the benefits of increased food production do not reach the poor people directly these people will remain hungry or malnourished, and bypassed by development.

The initial capital resources of the Fund are over $1 billion ($1.022.1 million). They were made available through voluntary contributions from the OECD countries ($567.3 million), the OPEC developing countries ($435.5 million) and the developing recipient nations ($19.3 million).

Sri Lanka Project

The main objective of the Kirindi Oya Irrigation and Settlement Project, co-financed with the Asian Development Bank, is to rehabilitate and expand irrigation systems in an area of about 12,900 hectares to increase food production and provide homes, land and basic social services to about 8,320 farm families in newly opened areas. The project is part of the Government programme to develop the vast "dry zone" of the country. It will also create employment and raise the income and living conditions of farmers. The "dry zone" has good agricultural potential but lacks adequate irrigation facilities. The Government accords high priority to the project. The total investment cost of it is estimated at $39.2 million.

Project works will include the rehabilitation of the existing irrigation system, construction of a dam, canals, distributaries, farm ditches and drains. New land will be developed for cultivation, and the project reservoir will make possible irrigation for multiple cropping of paddy, cotton and subsidiary food crops.

As a result of the project, production of paddy is estimated to increase by 41,760 metric tons a year, and there will be additional employment for about 6.2 million man–days during the seven–year period of construction and 800,000 man–days a year after the completion of the project. The major beneficiaries will be the small farmers in the areas, most of whom are landless labourers or shifting cultivators. They will be provided with land and homes, and will benefit from the provision of water supply, public health care and schools. On completion of the project, it will be possible for a farmer to have two crops on the irrigated land, and his annual net income is expected to increase twofold.

Tanzania Project

The Mwanza/Shinyanga Rural Development Project, which is expected to be co–financed with the International Development Association (IDA) of the World Bank Group, will constitute the first phase of a long–term Government programme designed to improve the social and economic conditions of rural populations in those two regions of the country. The main objectives of the programme will be to increase productivity in agriculture, forestry, livestock and small–scale industries, to improve health, education and water sypply, and to strengthen the supporting infrastructure and technical services. The programme will place the recently constituted villages at the centre of the development process by mobilizing the villagers to participate in the planning and imple- mentation of the infrastructure and services. The village self–help programme is a new approach to development being implemented by the Government. The total project costs over a five–year period of investment are estimated at $30.3 million.

The project will finance a road network, agricultural inputs, seed production, village–level trails, improved village poultry production, develop- ment of forestry plantation, reorganization of agricultural and livestock extension services, research on cassava, oxen–drawn equipment, and credit for village investments.

At the completion of the first five–year period, the estimated value of increased production will be $2.1 million for crop products (an increase of 81 per cent). Maize and sorghum production will be augmented through the intro- duction of improved seed and seed dressing, and that of cassava through improved planting materials of high–yield varieties. These technical improve- ments will generate an estimated increased production of 13,600 tons of maize, 13,500 tons of sorghum and 29,600 tons of cassava.

All farm holdings, irrespective of size, will benefit from the project activities. However, the target groups to which the project will deliver the largest benefits are the small farmers. The project will aim at increasing the per capita crop income of the farmers by an average of 25 per cent and the number of direct beneficiaries of the project could well reach 700,000 persons.

53

FOOD AND AGRICULTURE ORGANIZATION AND WORLD FOOD PROGRAM

$10 MILLION-A-MINUTE PLEDGES TO
WFP AT NEW YORK CONFERENCE

In little more than two hours some 54 countries pledged the record amount of nearly $631 million to the World Food Programme at its Pledging Conference for 1979-80 at United Nations headquarters in New York at the end of February. This amount, which represents two thirds of the $950 million target figure, is reported to be the highest in value terms ever pledged at a one-day conference for any United Nations agency or programme.

Some $495 million worth of the pledges announced comprised commodities, while the remaining $136 million were in cash and services.

The Executive Director, Mr. G.N. Vogel, described himself as "happy" at the outcome on his return to Rome.

"When you consider that more was pledged to the Programme in a single day than has been pledged to date for the current 1977-78 biennium ($613 million), I think we did very well," he said.

He cautioned, however, against over-optimism.

"Even if we get large pledges from those donors who have not yet announced their intentions, it is unlikely that these will make good the shortfall of $319 million," he said. "The Programme must have supplementary pledges if we are to reach the target."

On an earlier occasion Mr. Vogel pointed out that the Programme could achieve its target if donors who currently provided $2 000 million worth of food aid a year bilat-erally were simply to channel $100 million of that aid through the Programme.

The largest donors again were the United States and Canada — $220 million and $190 million respectively. Because of the depreciation of its currency by 10 percent in the past year, however, Canada's pledge has been officially registered at $173 million (U.S. dollars) — some $17 million less than Canada had intended. There is always the possibility, of course, that by the time Canada's contribution is taken up the exchange rate may have moved upward in the Programme's favour.

For the first time the U.S. pledge was unqualified by a matching clause under which her previous contributions were conditional on the total amount pledged by other nations.

In common with some other donor countries, Saudi Arabia, which has contributed a total of $100 million in cash between 1975 and 1978, has yet to announce her pledge. The Programme's third largest donor, the EEC, was represented at the Conference but the Community's delegate said that while it had every intention of pledging, it was not yet in a position to announce the size of its contribution.

Other major donors who pledged included: Australia ($10.7 million); Denmark ($35.6 million); German FR ($35.4 million); Japan ($10 million); Netherlands ($46.3 million); Norway ($34 million); Sweden ($25 million); United Kingdom ($15.6 million).

Once again a number of developing countries which have received WFP assistance demonstrated what

the Executive Director has described as "an unusual and heart-warming feature of the Programme", by pledging as much as they were able in commodities or cash. Bangladesh pledged $200 000 worth of commodities; Bhutan $1 000 (cash); Colombia $465 000 ($10 000 cash); Cuba $1 250 000 (commodities); Cyprus $1 305 (cash); The Gambia $5 000 (cash); Iceland $16 000 (cash); Lao $1 000 (cash); Malta $2 500 (cash); Swaziland $2 300 (cash); Tunisia $50 000 (cash).

The U.N. Secretary-General, Dr. Kurt Waldheim, who opened the Conference, reminded donors of the Programme's need to know their intended contributions as early as possible.

"Food aid needs a more dependable base," he declared. "It would be helpful if food-surplus countries would make more specific and longer-term commitments than they do at present to facilitate systematic and effective planning."

In a statement which brought the Programme's activities up to date, Mr. Vogel said it had received support from 116 nations and contributed to the development of 112 countries in 882 projects for social and economic development and 336 emergency operations.

"In a world containing 700 million seriously malnourished people we are at best about to scratch the surface of alleviating world suffering and hunger," the Executive Director said.

The U.S. representative, Ms. Kathleen Bitterman, said that whereas the United States once matched the rest of the world's pledges to the Programme dollar for dollar, this was

World Food Programme News, April-June 1978, pp. 1-3.

no longer necessary.

"For WFP has developed strong international support, thus making it the joint effort and responsibility of many countries," she said. "We note with appreciation the efforts by many other donors to increase and to make their food aid more effective." The U.S. pledge for 1979-80 raised its total contribution to more than $1 thousand million.

In announcing Canada's pledge, the Minister of Agriculture, Mr. Eugene F. Whelan, described WFP as being "unique".

"It is different from the World Bank, UNDP, bilateral food aid or other international agencies," he said. "Its strength lies in being a people's programme with tens of millions of people in developing countries being involved."

The Minister added that Canada, which had on a number of occasions in the past given supplementary contributions in addition to its pledge, was reviewing its 1978 commodity pledge.

STOP PRESS

Saudi Arabia to pledge $55 million

Saudi Arabia has announced that it will pledge $55 million in cash to the Programme for 1979-80. This represents an increase of $5 million over the previous two pledging periods, for each of which it gave $50 million.

The Saudi Arabian intention was conveyed to Mr. Edouard Saouma, Director-General of FAO, by Crown Prince Fahd on behalf of King Khalid when the Director-General visited the country at the end of March.

This brings total pledges for the biennium to $686 million — 72 percent of the target — and increases cash contributions to $291 million.
(A recent report by the United Nations Commission for Trade Aid and Development [UNCTAD] shows that net disbursements of concessional aid to developing countries by OPEC amounted to $5.2 million in 1976. Saudi Arabia was the second largest bilateral aid donor, second only to the United States.)

PLEDGES 1979-80 BIENNIUM

. . . . (in U.S. dollars) . . . .

Donor country	Commodities	Cash	Services	Total
Australia	7 159 090	3 522 727	—	10 681 817
Austria	4 275 000	475 000	—	4 750 000
Bangladesh	200 000	—	—	200 000
Barbados	—	6 500	—	6 500
Belgium	1 857 575	930 303	—	2 787 878
Bhutan	—	1 000	—	1 000
Central African Empire	—	7 000	—	7 000
Canada	154 545 454	18 181 818	—	172 727 272
Chile	—	35 000	—	35 000
Colombia	455 000	10 000	—	465 000
Cuba	1 250 000	—	—	1 250 000
Cyprus	—	1 305	—	1 305
Denmark	24 347 826	12 173 913	—	36 521 739
Ecuador	—	50 000	—	50 000
Egypt, AR	350 000	—	—	350 000
Fiji	—	1 000	—	1 000
Finland	2 172 839	691 358	—	2 864 197
Gambia	—	5 000	—	5 000

PLEDGES 1979-80 BIENNIUM (continued) .... (in U.S. dollars) ....

Donor country	Commodities	Cash	Services	Total
Germany, FR	23 584 905	11 792 452	—	35 377 357
Greece	180 000	—	—	180 000
Honduras	—	10 000	—	10 000
Hungary	360 000	—	—	360 000
Iceland	—	16 000	—	16 000
India	—	1 250 000	—	1 250 000
Ireland	1 634 050	812 133	—	2 446 183
Italy	—	693 641	—	693 641
Japan	6 666 667	3 333 333	—	10 000 000
Jordan	—	45 000	—	45 000
Korea, Rep.	—	100 000	—	100 000
Kuwait	—	400 000	—	400 000
Lao	—	1 000	—	1 000
Lebanon	—	20 000	—	20 000
Madagascar	—	—	—	—
Malta	—	2 200	—	2 200
Mexico	100 000	100 000	—	200 000
Morocco	—	11 363	—	11 363
Netherlands	30 837 004	15 418 502	—	46 255 506
New Zealand	933 333	466 667	—	1 400 000
Norway	22 651 933	11 418 047	—	34 069 980
Pakistan	470 000	—	—	470 000
Panama	—	1 000	—	1 000
Philippines	—	95 238	—	95 238
Spain	—	400 000	—	400 000
Sudan	50 301	—	—	50 301
Swaziland	—	2 300	—	2 300
Sweden	17 204 301	8 602 150	—	25 806 451
Switzerland	1 515 151	757 575	—	2 272 726
Tanzania	—	44 191	—	44 191
Thailand	25 000	—	—	25 000
Tunisia	—	50 000	—	50 000
United Kingdom	10 437 050	5 218 526	—	15 655 576
United States of America	182 000 000	4 000 000	34 000 000	220 000 000
Viet Nam	10 000	—	—	10 000
Yugoslavia	400 000	—	—	400 000
Total	**495 672 479**	**101 153 242**	**34 000 000**	**630 825 721**

FAO COUNCIL GIVES IMPETUS
TO NEW ACTION PROGRAMS

by Martin Kriesberg

The FAO Council meeting held in Rome November 27-December 7 projected the image of a newly energized, action-oriented organization in the service of developing countries. This was the tenor of the opening speech by Director General Saouma as he cited the need for greater assistance, particularly to the poorest, least developed countries, to increase their food self-sufficiency and alleviate hunger and malnutrition.

Only one topic on the agenda was controversial: the FAO's Technical Co-operation Program (TCP) which is financed out of regular program funds. The U.S. Delegate led a group of major donor countries in questioning the use of assessed budget monies for this purpose and challenged the need for expanding the program. Developing countries strongly championed the TCP as providing a needed and unique form of ready assistance and extolled the "dynamic" Director General, who said it was a cornerstone of his administration. Agreement was reached on a continuation of the program, a second evaluation later, and muted language on new criteria for using the TCP. There was no agreement on funding levels, but the Director General indicated he would propose a larger budget allocation for TCP.

Most countries urged a stronger FAO commitment and program on food and nutrition matters. The United States offered to support FAO efforts through USAID's parallel bilateral program and, possibly, with technical personnel from USDA's new Human Nutrition Center. The United States also indicated that technical assistance resources should be provided through voluntary contributions rather than assessed contributions from donor countries. FAO's ad hoc Committee on Food and Nutrition Policies received support for its work, but approval of a new standing committee on the subject was delayed until after next Spring, when FAO's Committee on Agriculture will have food and nutrition as a major part of its agenda, to test whether the work should be continued in that body. Most developing countries speaking on the subject referred to the problem of malnutrition among the world's impoverished millions. Most developed countries referred to a need to assess the impact of current programs to focus on food and nutrition issues rather than on increasing production per se.

The topic of a new International Food Corps, first mentioned by U.S. Ambassador Young in a speech at the FAO Conference in 1977, sparked a lively discussion. Examples of related national programs were described by several developing countries and offers of assistance through bilateral volunteer groups were made. The FAO Secretariat agreed cautiously to further explorations of a coordinating and advisory role, pending a clarification on how such a program might be organized and funded. There was a wide range of experiences and concepts about food corps volunteers; the idea was clearly subject to

Newsletter of International Development Organizations, USDA Office of International Cooperation and Development, November-December 1978. Martin Kriesberg is Coordinator for International Organization Affairs.

different treatments.

Other topics discussed included an assessment of the food and agricultural situation. Most speakers on the subject welcomed the increased production of recent years and the growing stocks of grain that resulted. But many developing countries remained concerned by the concentration of reserve stock holdings and the absence of an international agreement which would institutionalize stock holdings.

Some differences on FAO's relationship with other U.N. Agencies and particularly with the UNDP surfaced in discussions on the topic of restructuring the U.N. system as it pertains to social and economic development.

MULTILATERAL TRADE NEGOTIATIONS

FOUR ISSUES SEEN SHAPING
FUTURE OF U.S. FARM TRADE

by Dr. G. Edward Schuh

Trade is important to any assessment of the outlook for either the U.S. economy or agriculture. The corollary, of course, is that developments in other countries, both in terms of policies and in terms of output, are important influences on how well both U.S. farmers and consumers will fare this next year.

The shape of that trade in the future will be influenced by:

• The multilateral trade negotiations;

• Changes in currency values;

• The need for positive adjustment policies; and

• Interactions between domestic and trade policies.

The Multilateral Trade Negotiations

After 4 years of rather protracted and difficult negotiations, this ambitious effort was to have been wrapped up by last July 15. Things did not work out that way, and the next target date is December 15.

Here are at least some of the general issues:

The first and perhaps foremost point to be noted is that in the current round of discussions an effort has been made from the beginning to make agriculture an integral part of the negotiations. In the Kennedy round, agriculture was negotiated on a separate track, with the result that at the last minute the overriding difficulties with this sector caused negotiations to be closed with little progress on agricultural issues. This time the U.S. Government has repeatedly stated, "No progress in agricultural matters, no MTN."

U.S. strategy on agricultural trade has focused on two main objectives:

• A reduction in both tariff and nontariff barriers to trade, and

• An attempt to establish stronger "rules of the game" on trade matters.

The latter has had two main elements: Attempts to agree on rules that will provide more discipline on policy measures such as export subsidies; and attempts to negotiate commodity agreements, with the emphasis, of course, on an International Wheat Agreement.

In attempting to obtain trade liberalization per se, principal interest has focused on the complex bundle of issues among industrialized countries. A similarity of climate among these countries causes them to have a broad overlap in commodity mix, which intensifies agricultural trade disputes. This problem is exacerbated by the tendency of advanced countries to protect their agriculture, and to deal with the income problem of that sector by means of interventions in the product markets. The European Community's Common Agricultural Policy is a prominent example of such protection; the United States does the same thing with dairy, sugar, and a few other commodities.

The conflict between the EC and the United States has been particularly acrimonious, and is a continuing source of friction and political difficulties. The United States would like to have greater access to the Community's markets. But the problem is not just one of access. With product prices set above market clearing levels, the Community often has to resort to export subsidies to dispose of the surpluses it produces as a result of those high prices. These subsidies tend to be disruptive of U.S. markets and are viewed as unfair competition by U.S. producers. We have lost a large portion of our Middle East markets in poultry because of these policies, and this year once again finds U.S. grain markets threatened by subsidized exports from the Community.

Protective measures give rise to other problems as well. The use of quotas and other nontariff barriers to trade, and such policies as the variable levy as practiced by the European Community, in effect isolate national and/or regional economies from market forces. When combined with export subsidies, these policies impose a great deal of instability on international markets because they reduce the scope for market forces to work, while at the same time imposing additional shocks on the system.

Market instability, of course, gives rise to pressures for further intervention in self-defeating attempts to protect domestic agriculture from external shocks. It also generates strong incentives for self-sufficiency, which leads to inefficient use of resources and a reduction in longer term potential trade.

One can easily despair at obtaining trade liberalization among industrialized countries, since the battle has been long and progress at times quite fitful and slow. But the alternatives are bleak indeed. As a relatively open econ-

Foreign Agriculture, December 4, 1978, pp. 1-5, 16. Dr. G. Edward Schuh is Deputy Assistant Secretary of Agriculture.

omy, U.S. consumers and producers bear a disproportionate share of the instability in international commodity markets. This instability poses a threat to U.S. domestic policies and to the U.S. stance in favor of freer trade.

Equally as important, failure to make progress in liberalizing agricultural trade poses a threat to the relatively open trade we have in industrial products. In fact, a very real danger we now face is the threat posed by the urge to retaliate by becoming more protectionist on industrial products. Such policies would undo the considerable progress we have made in liberalizing trade in industrial products in the post-World War II period, and cause us to sacrifice the very real gains we have realized from such trade.

The attempt to negotiate international commodity agreements is an important element in U.S. attempts to obtain better functioning international markets. We have signed an International Sugar Agreement, although Congress has not yet ratified it, and are actively engaged in negotiating an International Wheat Agreement.

Commodity agreements are not directly trade expansionist. But if they are successful in adding stability to international markets, their longer run effects can be in that direction. Supply assurance reduces the incentive for high-cost self-sufficiency.

In the case of the proposed wheat agreement, the U.S. goal has been to obtain a wider sharing of the burden of adjustment to changing conditions in the market. In the past, the United States has been forced to bear a disproportionate share of the burden. Hopefully, an agreement will establish mechanisms for a wider sharing of the burden.

The past record with international commodity agreements causes many to be less than sanguine about their efficacy and longevity. One cause of the past failures, however, has been the establishment of agreements that are too ambitious. In the agreements now under discussion, the goals have been kept rather modest. The attempt is to obtain concerted actions in a flexible way, with buffer stocks providing the means to offset short-term fluctuations in market forces.

The final element of the trade negotiations is the attempt to establish well-defined rules for trade interventions. The effort here focuses on rules for the evaluation of products by customs, rules for government procurement, safeguards, export subsidies, and countervailing duties. The latter two are probably the most important from an agricultural standpoint.

Export subsidies are extensively used for agricultural products, and countervailing duties are the logical countermeasure. Agreement on rules that provide some discipline in the use of these measures can limit the extent to which they are used and reduce the often capricious way in which both are implemented. Success in this endeavor will reduce both the frequency and size of shocks to international markets and thereby add to stability.

Changes in Currency Values

Discussions of monetary exchange rates have dominated the news this past year as the dollar has fallen on international markets. Exchange rates are important since they influence the extent to which a country realizes its comparative advantage in international trade. Interventions in foreign exchange markets are an important means of taxing or subsidizing agriculture, and can be an important source of disturbances to international commodity markets. By the same token, changes in the exchange rate can be an important means by which changing conditions in the international markets are transmitted to the domestic economy.

To understand the role of exchange rates, it is important to recognize that distortions in these rates are equivalent to explicit tariffs and subsidies. Trade theory teaches us that a correct measurement of trade intervention must take account of both the tariff or subsidy and the degree of distortion in the exchange markets. An overvalued currency is a subsidy on imports and a tax on exports, while an undervalued currency is equivalent to a subsidy on exports and a tariff on imports.

Despite this equivalence between distortion in the exchange markets and interventions in trade, exchange rates have received little attention in the current round of trade negotiations. However, the United States does favor floating exchange rates, and has defended such a policy in international forums. Its belief in the efficacy of such a policy may be one of the reasons for neglecting it in trade discussions, although history amply demonstrates how important distortions in exchange rates can be.

A number of issues involving exchange rate policies are now before us. Perhaps most important is the persistent decline in the value of the dollar. The dollar's sharp drop in recent months has increased the cries for protectionist measures in other countries. The problem here is not only the improved competitive position that such a decline gives the United States, but the advantage it gives to countries that keep their currencies tied to the dollar. Hence, Germany and other European countries face not only stronger competition from the United States, but competition from Brazil, Mexico, and South Korea as well. When inundated by goods from these countries, at the same time that their own export industries experience reduced demand from abroad, the appeals for protection are understandable. But these pressures make trade liberalization quite difficult, and may eventually prejudice the multilateral trade negotiations.

The fall in the value of the dollar also poses a threat to international capital markets. These capital markets have become an important instrument of economic intercourse, and are increasingly a means by which nation-states finance their economic development. But the sharp decline of the dollar has created substantial problems for banks, insurance companies, and other financial institutions. The losses on their dollar assets have in some cases been huge, with the result that the perceived risk in these markets is now larger.

The decline in the value of the dollar may also be giving false signals to U.S. agriculture. It seems clear that the strength of U.S. agricultural exports this past year is due in no small measure to the fall of the dollar. If the new rates are in fact equilibrium values, all will be well and good. But if the dollar is now undervalued, as many believe, these strong export markets may be in part an illusion. As the dollar recovers to its equilibrium level, a rather sizable adjustment problem may be forced on the agricultural sector.

The dollar's decline has also made the present and recent participants in the Common Market "snake" more desirous of using that device to insulate themselves from the gyrations of the dollar. The "snake" is a scheme whereby the currencies of the six member countries are linked together for a common float against other currencies. Each member currency is supposed to hold within 2¼ percent above or below its fixed level against each other currency, but the bloc of currencies is free to float against outside currencies.

Because of the fluctuations of the dollar, discussions are now underway to create an eventual European Monetary Union with a common currency managed by one central bank.

The difficulty with this proposal is that it has the cart before the horse. There are as yet no clear arrangements for pursuing a common economic policy. Moreover, there are substantial differentials in the rates of inflation among the proposed member countries. Under these conditions, the stability of the new European currency unit will require sizable interventions in exchange markets. Such interventions will tend to generate world inflation and damage sound monetary and fiscal policies followed by other countries. This in turn will nurture protectionist sentiments and the desire to be isolated from international market forces.

If such a common currency could be established, it might have a salutory effect on U.S. policy. The emergence of a viable competitive currency might impose a discipline on U.S. economic policy that was lost when the value of the dollar was severed from gold. But whether this ambitious scheme can be realized remains to be seen.

A more likely longer term solution to the problem of international monetary disturbance is the establishment of a true world bank. Such a bank would provide for the world the same functions that central banks provide for individual countries. It would manage the world stocks of money, hopefully in a sound fashion, and provide the means whereby individual countries would deal with their balance-of-payments problems. Although the International Monetary Fund is a world bank of sorts, we are still a long way from having a true central bank function.

The final exchange rate issue for agriculture is the emergence of the Green Currencies in Europe. These currencies constitute a multiple exchange rate system whereby members of the European Community were able to back away from the common prices for agricultural products that in the beginning were a central element of the Common Agricultural Policy. All but one of the nine member countries (Denmark) now maintain an exchange rate for agricultural products that is different than the exchange rate for trade in other products and for financial transactions.

The significance of these exchange rates for U.S. agriculture is that they have reduced the incentive for adjustment within the Community. Any delay in making that adjustment only furthers the day when trade liberalization will come to the Community, with the attendant advantages discussed earlier.

Need for Positive Adjustment Policies

Positive adjustment policies are a much neglected aspect of trade policy. The concept itself is straightforward. Efficient trade benefits society as a whole, with larger exports financing a higher rate of economic growth in the aggregate and imports providing lower cost goods to consumers and cheaper raw materials to the producer sectors. The problem is that these benefits are widely dispersed in society, while individual sectors in the economy may be harmed by low-priced imports.

Efficient policy would require that resources be transferred from those sectors that are no longer competitive to those where their contribution to society is higher. These adjustments give rise to the international division of labor, which plays such a prominent role in trade theory, and which is the source of the gains from trade. Moreover, the gains from trade to society at large are expected to be sufficiently large that resource owners can be compensated for their adjustment costs in transferring to more productive sectors from the sectors that cannot compete with lower priced imports.

So much for principle. In practice, the problem is a great deal more difficult. Few people like to leave their chosen vocation or profession, especially if the need for adjustment comes late in life. Hence adjustment programs are often referred to disparagingly as "burial expenses."

Similarly, there are serious questions about just how far the international division of labor should be allowed to go. Legitimate questions about national security are raised when a nation's steel industry threatens to go down the tube, or when the United States sees an important share of its electronic industry transferred to other lands. Countries, such as Japan, which now imports more than 50 percent of its caloric intake, reasonably ask just how much further they should go in becoming more dependent on other countries for their supply of foods, just as many in the United States question how dependent we should permit ourselves to become on foreign sources of petroleum.

Two problems complicate the adjustment process. First, the transfer of labor is more difficult when the economy is operating at less than full employment. And, in fact, an important source of the growing pressures for protectionism in recent years is due to the sluggish growth in industrialized countries and the relatively high rate of unemployment. Unfortunately, this sluggish growth has occurred at the same time that there has been a major realinement of exchange rates, and with it some major shifts in competitive advantages.

Competitive threats from foreign countries have become more severe at the precise time that countries find it more difficult to make the necessary shifts in their domestic economies.

The second complicating problem is when foreign competition threatens a sector that inherently faces adjustment as development proceeds. This is the case with agriculture and helps to explain why trade interventions tend to be more severe for this sector of the economy than they do for others. The nature of the development process is such that labor resources typically have to be transferred from agriculture to other sectors as development proceeds. This adjustment process can be difficult in its own right, as our own historical experience amply demonstrates. When a trade adjustment is placed on top of that "development" adjustment, the problem can be doubly severe.

This perspective can help in understanding the high protective barriers the European Community has put around its agricultural sector. Member countries have been in that stage of their development that required a net reduction in their agricultural labor force, especially in light of the existing potential for technological modernization.

In the case of the EC, this problem has been exacerbated by what are referred to as structural factors. As with the United States in the late 1950's and early 1960's, the owner-operators in agriculture were older than the rest of the population because of the selective effects of past outmigration.

More importantly, however, land holdings in member countries are particularly fractionated and dominated by small parcels. When combined with the attachment to land ownership that characterizes Europe because of political instability over the years, the adjustment problem has been especially difficult.

Unfortunately, the Community missed a golden opportunity to deal with this adjustment problem during its post-World War II economic boom. When demand for labor for its expanding nonfarm sector was growing rapidly, the EC opened its borders to migrant labor from other countries in order to alternate wage pressures. In the absence of such policies, outmigration from agriculture would undoubtedly have been greater and a more rapid reorganization of agriculture would have taken place. The demands for protectionism would in turn have been substantially less.

Devising innovative means to deal with the adjustment problem, both here and abroad, is the key to obtaining further significant gains in trade liberalization. Many of these policies have to be devised nationally to suit local conditions. They will need to focus on the labor markets, but in some countries of the EC they will have to deal as well with rather difficult land tenure problems.

There is also a place for international cooperation in dealing with the adjustment problem. An International Adjustment Fund—which I have recommended before—would help finance projects designed to facilitate the adjustment process. The rationale for such a fund is that the world at large benefits from freer trade. Yet an individual country finds it difficult to internalize the political trade-off from such trade since the economic exchange is seldom perceived as between domestic producers and consumers, but rather as a loss by domestic producers to the benefit of foreign producers.

Resources for this fund would come from individual countries, perhaps based on their gross national product, since this would be a reasonable proxy for consumer benefits. Use of the funds from this source would be an application of the well-known compensation principle of welfare-economics fame. Its strength would be the use of international funds to solve what is perceived as an international problem.

Linkages Between Domestic and Trade Policies

Domestic U.S. agricultural commodity programs were predicated on strong export markets. However, the maintenance of strong export markets is equally dependent on maintaining appropriate domestic policies. Domestic policies that price U.S. commodities out of international markets can alter the U.S. trade situation rather significantly.

Fortunately, both the 1973 and the 1977 Food and Agriculture Acts took long strides toward domestic commodity policies that help us to remain competitive in international markets. The establishment of broad price corridors for products that are important in international trade is an important example. Market forces are allowed to work within these corridors with the result that there is less of a tendency for the United States to price itself out of foreign markets.

The growing separation of income policies from commodity policies is another positive aspect of the policy framework. The use of the target price concept permits market prices to seek their market-clearing levels, within the limits of the price corridor, and income problems are dealt with by means of direct deficiency payments to producers. Through these mechanisms U.S. products remain competitive in international markets.

Finally, the farmer-held reserves provide buffer stocks that give the United States a reasonable chance of remaining a reliable supplier to foreign countries, and make

62

some contribution to developing more stable international markets. This increased stability reduces the incentive for self-sufficiency on the part of other countries. The turning away from self-sufficiency provides more market potential for the United States and other exporting countries in the future.

Although domestic policy has evolved in the direction of making the United States more competitive in international markets, there will be continuing difficulties in preserving that policy framework. Farmers will perceive a strong link between the prices they receive and their incomes. The political pressures to raise the loan level and with it market prices will be great. Similarly, it remains to be seen whether it will be possible politically prices rise.

One of our major challenges is to help U.S. citizens overcome their fear of development and progress in other countries. The recent emergence of competitive threats from countries such as Brazil, South Korea, Taiwan, and Singapore has given rise to demands that the United States limit its technical assistance to other countries and reduce the foreign aid budget even further than it already has been.

To do that would be extremely shortsighted. U.S. prosperity will be determined in large part by economic progress in other countries. A retreat to Fortress America is no longer a viable alternative.

SPEECH TO THE NATIONAL FOREIGN TRADE CONVENTION

by Christopher Tugendhat

The interdependence of the U.S. and Europe in matters of trade exists at two separate but related levels.

The first level is that of bilateral trade. The United States provides the members of the European Community with their largest export market outside the Community's frontiers, taking in 1977 some 12.6 percent of their non-Community exports. Similarly, the Community provides the USA with its largest export market, taking in 1977 as much as 22 percent of U.S. exports. Indeed, in passing I would point out that at a time when the overall U.S. trade balance is in serious deficit, the U.S. surplus on trade with the Community is positive to the tune of 4.1 billion dollars (1977). The existence of such a surplus demonstrates, I think, the extent to which the Community has succeeded in effectively resisting pressures to adopt protectionist policies towards American exports.

The fact that we are each other's best customers makes trade between us enormously important for our respective industries, farmers and consumers and it is essential that is remembered on both sides in the conduct of our bilateral relations. But the importance of our relationship is not limited to the bilateral dimension, we are also critically dependent upon each other at the higher level of the overall world trading system.

The European Community is the world's largest trading entity. We account for some 24 percent (1976) of the world's imports and exports. The U.S. also

European Community News, November 14, 1978, 4pp. Speech delivered November 14, 1978 in New York City. Christopher Tugendhat is a member of the Commission of the European Economic Community.

accounts for a very significant, although smaller, proportion of the total. The sheer weight of our mutual involvement in world trade requires us, together with Japan, to act jointly and responsibly in the interests of the trading system as a whole. If we were ever to depart from this principle of joint and shared responsibility in the conduct of our trade policies at world level the consequences could be most serious. If the American and European giants were ever to fall out they could do a lot of damage both to each other and to many bystanders.

Multilateral Trade Negotiations (M.T.N.)

Nowhere is this principle of shared responsibility better illustrated than in the realm of the MTN.

These negotiations which are more ambitious in scope than any previous negotiations on trade undertaken since the establishment of the GATT in 1977, are at the center of our efforts to preserve and strengthen the foundations of the present trading system. They are designed to provide further liberalization, new rules, new procedures and new mechanisms for solving disputes which together would constitute a reinforced framework for international cooperation for at least the next decade. The negotiations have become a symbol of our commitment to an open trading system and the rejection of protectionism. Our governments are pledged at the highest level to achieve success. Failure is politically unthinkable. There is every reason to fear that if our efforts do not succeed we shall be unable to resist or control a cumulative process by which a crucial pillar of our prosperity would be gradually eroded and the tide toward increased mutual interdependence could be checked and reversed. One has only to pause and think of the consequences that have flowed from the break up of the Bretton Woods System to realize how vital it is to avoid the trading system falling prey to a similar fate.

We are now in the very final stages of these negotiations and the fact that we are within reach of success is in no small way due to the commitment and energies of the U.S. administration--and in particular to the driving force of the President's Special Trade Representative, Bob Strauss, who has played a vital part in bringing us to the point we have now reached. From the moment he took office, he was instrumental in forging a close partnership between the so-called big three--the U.S., the EEC and Japan--a partnership which has successfully ensured that offers were put on the table in January this year and that an overall package was outlined by July. Now what remains is to conclude the final political negotiations.

Let me briefly summarize the outcome which the Community wishes to see.

Industrial Tariffs

First, the Community wants a significant further liberalization of trade via a harmonized reduction of tariffs. Our consistent aim in the current negotiations has been to achieve harmonized reductions that bring down not only average levels of protection but in particular the prohibitive peaks of protection. After implementation, we would expect to see tariffs between the main industrial countries of an average level of 5-7 percent and an absence of duties at levels of 20 percent and over.

Agriculture

As far as agriculture is concerned, the Tokyo Round far exceeds anything attempted in previous negotiations. The Community's approach has been strongly to favor including agriculture in the MTNs but to insist that there can be no effective negotiations unless all the parties recognize that government involvement and support for farming is an undeniable fact throughout the world which sharply distinguishes the agricultural from the industrial sector. I am glad to say that there now appears to be a good chance of achieving international agreements on key commodities in agricultural trade--cereals, dairy products and meat-- which will not only stabilize trade but facilitate the expansion of trade in these commodities. On other products, where this is feasible and appropriate, there will be direct liberalization on a reciprocal tariff cutting basis. Finally, the Community is not intending to duck the sensitive issue of agricultural export subsidies. I hope there will be provisions affecting pricing policies in the international commodity agreements, to which I have referred, as well as provisions in the context of a new code on subsidies and countervailing duties, which will contribute to avoidance of the disruption in trade which excess subsidies can cause.

Non Tariff Barriers

Mention of a code on subsidies and countervailing duties brings me to another important aspect of these negotiations, namely the attempt to deal with a range of major non-tariff barriers which have either so far escaped international disciplines or which are subject to rules that need review and elaboration. Although it is pursuing its own internal policies of removing non-tariff barriers to trade, the European Community has not shirked its responsibilities for contributing to international progress in these areas. For example, we are well on the way to establishing codes to prevent obstacles to trade arising from policies of standardization and to eliminate discrimination in the field of government purchases. We are looking, too, for a new safeguards code which, in return for subjecting emergency safeguard action to increased international discipline and surveillance, would permit selective action against the source of injury and would thereby help keep trade disturbance to a minimum.

As you may know, our approach to the issue of non tariff barriers has also led us to take issue with long-standing U.S. protective practices. I am referring to efforts to establish a new harmonized system of customs valuation that would bring an end to such U.S. valuation systems as the American selling price and the final list, and also to efforts in the context of the proposal I have already mentioned for a code dealing with subsidies and countervailing duties to bring us legislation on countervail (which dates back to the 19th century) into line with GATT requirements for a material injury test.

These remarks prompt me to make a final observation about our approach to trade issues in the MTN. We are seeking in these negotiations to bring about a framework for international trade in which the main participants, at least, accept a commitment to the uniform application of GATT rules. I know this is a potentially controversial theme since in the U.S. Congress there has always been a tenacious defense of derogations enjoyed by the U.S. under the GATT. However, we are convinced that the uniform application of GATT rules is the only precept on which to build a reinforced GATT that can command effective and universal acceptance as a framework for trade rules in the future.

Monetary Problems

I referred earlier to the world's present monetary disorders, the full potential benefits for both the developed and the developing world of a successful outcome to the MTNs will, of course, only be realized if those disorders are removed. It may therefore be of interest to this audience if I briefly outline the proposals which the European Community is currently considering for creating a European zone of monetary stability.

Such a zone would be established and maintained by means of a European Monetary System (EMS). Under this system, fluctuations in the value of each of the member states' currencies in terms of the currencies of its partners would not be permitted to exceed fixed margins on either side of agreed central rates. (It should be noted however, that the central rates themselves could be changed by mutual consent.)

In order to help the member states to maintain these rates, a substantial European Monetary Fund is envisaged from which they would be able to borrow on appropriate terms.

But from the outset is has been recognized that whatever the arrangements made for direct intervention, EMS will not endure unless the member states pursue national policies which ensure much greater convergence than in the recent past in the performance of their economies, particularly with respect to inflation.

One of the main reasons why the member states wish to stabilize the relationship between their currencies is that their nine national economies are now very closely linked to each other by ties of investment and trade. I said earlier that the USA provides the member states with their largest non-Community export market, but the Community itself is now a full customs union and for each of the member states, the most important export market of all is that provided by its partners. The United Kingdom now sends 36 percent of her total exports to the rest of the Community, Germany 46 percent, and France 51 percent. For the smaller member states the figures are even higher.

In these circumstances of very high mutual dependence, the severe fluctuations of recent years in the relative value of the member states' currencies combined with external pressures have caused major strains in their national economies, thus distorting monetary and fiscal policy, and also inevitably inhibiting investment.

The fall in the dollar in recent weeks has been on a scale that has major implications for the U.S. economy. But it may not be widely realized by Americans that your country has hitherto suffered much less from the breakdown of the Bretton Woods System than has the European Community. This has been to a great extent because so much of the economic activity of the United States is internal, and thus covered by a single currency. EMS could, I believe, provide the Community's internal trade with similar, though obviously less complete protection from the consequences of monetary turbulence. And in so doing would greatly assist the Community countries in their efforts to achieve sustained and inflation free growth.

It is of course very much in the United States' interest that we succeed in reviving growth in the Community because it will help the U.S. to overcome her own balance of payments problems.

Moreover, in addition to reducing monetary fluctuations within Europe, EMS should also help to restore stability at a global level to the obvious advantage of all the world's trading nations. At the moment one of the main causes of instability in the world's currency markets is that speculators wishing to move out of dollars know that they can swiftly push up the value of the stronger European currencies, particularly the Deutschmark. However, speculators are less likely to be able to push up all the parities of an EMS together, and the incentive to sell dollars for quick profit would therefore be correspondingly diminished by its existence.

Those who are responsible for the management of the EMS will, of course, have to adopt a coherent policy toward the dollar, just as those who manage the dollar will have to adopt such a policy toward the EMS. But since the existence of the EMS will be a force for stability, I am wholly confident that it will be possible to establish a mutually satisfactory monetary relationship between us.

Recognizing that an effective and sensible EMS is not only in the European but also the general interest, the American government has publicly voiced its strong support for the Community's efforts to solve the technical and political problems that must be overcome if it is to become a reality. I would like here tonight, as a member of the European Commission, to express our appreciation of the Administration's constructive response.

Conclusion

In this presentation I have tried to show something of the importance of the Community in international trade and our approach to trade and monetary problems. What I have sought to convey is a picture of the Community which, although deeply involved with its own economic and political integration, nonetheless combines this with a sense of international responsibility and a sincere commitment to multilateralism. Since the Community is the sum of its member states it is not surprising. European countries by tradition are outward looking and accustomed to playing a constructive role in world affairs. But, being also more than the sum of its member states, the Community is now developing a common international identity and policies that befits our actual and potential strength.

I am confident that we shall discharge our international role with wisdom and responsibility--and in close partnership with the United States.

67

THE NTBs TO FREE TRADE

by Robert J. Samuelson

The Europeans are stealing U.S. wheat exports. And not just a few bushels, either. Something like 3.3 million tons—about 10 per cent of normal U.S. exports—are involved, and the value, depending on the method of calculation, ranges from $400 million to nearly $1 billion.

That's not small change, and midwestern grain interests are livid. To them, it's an open-and-shut case of theft. American farmers grow wheat more efficiently than their European competitors. In a simple faceoff, grain buyers would clearly choose the low-cost supplier.

But the real world works differently. The European Community sets artificially high prices for its farmers' wheat and, when they produce a surplus, unloads it by subsidizing exports. Without the subsidy, European wheat would sell at nearly twice the world price. The losers are not only U.S. wheat farmers, but also European consumers, who pay the subsidy in higher prices.

We mention this practice because it's precisely the sort of non-tariff barrier—known as an NTB among the technicians—that was supposed to lie at the heart of the multilateral trade negotiations now concluding in Geneva. Ever since the Kennedy Round of trade talks (1963-67), which reduced tariffs by about a third, a growing number of NTBs, ranging from subsidies to discriminatory government procurement procedures, have constituted the chief obstacles to free trade. (For a report on Buy American laws, see this issue, p. 60.)

By dismantling the NTBs, the Geneva trade agreement was supposed to reassert free trade's logic: producers competing on the basis of efficiency, consumers buying at the lowest prices. But, after five years of tedious negotiations, that hope remains largely unfulfilled.

This is no one's fault except history's. Free trade is never painless; competition implies winners and losers. As long as the world economy grew rapidly, countries could assist the losers, mostly by absorbing them into new jobs. Prosperity fostered free trade.

Now, the climate has changed. Slower growth and higher unemployment have helped create a mean-spirited mercantilism. Countries constantly seek to protect themselves from imports and to promote their exports. And yet they dare not completely destroy the fabric of international trade on which everyone depends. These contradictory pressures have produced their natural result in the new trade agreement: an opaque compromise that can increase or diminish protectionism.

Although tariffs again will be cut—probably by about 30 per cent over eight to 10 years—these reductions are secondary. The Kennedy Round had already brought the average industrial tariff down to about 8 to 10 per cent. The agreement's significance lies in a series of new "codes" that are supposed to reform the General Agreement on Tariffs and Trade (GATT). In effect, the GATT is a loose criminal code for international trade: a list of the do's and don'ts by which all the world's traders agree to abide.

But it's not that simple. All such agreements require nations to sacrifice domestic sovereignty to international control, subordinating short-run interests to long-run ones. But in today's climate, such concessions come grudgingly, if at all.

The ambiguities emerge clearly in the grain case. In a world of free trade, many of Europe's grain farmers would vanish, ejected from the market by less expensive U.S. and Canadian wheat. But the European Community could never accept that result. Not only might it leave Europe vulnerable during periods of shortage, but it would create social and political disorder: what to do with the displaced farmers?

Had the United States demanded the abolition of the community's Common Agricultural Policy (CAP), which sets high domestic farm prices and raises import prices to the same level, there simply would have been no trade agreement. The U.S. objective was more modest: limit export subsidies.

The new subsidies code, U.S. officials say, achieves this. But their claim is uncertain. The new code does not ban farm export subsidies. To do so would have prevented the Europeans from selling their surpluses and, therefore, would have been unacceptable. Rather, the code insists that subsidies not be used to gain "more than an equitable" share of trade. Further, the code says a "more than equitable share" should be measured against the last three years of "normal" trade.

Like anything drafted by lawyers, this provision reeks of ambiguity. To Americans, the code means a country can't use subsidies to increase its share of another country's market. But, on a case-by-case basis, no one knows how a GATT panel—which must make the final decision—will interpret that view.

The Europeans, not surprisingly, insist that their current wave of subsidized sales would be acceptable under the new code. Americans see the Europeans increasing their market share in Brazil, Morocco, Egypt and Portugal. Just how any large new markets (i.e. China) might be treated is anyone's guess. The basic problem inevitably arises in years of good harvests and grain surpluses. Although Europe's share of world wheat exports is rising from 8 to 12 per cent (against 40 per cent for the United States), American wheat exports still have increased.

No one, however, should picture the United States as a bastion of free trade opposing European protectionism. To muster necessary congressional support to pass the Geneva agreement, Robert S. Strauss, the U.S. Special Representative for Trade Negotiations, will face strong pressures to make administrative concessions—technically, outside the agreement—to groups that want protection.

Textile firms and unions want tighter regulation of imports under the Multifiber Arrangement, the international agreement that limits clothing imports. Specialty steel firms want a continuation of existing quotas. Television manufacturers may want voluntary quotas from Japan extended elsewhere.

America has an interest in free trade. Exports create jobs and imports remain an effective form of price competition. But free trade is built not on morality but politics. And, as the Geneva agreement indicates, free trade's political foundation is very shaky indeed.

GRAIN RESERVE TALKS ARE STARVED FOR PROGRESS

It's been just about four years since the World Food Conference called for the creation of an international grain reserve to stabilize prices and provide developing countries with a measure of food security. But the way the international wheat talks are going these days, some experts say, such a reserve doesn't appear to be in the cards.

Grain expert D. Gale Johnson of the University of Chicago, for example, has already written off the talks as a failure. "I do not believe that it will be possible to negotiate a set of rules for the management of grain reserves under international auspices," Johnson wrote in the latest issue of The World Economy.

Barbara Huddleston, an expert on the grain trade at the Washington-based International Food Policy Research Institute, also agrees that the chances of successfully negotiating a reserve "are not too good."

Privately, US Agriculture Department officials are pessimistic, too. And they say that the US will abandon the talks if no headway is made in a November conference to be held under the auspices of the United Nations Conference on Trade and Development.

While one US official reports "incremental gains" in the London talks held this June with representatives from 20 grain-exporting and importing nations, he says that "the real tough issues are yet to come."

And when it comes to these gut issues, no saving compromises appear to be in the offing.

Central to any agreement on a reserve is determining at what price levels the reserve would be obliged to take in surplus grain or turn its stores of grain loose to keep the cost of grain from going too high. But Canada, a major grain exporter, is insisting that no grain be released from a reserve until its selling price is "in the high price range," a US official says. Japan and the European Economic Community (EEC), on the other hand, want much lower prices to trigger the release of reserve grain.

In addition to this dispute, the US and the EEC are at odds over the very size of the reserve. The US favors one at 30-million-tons to be held in bits and pieces by grain-exporting and importing countries. But the EEC, which is concerned about the expense of storing large quantities of grain, wants a 15-million-ton reserve.

Sharing the costs of acquiring grain for a reserve in the first place is also a touchy subject on which there seems to be little agreement. US Agriculture Department officials estimate that purchasing grain for a 30-million-ton reserve would take more than $3 billion. But some developing countries have indicated that they will only participate in a wheat agreement if the industrialized countries pick up the cost—a burden which the US, for one, does not want

to assume. "We don't want to create a special facility to take care of financing developing-country participation in the reserve," says another official. "We've already got the World Bank and the International Monetary Fund to do that."

The separate US trade talks with European countries over gaining access to European markets for US produce and beef are also complicating the effort to create a reserve. While France seems genuinely interested in a reserve to stabilize prices, for example, it is asking for US concessions on the matter of a grain reserve in return for opening up its market a little more to US agricultural goods.

The Inter-Dependent, September 1978, p. 2.

FOOD SECURITY:
AN INSURANCE APPROACH

by Panol Konandreas, Barbara Huddleston,
and Virabongsa Ramangkura

This paper suggests an approach by which the international community can contribute to the food security of food deficit, developing countries without having to create large buffer stocks and stabilize world grain prices. The international community is considering an agreement which would establish minimum and maximum indicator prices for wheat, and use buffer stocks to defend them. But important differences among major participants about commodity coverage and the use of production adjustment and trade policy measures make agreement unlikely. A more acceptable alternative may be a scheme based on insurance principles specifically designed to assist food deficit, developing countries. The objective of such a scheme would be to permit developing countries to stabilize cereal consumption within a range of projected demand at a relatively stable cost.

Two alternative insurance schemes were evaluated for sixty-five food deficit, developing countries for the period 1978 to 1982: a purely compensatory financing mechanism, and a financing mechanism combined with a physical wheat reserve. In the latter case, stocks would be released only during very high-price years (price above $200 per metric ton (MT) or $5.45 per bushel of wheat) and only to countries experiencing a production shortfall of more than 5 percent during those years. On the basis of present market conditions it was assumed that a physical reserve could be acquired from this year's crop at the prevailing price. Reserve levels of 4, 8, 12, 16, and 20 million tons were considered.

Five years was considered a reasonable period for making realistic statistical estimates. An agreement could be negotiated for a five-year period, but the anticipated duration would have to be considerably longer for the scheme to operate effectively.

Compensation from the scheme would be permitted whenever a developing country's cereal import bill exceeded a specified percentage of the trend import bill (e.g., 110, 120, or 130 percent of trend). The consumption level defended by the scheme at a given year depends on a country's cereal production during that year. Thus, if its domestic production shortfall is more than 5 percent below trend, the country's actual bill would be calculated for the quantity of imports that would maintain 95 percent of projected demand. If the shortfall is between 95 and 100 percent of trend production, consumption would be maintained at the same percentage of projected demand. Finally, if production exceeded trend, consumption would be maintained at 100 percent of projected demand. These rules would ensure that each country could maintain a consumption level between 95 and 100 percent of projected demand in all years, depending on the performance of its own cereal production. However, consumption is not restricted to the guaranteed level. A country can maintain its own supplementary reserves and/or allocate additional foreign exchange to food imports if it wishes to support a higher consumption level.

Because of the sharp fluctuations in domestic production in many developing countries, there would be at least some countries

Research Report 4, International Food Policy Research Institute, September 1978, pp. 13-16.

eligible for compensation each year. Once a country's domestic production for a given crop year was known and enough information was available to permit an estimate of the expected world market price, the probable cost of import requirements could be estimated. Funds could then be made available to eligible countries. Some mechanism would have to be devised to tie these funds to the purchase of the specified quantity of grains for food consumption. Since in most years the world price would not be high enough to trigger release of grain from the reserve, the assistance to eligible countries would be in the form of compensatory financing. The wheat reserve would be drawn upon when world market prices exceeded the release price, and would be used only to compensate for production shortfalls of 5 percent or more below trend production in those years. This released grain would be valued at the prevailing world price, and the amount subtracted from the total compensation for which each country is eligible. The remainder of the payments due to countries would be provided through compensatory financing. In the event that production shortfalls and/or price increases were so extreme that resources would be exhausted before meeting the requirements of all eligible countries, the consumption level defended by the scheme would be reduced for each country and the additional consumption adjustments necessary would be shared proportionately by all participating countries.

The scheme is least costly with a grain reserve of about 8 million tons; with a reserve of about 16 million tons the cost is equal to that of a scheme operating solely as a compensatory financing mechanism. However, the differences between total expected costs at various reserve levels are so slight that they have no practical significance as a measure for deciding which alternative is preferable. More important is the effect of the reserve on the distribution of the cost of the scheme: the larger the grain reserve held in the system, the lower the

probability of very high cost. Consequently, for a given level of funding, the larger the grain reserve, the greater the probability of achieving the objectives of the scheme. In addition, a larger grain reserve provides a higher and more equitable probability over the years of covering production shortfalls of 5 percent or more below trend production during high-price years. For these reasons if a grain reserve was established in conjunction with a compensatory financing mechanism, 20 million tons of grain would be the suggested reserve level for developing countries.

In addition to these technical considerations, a scheme with both funds and stocks has the advantage of providing a supply guarantee to back up the financial insurance, and is likely to be preferred by potential developed country contributors. Without a physical reserve, the additional purchasing power acquired by developing countries could, in periods of particularly short supply, pressure developed countries to make politically unacceptable adjustments in their own domestic consumption or cause the scheme to fail because of the imposition of export controls. The physical reserve could also provide an outlet for surplus stocks which tend to accumulate in certain exporting countries.

Alternative insurance levels for a scheme with a 20 million ton wheat reserve were evaluated and their costs compared to those for a scheme involving a compensatory financing mechanism only. The financial capacity needed to attain a given probability that the scheme will achieve its objectives under various alternatives is also calculated. Two important findings are worth mentioning here. First, a given level of funds provides a higher probability that the scheme will achieve its objectives when the scheme involves grain reserves in addition to compensatory financing. Second, the marginal funds needed to increase the probability of the scheme achieving its objectives are larger the higher the probability level.

It should be noted that for a given level of funding, higher insurance coverage implies a greater risk of depleting funds during the last years of the five-year period; therefore, benefits are unevenly distributed over time and among countries, favoring countries that happen to draw early during the five-year period. For this reason, for a given level of funds the insurance coverage should be set at a level that would imply a high probability for the scheme achieving its objectives over the five-year period. Assuming that for most countries concerned a cereal import bill up to 130 percent of trend during some years would not be a formidable obstacle in meeting their consumption targets, a fund of $3.7 billion would cover the expected cost of a food insurance scheme. * Such a level of funding would assure at least a 75 percent probability of the scheme achieving its objectives. Additional funding of about $2.4 billion would increase this probability to about 90 percent.

The share of each country's benefits from the system has also been estimated based on the expected total withdrawals for a given country and the expected total cost of the scheme for the five-year period. India receives more than 20 percent of the benefits, followed by Morocco, Mexico, and Turkey. Six or seven countries account for almost 50 percent of the cost of the system.

Crucial components in the success of any management of funds needed for its operation. One option is a scheme self-financed by the member countries. For example, if India had to pay an equal annual premium for the next five years based on its expected withdrawals, the premium would range from about $206 million to about $245 million, depending on the level of insurance provided by the scheme. In practice, however, most low income countries could probably not afford to participate unless the scheme were subsidized by developed countries. Developed countries could make their contributions either bilaterally or through a multilateral mechanism. Ideally, developed country assistance would be most effective and desirable from the point of view of recipient countries if it was a collective contribution that would be paid through an agreed upon cost-sharing arrangement. Donor countries could subsidize the premium payments of low income countries or make concessional food aid available to lower the cost of imports for recipient countries and thereby help them meet their food security premiums. Alternatively, funding countries could simply agree on the level of financial commitment they were willing to undertake collectively, and a scheme could be designed accordingly.

Whether funded by a schedule of premium payments or by a schedule of donor country contributions, the scheme should be funded to cover at least its expected cost at a given insurance level. Borrowing might be necessary if its cost exceeds the amount of funds available.

Finally the scheme could be funded through the compensatory financing facility of the International Monetary Fund (IMF) by including cereal import expenditures in the IMF's existing compensatory financing facility for commodity exports or by creating a new facility. Funding the scheme through the IMF may be the most desirable approach, both because the IMF could handle the necessary financing arrangements and because the bureaucracy needed to operate it already exists.

---

* This figure also includes the cost of $1.1 billion needed for the operation of the 20 million ton grain reserve.

INTERNATIONAL COMMODITY POLICY NEGOTIATIONS--
THE GROUP OF 77 AND UNCTAD

INTERNATIONAL COMMODITY POLICY

by Julius L. Katz

I am pleased to have this opportunity to testify before your subcommittee in support of H.R. 9486, a bill to authorize a contribution of up to 5,000 metric tons of tin metal to the buffer stock operated by the International Tin Agreement. To set this question in its proper context, I would like to outline the administration's general international commodity policy and the status of current international discussions on several other key commodities.

The United States is a major consumer and producer of many critical raw materials—both mineral and agricultural. We have a stake in the efficient functioning of the international markets for such commodities. Our objectives are two-fold and address short-term and long-term problems of balance between market supply and demand.

In the short term we recognize that extreme and erratic fluctuations in commodity prices can damage our interests and those of developing countries which depend on the export of a few major commodities. This problem was made clear during the great commodity boom-bust cycle of 1973–75 which paralleled the onset of the petroleum crisis. Sharp boosts in commodity prices can add impetus to domestic inflation in our economy through pressure on manufacturing costs and wages. The rise in costs becomes embedded in the economic structure and persists long after commodity prices move downward. The sharp declines in raw material prices, which usually follow peaks in the commodity price cycle, also injure producers and cause major drops in the foreign exchange earnings of developing country producers.

In the longer term we have an interest in assuring needed supplies of basic raw materials at reasonable prices. This requires adequate flows of new investment to insure that new supplies can be brought into the market to keep pace with rising demand. Excessive price instability works against this interest by creating uncertainty on the part of investors about expected returns from projects.

This long-term global supply challenge—in agricultural and nonagricultural commodities—is being met partly through domestic investment but also through a variety of international mechanisms, including bilateral aid, investment insurance, international financial institutions, and private foreign investment.

Sources of Financing

Private multinational corporations will undoubtedly remain essential to achieving adequate supplies of raw materials for the global economy in the foreseeable future. Recognizing that prospect, and the fact that developing countries are likely to provide a growing share of global reserves of key raw materials, investment insurance programs, such as those of the Overseas Private Investment Corporation (OPIC), help create conditions conducive to sound investments. By ameliorating political risk factors, OPIC enables prospective investors to make decisions based mainly on economic criteria and in this way contributes to a more efficient allocation of capital resources.

Despite the continued importance of foreign investment, national resource exploitation in developing countries has, in recent years, been marked by a growing role for national governments. The traditional long-term concession agreement between the host country and foreign investor has given way to a variety of complex contractual arrangements which have resulted in more active government participation, if not control. Furthermore, in the face of rapidly escalating costs, the major source of financing has shifted from internally generated capital of private corporations to debt.

Under these changing circumstances, international financial institutions, such as the World Bank, with our support are providing new sources of investment capital. World Bank participation can also act as a catalyst to private investment in some cases by providing a buffer between the host government and prospective private operators or commercial creditors.

The Integrated Program

The United States is now engaged internationally in a comprehensive effort to deal with these problems of commodity trade in the so-called Integrated Program for Commodities. This program was first put forward in 1975 in the United Nations Conference on Trade and Development (UNCTAD) by the UNCTAD Secretariat with the strong support of the developing countries. Implementation of the program was called for at UNCTAD IV in Nairobi in May 1976.

The program involves technical discussions in UNCTAD of market conditions for 18 major commodities. These technical discussions are to be followed where appropriate by efforts to negotiate international price stabilization agreements and other measures to improve the functioning of the market. We have been participating actively in these discussions since 1976, and they will continue throughout 1978.

The Administration believes that in-

Bulletin Reprint, U.S. Department of State, March 1978, 8 pp. Based on a statement made before the Subcommittee on International Economic Policy and Trade of the House Committee on International Relations, February 21, 1978. Julius L. Katz is Assistant Secretary for Economic and Business Affairs.

ternational price stabilization arrangements should be considered for specific commodities where such arrangements are feasible and appropriate. Where markets do not permit smooth adjustments to shifts in supply and demand, there may be a case for international agreements to improve the way in which a particular commodity market operates. We prefer to use instruments which enhance, rather than replace, market mechanisms. The technical objective in any given case would be to stabilize the market price of the commodity around its long-term trend, as determined by the forces of supply and demand. We are opposed to arrangements which introduce artificially rigid mechanisms to replace fully operative markets or which try to peg prices at artificially high levels.

Ideally, we would prefer to stabilize commodity prices through the operation of internationally constituted and financed buffer stocks. Such buffer stocks would seek to reduce price fluctuations around long-term market trends. A buffer stock would buy the commodity to defend the minimum price objectives and would release stocks to the market to protect the maximum price objectives. This technique permits market forces to operate within the agreed price objectives. Distortions of the market can thus be minimized so that producers and investors can respond to market signals in making decisions on investment and resource allocations.

But the establishment of buffer stocks is not a simple matter, given the complexities of the particular market and the international negotiation process. It is often difficult, in practice, to formulate a stabilization system based on a pure buffer stock model. Long-term market trends are frequently difficult to determine. The width of the price band and the calculation of the size of the buffer stock required to defend the band can be difficult technical problems. These problems are compounded when one tries to decide on such details in negotiations with other governments which often have differing views on these issues.

Objective conditions prevailing in particular markets may also require the use of other mechanisms. "Pure" buffer stocks are not always appropriate. Not all commodities can be easily stored, and costs may sometimes make

an international stocking arrangement infeasible. In such instances, as in the case of the new International Sugar Agreement, it may be necessary to adopt market-sharing arrangements, with export quotas for producers backed by nationally held and internationally coordinated reserve stocks. Such a system provides for stocks to absorb a portion of surplus production which is then available to protect the ceiling price in the agreement. Arbitrary and rigid controls on production can thus be avoided. Such controls, as I will later mention with respect to the tin agreement, are generally destabilizing. By holding down production and investment, they prevent the buildup of stocks which respond to excessive price increases.

I might point out here that, in the debate over the relative merits of buffer stocking as opposed to supply management, the issue of the cost of buffer stocking is often overstated. The capital costs of a buffer stock (e.g., copper) are often thrown up as a major argument against such devices. A balanced argument, however, must take into account the economic benefits which might flow from such a stock as well as the costs. Stabilization through such a mechanism may give rise to net benefits through reduced inflation; greater assurance of adequate supply at reasonable prices; and, over the long run, more stable export earnings for producers.

Price stabilization measures, however, are not necessary or appropriate for all commodities. For example, there are some commodities, such as jute, which suffer from a long-term decline in demand. In such cases, other measures may be called for, such as market promotion and research and development for new products or new uses. In the case of commodities, which are in chronic oversupply, diversification programs to promote production of other commodities may be needed.

The choice among these approaches will depend on a rigorous analysis of each commodity market to determine what imperfections exist and what techniques might be most suitable to correct them. There is no single formula that can be applied in every case. Whatever the approach, our commitment is to work seriously with other governments to develop workable,

beneficial means of handling commodity trade problems.

Compensatory Finance

Aside from the commodity-specific framework of UNCTAD, we have also been addressing the more general balance-of-payments problems which developing countries often confront in unstable raw material markets. Since it was liberalized in 1975, the International Monetary Fund (IMF) Compensatory Finance Facility has provided effective relief in the form of loan funds to countries experiencing short-term export earnings shortfalls. If, for example, a country's overall export earnings decline for a particular year as a result of a cyclical slump in world prices or demand for raw materials, that country can receive IMF financing to help compensate for the shortfall. This mechanism thus alleviates the impact of commodity market fluctuations on foreign exchange earnings and permits governments to plan their own development programs with greater certainty about the resources that will be available.

Specific Commodity Issues

I want to turn now to some examples of specific commodity agreements and negotiations in which we are involved to illustrate the problems that arise in moving from general principles to the practical problems of commodity markets.

Tin. The United States joined the Fifth International Tin Agreement (ITA) in 1976, and we have participated actively since then in the International Tin Council (ITC), the ITA's executive body. We entered the agreement because we judged that U.S. participation would help to further our international economic and political interests. On the economic side, the United States is the leading consumer of tin. We acquire more than 80% of our current tin consumption from abroad, with the remainder coming from domestic secondary production. The metal is an important basic input for key industrial uses, especially in the steel and solder industries.

The tin trade is even more important for the exporting countries in the ITA—particularly Malaysia, Bolivia, and Thailand—where it is a major source of domestic employment, government revenue, and export earnings. By joining the tin council, the United States put itself in a better position to influence the council's policies affecting the long-term supply of tin, thus protecting both American industry and consumers. Our decision clearly demonstrated our commitment to the idea of joint producer-consumer cooperation on international raw materials problems and also reaffirmed our willingness to respond forthrightly to the legitimate needs of the developing world.

The intent of the ITA is to balance international supply and demand of tin, stabilizing the price within an agreed band at levels deemed to be both remunerative for producers and fair to consumers. To the extent that the ITA can be effective in achieving those objectives, it can contribute to the economic health of the participating countries and also demonstrate the feasibility of international cooperation in dealing with major trade and developmental problems.

The purpose of the bill now before the committee is to help rectify several major problems which have hampered the ITA historically. The most important of these is that the buffer stock operated by the agreement has been too small to stabilize the world tin price effectively. In periods of slack demand and falling prices, the buffer stock could not absorb enough metal from the market to defend the floor price. This has led the tin council to rely excessively on export controls, the other major component of the ITA's stabilization machinery, to keep the price above the floor level. Conversely, when shortages have appeared and prices have hit the price ceiling, the buffer stock has had insufficient metal to release into the market to dampen the price rise.

Application of these controls has tended to inhibit production and discourage new investment in the tin industry. Over the short term, export controls are inherently more cumbersome and slower to take effect in the market than are buffer stock purchases and sales. There are long lags between the imposition and subsequent relaxation of such controls and any actual impact on market supplies and prices. The result has been the development of chronic tin shortages and a tripling of the tin price over the past 5 years. This

situation has been made worse, of course, by the exhaustion of the ITA's buffer stock in the face of such price increases.

Another important factor which interferes with price stabilization and supply growth is the imposition of excessively high production taxes and restrictive licensing practices by some producing country governments.

The combination of export controls and production limitations, together with restrictive domestic tax and investment policies, has produced a persistent deficit between tin metal production and consumption. Production of tin concentrates has dropped from a peak of 196,000 metric tons in 1972 to 185,000 tons in 1977. In 1977 the gap between current world tin metal production and consumption was approximately 20,000 metric tons, a figure which is not expected to decline appreciably in 1978.

This deficit will persist at least until 1980 and will generate continued pressure on tin prices, in the absence of infusions of metal into the market from the General Services Administration (GSA) stockpile and other sources. While the average New York price in 1972 was $1.77 per pound, the latest price is around $5.30 a pound. This is above the $4.60 ceiling price of the ITA's price band, a situation which has prevailed for the last 14 months in spite of several upward shifts in the band during that period. The obvious failure of supply to respond to these price increases clearly shows the effects of the export control policies followed by the ITA and the major producers. In sum, the world tin market is not functioning efficiently.

The contribution to the tin buffer stock which H.R. 9486 would authorize is intended to help alleviate this situation and to make the ITA a more effective stabilization instrument. It should also support the efforts of importing countries to persuade the major producers that a modification of their tax and investment policies is essential to our joint efforts to insure stable long-run growth in the tin market.

The ITA provides for a buffer stock with a nominal level of 40,000 metric tons. Half of this is to be in the form of mandatory contributions from producers with the rest made up of voluntary contributions of metal or the cash equivalent from consuming countries.

Six other consuming countries have thus far contributed or pledged the equivalent of about 4,000 metric tons. Our contribution would, we believe, encourage other consumers to contribute. It would also demonstrate, in concrete fashion, the seriousness of our commitment to participate in workable international commodity arrangements.

Since we consider that the ITA has economic benefits for us, both with respect to short-term stabilization and long-term assurance of reasonably priced supplies, we should share the cost of making it work. We have stated that the same principle of mutual producer-consumer responsibility applies as well to other commodity agreements which we have recently joined or may join.

An increase in the buffer stock will also strengthen our arguments within the tin council against the excessive and prolonged use of export controls. A larger buffer stock should permit the ITA to moderate the price volatility which has plagued the tin industry during the 1970's. Over the longer run, such enhanced price stability, along with appropriate tax and investment policies in producing countries, should help bring about the new investment necessary to assure adequate supplies of tin in the 1980's and beyond.

The provisions of H.R. 9486 would assist us to carry out our objectives with regard to the ITA. The bill would authorize the President to direct the Administrator of the General Services Administration to transfer up to 5,000 metric tons of tin metal to the International Tin Council. The contribution would be made from metal which is surplus to our needs under the Strategic and Critical Materials Stock Piling Act. At the moment, GSA holds some 168,000 tons of surplus tin out of a total stockpile of 201,000 tons, so that the bill would have no impact on our strategic needs for the metal.

Based on the number of votes we have in the tin council (26% of total consumer votes) our pro rata share of the 20,000 tons of consumer contributions provided for in the agreement is 5,220 tons. This quantity at the current ITC floor price would have a value of $43.5 million which is the valuation given to our contribution for purposes of liquidation and repayment to the United States upon termination of the agreement. At current market prices, however, $43.5 million would equate to approximately 3,500 tons of tin metal. It is this quantity, therefore, that the United States would contribute in the present circumstances. Should either the market or ITC floor price change prior to the contribution, however, the amount of the contribution would be adjusted accordingly. We anticipate that the tin will remain physically in the United States and will be sold here.

This contribution will not disrupt the tin market. As I noted earlier, the market price is substantially above the ITA's present price ban. The release of additional tin metal through our contribution will help to dampen these high market prices. Some producer countries themselves, realizing that excessively high prices will cause a long-term shift in consumption away from tin, welcome our proposed addition to the tin buffer stock.

I would note here that while we have used the term "contribution," we are in effect making an investment in the tin buffer stock. This investment will be returned to us at the termination of the agreement in 1981, along with our pro rata share of any profits resulting from buffer stock operations. While a profit is not guaranteed, contributions have earned an average return of 8% per annum in past agreements.

Wheat. As you know, a negotiating conference convened in Geneva last week to begin negotiations on a new International Wheat Agreement that would replace the 1971 International Wheat Agreement, which lapses this June. The conference will consider both a new wheat trade convention and a new agreement of food aid to food-deficit developing countries. Our principal objective in these talks is to obtain an agreement that will help to stabilize world wheat prices, expand trade in wheat, and enhance world food security.

We are the largest wheat-exporting country. Our share in total world wheat exports for the current crop year will be around 40%—down from 47% in 1972–75 but still crucial for our overall trade position and the well-being of our domestic producers. Our dominant position in wheat trade, however, has carried with it certain costs. Because some countries insulate their domestic markets from world trade, we have borne a disproportionate share of the burden of

adjusting world supplies to shifts in demand. We have held the world's wheat reserve stock, and it is our farmers who have had to adjust production to meet major variations in world demand for wheat.

I cannot now describe in detail the provisions which will emerge from the negotiations. The text under consideration, however, includes all the major elements we proposed in the International Wheat Council last year. The system, in our view, should be based upon nationally held, internationally coordinated wheat reserve stocks which would be used to stabilize the world wheat price within a wide price band. We are opposed to setting rigid maximum and minimum trading prices since experience shows that such rigid limits could not work without equally rigid market-sharing provisions. Such an agreement would not be acceptable to any of the major participants in the negotiations.

Any wheat agreement needs to be accompanied by provisions for liberalizing the world grain trade. We should insure that efficient producers have an incentive to maintain productive capacity. One or two countries should not be forced to carry the major burden of adjustment to market changes.

Coffee. Coffee is a commodity for which we already have an agreement. In fact, the United States has participated in three International Coffee Agreements since 1962. The characteristics of the coffee economy and its market conditions dictated a market-sharing approach in this case rather than a buffer stock approach. Coffee agreements have relied primarily on export quotas to insure orderly marketing of surplus production and stocks which prevailed for most of the 1960's. The 1962 and 1968 agreements succeeded in their objectives of preventing a collapse of coffee prices to disaster levels and of encouraging exporters to move into other products offering higher returns. In retrospect it seems that the disincentives to new investments were excessive as was the decline in stocks during this period. Thus the world was ill-prepared for the sharp production losses in Brazil and elsewhere in 1975, resulting in record high prices.

The 1976 International Coffee Agreement is essentially a standby

agreement, intended to encourage a recovery of production from the tight supply situation brought on by the 1975 Brazilian frost and temporary declines in production in other producing countries. The export quotas provided for in the agreement are in suspense and will not come into effect until the market price descends to the trigger levels set in the agreement.

The formula employed currently would place the trigger levels between 63.5¢ and 77.5¢ per pound, although they can be adjusted by mutual agreement of producing and consuming countries. Export quotas would be distributed among producers largely on the basis of their historical export performance in the postfrost period and also according to their proportion of total world stocks.

This arrangement is meant to encourage producers to market available supplies in the short run and in the longer term to follow more rational stocking policies. The latter point is especially important because a buildup of carryover stocks will moderate future price escalation. The agreement also includes a provision for the suspension of export quotas when the market price has risen 15% above either the average for the previous year or an agreed price range. This provision should permit accumulated stocks to enter the market and moderate the price rise. The existence of adequate stocks in producer countries will be crucial to the success of this mechanism.

The members of the agreement have also begun a study of the feasibility of putting national stocks under some form of international control. This study is provided for by one of the provisions of the agreement. We participated fully in the first meeting of the study group. There are many problems that need to be explored in detail. Still, we welcome a thorough examination of all the possibilities for pursuing the goals of the agreement through international stocking arrangements.

While prices reached extraordinarily high levels during 1977 as a result of catastrophic frost in Brazil and production disturbances in other countries, coffee production is now recovering from the low levels of 1975, 1976, and 1977, especially in Brazil. As a result, prices have begun to decline.

Rubber. International discussions on

DEVELOPING COUNTRY DEPENDENCE ON PRIMARY PRODUCTS FOR FOREIGN EXCHANGE EARNINGS

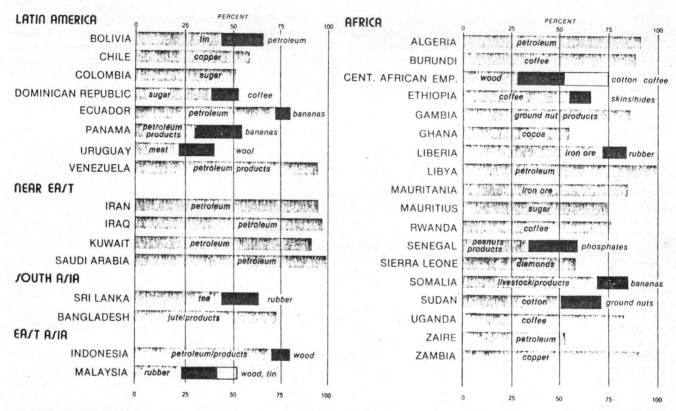

Source: International Financial Statistics, 1976.

the stabilization of the world market for natural rubber have been going on since early 1977 under the sponsorship of UNCTAD. Technical work on the operation of the market and possible elements of a workable stabilization agreement are well advanced, and at their next meeting beginning February 27, producing and consuming countries are expected to decide to convene negotiations on an agreement later this year.

Our interest in such an agreement would be to seek to stabilize the price of natural rubber and to encourage the investment we believe will be needed to increase production in the mid-1980's when shortages of natural rubber are forecast. Higher synthetic rubber prices and greater use of radial tires have increased demand for natural rubber, and we have an interest in helping to assure a growing supply of natural rubber at stable prices.

There is still no consensus among producers and consumers, however, about the details of an acceptable rubber agreement. On the basis of the studies done within the executive branch, as well as the international consultations which have been held, we have concluded that it could be feasible to establish an international buffer stock for natural rubber which could stabilize prices within a reasonable range. We are, therefore, prepared to participate actively in the negotiations for a natural rubber agreement and to recommend U.S. participation if a satisfactory agreement is concluded.

Copper. International discussions on the need for stabilization of the world copper market have been going on for more than a year under UNCTAD sponsorship. Copper is one of the major commodities in international trade, with more than $5 billion traded in 1976. We are the world's largest

producer and consumer of copper. Although we are not heavily dependent on foreign sources of supply, excessive instability in the world copper market does have a serious effect on our producers and consumers of copper.

Prices worldwide are currently depressed as a result of slow economic growth in major consuming countries and continued high levels of production, particularly by developing country producers. The large overhang of supply has pushed prices below average U.S. production costs and has led to a recent upswing in imports. Our net imports of copper amounted to about 20% of our consumption in 1976–77, up from about 12% over the previous several years. This situation is a phase of a typical copper cycle; the copper market has tended to be closely tied to the general business cycle and has long been marked by wide swings in prices.

We are now engaged within the government and in the UNCTAD talks in the analysis of the underlying problems of the copper market and the feasibility of international measures to correct them. The feasibility of an international buffer stock to moderate price fluctuations will depend largely on technical factors—including competition from substitutes and the identification of an acceptable price indicator. We would particularly want to assure ourselves that any international stabilization measures on copper take full account of the interests of our domestic industry and do not encourage uneconomic shifts of consumption from copper to other products.

Earlier this month, the third UNCTAD preparatory meeting on copper agreed to establish a producer-consumer forum to continue this international study of the copper situation. The producer-consumer forum will carry out additional technical analyses of the copper market and study alternative stabilization schemes. It will also serve to improve the quality and flow of information concerning conditions in the market. This latter step alone could contribute to improved functioning of the market. If the producer-consumer forum later determines that additional international action may be feasible, it could recommend the convening of negotiations for an international stabilization agreement.

Sugar. With respect to sugar, the President sent the new International Sugar Agreement to the Senate last month [January 25, 1978] for advice and consent to ratification. We intend to submit implementing legislation to the Congress shortly. The agreement was concluded last October, after very difficult negotiations, and entered into force provisionally on January 1. It is intended to stabilize the world market price of sugar.

In contrast to the situation in coffee, the sugar agreement must initiate action that will cause the depressed market price to rise up into the agreed range of 11–21¢ per pound. Later, it will function to prevent the sort of extreme price peak experienced in 1974 when prices rose above 60¢. The agreement depends on a system of nationally held, internationally coordinated stocks combined with export controls. A special stock of 2.5 million tons—built up over a 3-year period when prices are low—would be placed

on the market when the world price rose above 19¢, thus helping to protect consumers against excessive price increases.

Of particular interest is an innovative scheme for financing sugar stocks. Each time sugar is traded on the free market by a member country of the agreement, a nominal fee will be collected for the stock financing fund. This fee—about ⅓ of a cent per pound—amounts to only 1/100 of the retail price of sugar in the United States. Collection of these fees will build a fund amounting to $400–500 million over a 5-year period. Interest-free loans from this fund will be made to exporters for the cost of carrying special sugar stocks. The exporters will receive 1.5¢ each year for each pound of sugar held in the special stock. The loans will be repayable when the stocks are released at a time of high sugar prices.

The stock-financing plan demonstrates that financing need not be a problem in international commodity agreements. The sugar plan involves no cost to the U.S. Government and only an insignificant cost to the U.S. consumer. In return it provides strong protection against high sugar prices.

We expect the agreement to bring supply into balance with demand in 1978 and the world price to rise from the 7¢ a pound level which prevailed late last year to the 11¢ minimum. The U.S. import price should thereby rise to a level that would permit both U.S. and foreign producers to earn a reasonable return on their investment. When this level is reached, the President will be able to lift at least part of the 5.5¢ per pound import charges which he recently imposed as part of our domestic price support program.

The International Sugar Agreement is superior to a domestic program in several respects. The agreement can provide the same price stabilization benefits to producers as a domestic program without significant budgetary expenditures or without the high tariffs that lead to problems in our foreign relations. Further, the agreement can provide protection for consumers against high sugar prices. Domestic programs do not have the ability to limit sugar price increases.

The Common Fund

In addition to the discussions on individual commodities, the UNCTAD

Integrated Program for Commodities includes a proposal to set up a common fund to support international commodity agreements. The Administration supports a fund that would facilitate the efficient financing of international buffer stock agreements.

With that objective in mind, the United States and other industrialized countries agreed at last year's economic summit conference in London that there should be a common fund. This conclusion was underscored at the Paris Conference on International Economic Cooperation [May 30–June 2, 1977], at which we approved a final communique affirming that a common fund should be established, with its "purposes, objectives and other constituent elements" to be negotiated in UNCTAD.

In preparation for these negotiations, the industrialized countries developed a proposal in the Organization for Economic Cooperation and Development for a financially viable common fund that would consolidate the financial activities of participating international commodity agreements by pooling their cash resources and borrowing against callable capital or guarantees pledged to the fund through the individual agreements. The latter would retain basic responsibility for raising the necessary finance for buffer stocking and would also be autonomous in their policy and operational decisions.

There are two ways in which this scheme would lighten the burden of buffer stocking operations for all concerned.

• First, it would realize financial economies as a result of the offsetting price movements of different commodities associated with the fund. These economies derive from the fact under normal circumstances, price cycles do not coincide for all commodities, so that an international commodity agreement in a buying phase and needing cash could—through the fund—borrow from another commodity agreement in a selling phase and accumulating cash.

• Second, by consolidating the borrowing operations of participating agreements, the fund would realize financial savings in borrowing on capital markets.

With regard to measures other than

price-stabilizing buffer stocks, the industrialized countries have stressed their importance—particularly for commodities facing declining demand—but have argued that such measures can be effectively handled through producer-consumer commodity organizations, existing international financial institutions such as the World Bank, U.N. agencies, and bilateral assistance programs. We do not exclude the possibility that some improvements in current activities in this area may be desirable, nor do we exclude some role—such as coordination of the activities of producer-consumer bodies—for a common fund.

The developing countries are seeking a common fund financed primarily by direct capital subscriptions from governments, as distinct from a pooling arrangement based on international commodity agreements. The fund would finance not only commodity stocks but also a wide range of other, nonbuffer stocking measures, some of which are of a development type.

The negotiations are currently at an impasse. The second session of the negotiating conference in Geneva last November was suspended at the request of the developing countries one day before its scheduled conclusion. We expressed regret at the suspension and are currently exploring with other governments and the UNCTAD Secretary General whether a satisfactory basis can be found for resumption of the negotiations later this year. We believe a satisfactory outcome to any future negotiations, however, will depend to a large extent on whether the developing countries are prepared to give serious consideration to the proposal the industrialized countries have on the table. □

TRADE AND COMMODITY POLICIES: WHAT HAPPENS TO PEOPLE?

by Guy F. Erb

Negotiations and decisions on trade policies that involve governments and private institutions will affect the distribution of income within and between societies and thus directly affect the welfare of individuals. In the developed countries, trade policy decisions can mean the difference between employment or joblessness for industrial workers. In the developing countries, the impact of trade policies can determine a person's opportunities to break out of the vicious circle of poverty.

In the developing countries, governments frequently have failed to ensure that the fruits of trade expansion or increased stability of commodity export earnings have reached the largest possible number of their people. Only recently have governments begun to consider policies that explicitly link such international measures as commodity agreements to the fulfillment of the basic needs of the poor in developing countries. To a certain extent, the lack of such a link has contributed to resistance in developed countries to the idea that the developing countries should earn more from international trade. Such resistance is attributable on the one hand to the public perception that there is little evidence that measures are or will be taken in developing countries to promote the welfare of their poorest people and, on the other hand, to considerable evidence that changes in the international trade systems are resulting in a loss of jobs in the industrialized world.

The present negotiations on trade barriers and on commodity policy are being conducted at a time when there is significant growth in support for development policies that directly benefit impoverished people. Some international organizations and developed-country governments now emphasize programs—mainly through development assistance programs—that aim to more directly meet the basic human needs of poor people. On trade and other issues, the governments of developing countries have stressed since 1974 the changes that their proposals for a new international economic order would bring to intergovernmental relations. Simultaneously, increasing recognition has been given to the need to evaluate trade and aid policies according to their impact, if any, on the standards of life of all people. While trade negotiations among governments by no means contradict a policy emphasis on meeting basic human needs, there is a potential conflict between policies directed toward the claims of *governments* of developing countries on the *governments* of industrialized nations and policies that focus on the welfare of *individuals*.

In the absence of measures designed to distribute equitably the benefits from international

Negotiations on Two Fronts: Manufactures and Commodities (Washington, D.C.: Overseas Development Council, March 1978), pp. 57-60. Guy L. Erb is a Research Analyst with the Overseas Development Council.

trade or investment, higher income groups historically have received the largest shares of increases in income. In any society, elite groups are obviously in a position to ensure that they benefit most from the gains resulting from economic growth. In the present context, that tendency on the part of elites—plus a resistance in developing countries to the policies and requirements of donor countries or lending institutions that appear to impinge on their sovereignty—has already aroused considerable skepticism in the Third World about development strategies that aim at meeting basic human needs.

Such a response—however understandable in the context of national attitudes formed by recent emergence from colonialism and/or a continuing independence on industrialized economies—could contribute to the erosion of support in developed countries for trade and aid policies that are responsive to Third World concerns. The concept that the U.S. government should not aid rich people in poor nations at the expense of poor people at home has considerable appeal in the United States. Those proposing trade liberalization for developing countries and new commodity policies will be challenged to show the likely results of such policies in terms of gains to small farmers, miners, and landless laborers in agriculture. Moreover, those opposed to adapting to the developing nations' increased trade and financial capabilities and those critical of development assistance programs could justify their opposition by citing the apparent reluctance of developing countries to implement programs that meet human needs.

The need to devise measures that ensure that trade policies and transfers of external resources bring tangible benefits to poor people is a major challenge to U.S. and other policymakers. Attempting to direct gains from changes in international economic policies to the poor is one of the most intractable of development problems. Yet both community and central government actions can contribute to that end. In Latin America, cooperatives have been established among coffee workers to enable them to obtain a greater share of the income generated by coffee exports. In some Asian countries, government policies have contributed to a shift in the internal terms of trade in favor of the peasant agricultural sector, although they have not yet successfully insulated rural producers and small landholders from the effects of commodity prices that have fluctuated around a downward trend. Further measures are required to prevent widening inequalities of income distribution within developing countries.

Measures to link policy changes that affect relations *between* developed and developing states to the satisfaction of the needs of the majority of individuals *within* developing nations will not be easy to determine, but certainly are not—as some have suggested—irrelevant or impossible. Any "people-oriented" development strategy will have to draw heavily on domestic resources, export earnings, and financial assistance. In most developing nations, progress toward improving low standards of living would be greatly facilitated by adequate export earnings and receipt of financial resources from abroad; even with a significant change in the domestic distribution of income—something very few countries have been able to accomplish—the need for external resources will continue to be relatively high. The real challenge to any government and to international officials is to design and implement development programs that distribute the gains from trade and aid more equitably—and to include in the process those who will be affected by its results.

Representatives of developing countries often advocate changes in interstate economic systems on behalf of the poor in the developing world. In contrast, representatives of industrialized countries frequently stress inequities in the distribution of wealth and income *within* developing nations. In fact, the record of both national and international policymakers in reaching poor people with development activities is far from satisfactory. Two kinds of changes are required: 1) in the developed countries, trade, aid, investment, and technology policies must be designed that will increase the stability and the amount of resources transferred to the developing world, and 2) in the developing countries, private and official institutions must channel additional resources to the poor. Both rich and poor nations are somewhat skeptical about each other's intentions and capabilities. But both sides can attempt to complement their efforts to bring trade liberalization and commodity negotiations to a successful conclusion—which will provide positive gain to both developed and developing countries—with measures that deliver benefits more directly to all people.

III. *U.S. Farm and Food Politics and Policies: in Pursuit of Whose Interest?*

INTRODUCTORY COMMENTS

In hindsight, it now seems demonstrably clear that U.S. agricultural policy has been an admixture of domestic and international considerations during and since World War II. And the evidence is even more marked during the decade of the 1970s. At home there is a new U.S. food policy agenda. Consumers, organized labor, welfare institutions, environmentalists, nutritionists, school boards and administrators, the poor, railroads, among many others, desired, sometimes demanded, to become involved in the enactment and implementation of farm policies--which, to most of those interests, were food policies. Internationally, the U.S. food policy agenda was different, but of growing importance: Food for Peace, the U.S.S.R. and detente, the Common Agricultural Policy of the European Community, the rise of Japan as an economic giant but deficient in food production, the advent of the People's Republic of China as a major food importer, the agricultural developments in Brazil, serious food deficits in some of the Third World nations, are among the important examples of the internationalizing of U.S. food policy. Domestic food policies often influenced what the U.S. Government was willing and able to do in developing international food policies; the reverse was nearly always true.

The first selection is from Fred Sanderson's insightful review of developments in U.S. farm and food policy during this decade. Sanderson is skeptical: "Whether anything has been learned from the food crisis of 1972-76 re-mains doubtful," in his opinion. Also, he poses some of the serious questions which will face the U.S. food industry next year and during the next decade.

The political truth of the matter seems to be that the United States has never had a national, even less an international, food policy. All four of the models sketched out recently by Fowler and Orenstein[1]--polyarch, pluralism, populism, and participatory democracy--have been at work in American agriculture during this century, and notably so since the technological revolution swept over the American farm in the 1930s, and especially after World War II. Even when the so-called iron triangle--composed of major farm groups, the agriculture committees in the House and Senate, and the dominant bureaus in the USDA--generally controlled policy directions in U.S. agriculture there have been many schisms, based on different economic interests and conflicting ideologies--which is, indeed the prescribed environment for pluralism. Sectional, commodity, social class, racial, and ideological differences have been more evident than admitted.

Recently Stanley Hoffman has observed that "the two central questions of politics" are: "who commands, and who benefits?"[2] And so they have been in U.S. farm and food politics, although insufficient research has been placed on answering the question of "who benefits?"; indeed, there are many contradictory opinions relative to the question of "who commands?"

The Carter-Bergland Administration has developed the rhetoric which would lead "toward a U.S. food policy," or such were its early claims. To use the typology of Fowler and Orenstein, U.S. food policy has been a rather quixotic combination of polyarchy and participatory democracy: "a more rational farm policy," to use Secretary Bergland's phrase, based on ". . .human nutrition,

around which we will build a food policy for this country and as much of the world as is interested."[3] These new policy directions are outlined in Carol Foreman's speech to the American Council on Consumer Interests, which is included in these readings.

However, realities of U.S. farm and food politics seem to be that pluralism (i.e., group interests) and populism continue to be the dominant "types" in this arena of American politics. The Secretary of Agriculture has to become a master juggler; if he succeeds in conciliating the principal interests of the dominant groups, then they applaud his performance. On the other hand, farmer populism is still alive in rural America, as the rise of the American Agriculture Movement (AAM) seems to prove. Two accounts of the AAM are included herein, one by a knowledgeable foreign observer of American farm politics and the other by an American agricultural economist who is also widely recognized a as an objective and perceptive student of U.S. farm politics. Moreover, and quite to the surprise of many reputed experts, the AAM was remarkably successful in 1978. To quote from an enlightening article by Leo Mayer, Senior Specialist for Agriculture in the Congressional Research Service, ". . .the unhappy farmers were responsible for two pieces of farm legislation, the Emergency Agriculture Act of 1978 and the Agricultural Credit Act of 1978, and several Executive actions."[4]

In democratic politics, success in achieving one's legislative goals makes it difficult to score a repeat performance. A successful strategy is almost surely undergirded with a particular set of conditions--time, place, circumstance, and leadership. As Mayer concluded: "The deciding factor determining whether the AAM will continue or fade into the landscape will be the price and cost situations."[5]

However, these price and cost situations are determined by the interplay of many factors which, in turn, evolve into political issues: that is, the resolution of these issues centers around the questions: who wins, who loses; who benefits, who pays the costs? Some of these issues have been on the national agenda for decades, even throughout our nation's history. But the content, significance, and efficacy of the issues do change as the political and economic structure of power in the United States changes, and it is continually in the process of transformation. The following sections in this chapter contain readings that mainly emphasize U.S. food issues which are mutually international and domestic in their impact and significance.

Importance of Farm Exports; the Politics of Food Imports

The United States has been facing a dangerous balance of payment deficit ever since the quadrupling of oil prices in late 1973 and early 1974. Fortunately, a steady increase in U.S. food exports has been of considerable value in keeping that total trade deficit within reasonable proportions. In 1978, the total value of U.S. food exports was $27.3 billion, and the USDA estimates a total of $29-30 billion for 1979. About 30 percent of all U.S. trade, in value, is now in farm exports; in tonnage, U.S. farmers now export three-fifths of their wheat, more than half of their soybeans, more than two-fifths of their rice and cotton, and three-tenths of their corn and tobacco. Probably no other sector of the American economy is as much affected by U.S. exports.

The readings were selected so as to provide background information, and an understanding of current trends. Some of these trends can hardly be viewed as satisfactory. For example, the developing nations are increasing their food imports from the United States, and in terms of their interest and ours, at least in the long run, this trend should be reversed.

Looking at the other side of the trade issue--i.e., imports--there has arisen a paradoxical although not unusual situation. The United States, like others, loves to export what are essentially surpluses, at least in terms of domestic demands. However, in the matter of imports, U.S. farm interest groups tend to move ideologically from free trade to protectionism, and politically from support for the Carter Administration to sharp denunciation of any move toward implementing a policy of comparative advantage. For example, consumers are more involved in the politics of sugar than we realize; in fact, sugar is a very interesting case study of U.S. foreign policy interests in conflict with U.S. domestic sugar interests. And much the same can be said for the continuing political battles over meat imports, although the developing nations still have considerably more economic (producer) interest in U.S. sugar policy than in the meat imports issue.

U.S. Development Assistance, Including Food Aid

The readings in these two important issue areas again stress the interweaving of U.S. foreign and domestic policies. U.S. development assistance policies and programs do, of course, extend much beyond issues concerning food and fiber. Nevertheless, the growth and development of the agricultural sector in the Third World nations is certainly a major consideration relative to the interests of U.S. agriculture, as well as the broader, more pervasive interests embodied in U.S. foreign policy. It is an increasingly interdependent world, but the politics of the interdependencies are complex, therefore difficult to reconcile politically.

Perhaps the most fascinating aspect of U.S. development assistance politics in 1978 was the way in which the funding process seemed to defy conventional wisdom; a political surprise which is reveiwed in Lanouette's short essay. Americans do seem to be turning inward, showing much more concern for domestic as compared to international issues. But the trend toward protectionism, if not isolationism, seems more individualistic than nationalistic. It is my pocketbook which must be the overriding social and political concern, or so the "meism" syndrome seems to indicate. Albeit, the results in this instance were heartening, hopefully propititious of things to come. When the "Foreign Aid Establishment" really went to work, explaining carefully and prudently the vital significance of foreign aid policies to the general welfare of the United States, there was a remarkable, and quite unexpected, display of support in Congress. Whether this strategy of personal education can be successfully repeated for fiscal 1980, and thereafter, is yet to be tested.

In 1954, Congress passed the Agricultural Trade Development and Assistance Act--usually referred to as P.L. 480, or Food for Peace. By the end of calendar 1977, over $30 billion worth of food, in terms of market value, had been shipped. However, P.L. 480 policies and programs have changed very considerably over the last 25 years. What was essentially a surplus-disposal program has gradually been transformed into a more orderly, humanitarian-based, economic assistance program for Third World nations, with more than a whiff of politics thrown in from time to time. The next 25 years of food aid will likely be measurably different than those of the last quarter century, and the recommendations of the Special Task Force seem to indicate future policy directions. The case of food aid to Egypt, as well as to Israel in an almost identical manner, is atypical. Much of the food assistance to both nations moves under the terms of the Foreign Assistance Act of 1961. And the "changing conditions" referred to in Parker's article relate much more closely to the U.S. endeavor to negotiate a long-lasting Egyptian-Israeli peace arrangement than they do to the development of Egypt as a "cash" market for U.S. agricultural products.

Building a U.S. Food Reserve

The Biblical story of Joseph in Egypt and his building of a food reserve in times of plenty in order to be prepared for periods of scarcity is to the point, but much too simplistic, relative to the varieties of food reserves issues now under debate.

The principal U.S. food reserve, and by far the largest, is the one held on the farms and in the elevators of America. This is mainly a price-stabilizing reserve, one held more in the interests of maintaining farm prices at a reasonable (admittedly a debatable adjective!) level, and largely paid for by the U.S. taxpayer. Recently, Secretary Bergland announced that by the end of 1978 this farmer-owned reserve held in storage some ". . .875 million bushels of feed grains, 410 million bushels of wheat, and 90,000 hundred-weight of rice." Price is the trigger that would cause the food to move from that reserve into the market; however, those commodities are neither owned, nor controlled, by the Commodity Credit Corporation.

The Carter Administration is also negotiating with other nations for the establishment of a world food reserve--an "International Undertaking on World Food Security," to use the title of Resolution XVII at the World Food Conference. As noted in the previous introduction, there are several reasons why these negotiations have not been consummated, not the least of which is the accumulation of sizable world food stocks and the consequent decline in the fears and anxieties which are caused by a world food shortfall. Also, there is continuing U.S. involvement in the negotiations to renew the Food Aid Convention and to establish a 500,000 ton Emergency Food Reserve under the control and jurisdiction of the WFP.

In other words, the United States is involved in multilateral, bilateral, and domestic food reserve programs. As examples, if some form of International Undertaking of World Food Security is finally agreed to by the negotiating nations, then the United States would be obligated to adhere to whatever those international rules are; if the 96th Congress should agree to the USDA's proposal to set up an International Emergency Wheat Reserve of up to 6 million metric tons of wheat, then the legislation would specify those rules concerning the building of stocks and their release. In the instance of the farmer-owned reserve, where Congress has set up a kind of de-subsidizing scale for moving food from storage to the market, the farmer would--at least in theory and probably in practice--make his/her own economic calcualtions as to whether to sell or continue to store.

Different interests are conducive to the molding of different attitudes and opinions. The readings explicate that particular point. The Interreligious Task Force on U.S. Food Policy, a particular coalition of churches, is arguing for a U.S. food reserve which would be owned by the U.S. Government and held primarily for the benefit of Third World nations in emergency situations. On the other hand, the National Association of Wheat Growers tends definitely toward the view that food reserves are price-depressing; ergo, they are opposed to them. The Congressional agriculture committees and farmer interest groups are skeptical of a USDA-controlled International Emergency Wheat Reserve. They are not so worried about the USDA going into the market in order to build the reserve, but there is some serious concern about the USDA

releasing the reserve into the world market because of the effect that movement might have on market prices. In turn, Bread for the World is deeply
skeptical of the American Farm Bureau Federation's (AFBF) food aid plan, which
was sponsored in the U.S. Senate by Senator Robert Dole (Rep., Dan.). Essentially, the AFBF proposal was to set up a dollar reserve which the U.S. Government would use to buy the requisite emergency food supplies. Brennon Jones'
analysis of that proposal seems to be precisely on target.

Organizing--Implementing--Participating

The last three sets of readings in this chapter were selected with three
quite different objectives in mind.

The first two readings emphasize the role of the President as the foremost
U.S. policymaker. However, the United States does not have an international
food policy, which is a quite typical condition in U.S. politics. Quite likely,
the final report of the U.S. Commission on World Food Hunger will elaborate at
length on that ostensible shortcoming, although it is doubtful that Congress
will do more than listen respectfully.

The reading which relates to the implementation of the 1976 amendments to
the U.S. Grain Standards Act is included for two reasons. The specific reason
is to indicate that the legislation has quite likely proved very beneficial in
terms of increasing U.S. grain sales abroad. The more general reason is that
implementation is a vital part of the policy process; a good law must be agres-
sively administered if its goals and objectives are to be achieved.

Finally, participatory democracy must be a part of any truly democratic
republic. There are definite dangers, to be sure; an uninformed citizenry
shouting banalities at timid and staring legislators is not an inspiring sight.

Albeit, an informed, articulate, active citizenry must always be one of the
nation's prime goals. The advice and counsel offered in this reading--"How to
Influence Your Members of Congress"--is a sensible statement on a significant
topic.

NOTES
    1. Robert Booth Fowler and Jeffrey R. Orenstein, <u>Contemporary Issues in
Political Theory</u> (New York: John Wiley and Sons, 1977). In briefest form,
polyarchy means the <u>representation</u> of citizens, not their participation, in
the political process.
    2. "Domestic Politics and Interdependence," in: OECD, <u>From Marshall Plan
to Global Interdependence</u> (Paris: OECD, 1978), pp. 181-82.
    3. Quoted in Carol Foreman's address at the USDA's 1978 Food and Agricul-
tural Outlook Conference--U.S. Senate Committee on Agriculture, Nutrition and
Forestry, <u>1978 Food and Agricultural Outlook</u> (Washington, D.C.: U.S. Government Printing Office, December 19, 1978), p. 10.
    4. "The Farm Strike," <u>Policy Research Notes</u>, published jointly by the
North Central Regional Public Policy Research Committee and the USDA's Economics, Statistics and Cooperative Service, July 1978, pp. 6-16.
    5. Ibid., p. 16.

AN OVERVIEW OF U.S. FARM AND FOOD POLICIES, 1972-1978

THE "WORLD FOOD CRISIS" OF 1972-1976

by Fred H. Sanderson

Did U.S. food policy meet the test of the recent food crisis? Defenders of the policy would point out that substantial reserves were released to meet the increased export demand, that acreage limitations were lifted (although with some delay), that the U.S., by and large, refrained from export restrictions (with the minor exception of the brief embargo on soybean exports in 1973 and the informal controls on grain sales to the Soviet Union and Eastern Europe in 1975); that American grain producers rose to the challenge by increasing acreage by 27 percent; and that production did catch up with demand, allowing prices of grains and soybeans to drop back to levels roughly equivalent, in real terms, to those prevailing before the crisis. The critics would point to the tripling of grain and soybean prices which became a major factor in launching the world-wide inflation that was subsequently intensified by the energy price explosion and the raw materials boom of 1973-74; the sharp reduction in U.S. feedgrain consumption which was necessary to make some 90 million tons of grain available to the rest of the world; the massive liquidation of livestock which is at the root of the current beef shortage; and the fact that the crisis could have been avoided if it had not been for the excessive acreage restrictions in the U.S. and Canada in 1967-72. If the

Extracted from "U.S. Agricultural Policy and Its Impact on the Rest of the World" (unpublished paper, June 17, 1978). Fred H. Sanderson is an economist with the Brookings Institution.

North American grain acreage had not been cut, another 100 million tons of grain would have been available in 1972.

Whether or not it was possible to foresee the unprecedented surge of export demand in 1972-75 (which was compounded by the North American crop shortfall in 1974), most observers would agree that there are lessons to be drawn from this experience. North American farmers cannot be counted upon to increase production quickly enough to avoid sharp price increases in the event of a series of major crop shortfalls: it took four years of extremely high prices before production caught up with demand. Substantial reserves are needed to meet such contingencies. There are differences of opinion about the probability of a recurrence of such events and the size of the required reserves. In the opinion of this author, instability in world grain markets is likely to increase because both Communist and developing countries are less likely than in the past to absorb crop failures by tightening their belts -- and less constrained to do so by the lack of foreign exchange. Therefore a reserve of 100 million tons of grain, over and above normal working stocks, would not seem to be excessive. There is a fairly broad consensus, on the other hand -- at least in the grain-exporting countries -- that the costs of carrying these stocks should be shared by exporting and importing countries.

U.S. Agricultural Policy in the Aftermath of the Crisis.

Whether anything has been learned from the food crisis remains doubtful. Following the sharp drop in world grain prices in the crop year 1976/77, American farm policy also returned to normalcy. Farmers, legislators and administrators once more became preoccupied with the problem of food surpluses -- even though stocks are still short of their 1972 levels which proved to be inadequate.

The 1977 farm legislation is essentially a replica of the legislative framework enacted in 1973, with support prices and target prices adjusted for the inflation of production costs which took place in the interim. However, two important innovations were introduced:

1. The target prices are now linked to cost-of-production escalators based on future increases in the prices of variable inputs. This is a potentially costly feature which protects farmers against increased costs without allowing for increased productivity. The burden of this provision is borne by the American taxpayer.

2. For the first time, the Congress has provided the legislative basis for a grain reserve aimed at price stabilization. The initiative for this provision came from the Carter Administration, which proposed a farmer-held reserve of 8 million tons of wheat and, subsequently, a reserve of 17-19 million tons of feedgrains, to be built up by offering farmers incentives to hold grain off the market for three years or until prices reach a specified release level and to sell when that level is reached or exceeded. The objective was to stabilize grain prices within a band between the acquisition price (equal to the support price) and the release price (140% of the support price for wheat and 125% for feedgrains). The legislation also provides that so long as this program is in effect, government-held stocks cannot be released at less than 150% of the support price (as compared with 115% in past legislation).

The measure found strong support among consumer and charitable organizations as well as livestock feeders, but was initially opposed by grain growers who favored a floor price but were reluctant to give up the chance for windfall profits in the event of crop shortfalls.

The Administration could have proceeded without new legislation. It already had the authority to acquire grains at the loan rate and could have followed its proposed guidelines for the release of government-held stocks. The government also could have revived the "reseal" (extended loan) programs of the past without new authority. But it decided instead to seek the grain growers' consent to legislation by offering various concessions, including (1) a generous payment for storage costs (20 cents per bushel, subsequently raised to 25 cents); (2) a low interest charge on the loan--which was subsequently waived entirely after the first year; (3) rather modest penalties for premature sale (the farmer, in this event, must repay both the loan and storage payments, with interest); (4) no penalty for failure to sell after the release price is reached, except that government storage payments cease at that point. The loan may be called only when the wheat market price reaches 175% of the current loan level (140% for feedgrains), but even at this point the producer can avoid selling by seeking a commercial loan. Another concession was the modest size of the reserve. The reserve program which finally emerged from the numerous compromises with the grain producers and their spokesmen in Congress is probably inadequate to cope with market instability and almost certainly less dependable and more costly than a government-held grain stabilization reserve would have been.

Domestic Political Pressures

The ink was hardly dry on the 1977 Farm Act when a new radical "American Agriculture Movement" began to stage "tractorcade" demonstrations and threatened a farmers' strike in support of demands for much higher prices than those provided in the 1977 legislation. An analysis of these demands by the Department of Agriculture concluded that the proposals would raise grain prices by 80-100%, soybean prices by 50%, cotton prices by 80% and retail food prices by about 20%. While the volume of U.S. exports would drop, the price increase would bring as much as $7.5 to $10 billion more. Farmers would almost double their net income but the gains would accrue largely in the form of increased land values benefitting present land owners. To bring crop supplies in line with the reduced demand at the higher prices, 75 million acres would have to be withdrawn from production.

Support for this radical program was limited to a small but noisy minority among farmers who were motivated, in the main, by temporary financial difficulties due to excessive debts incurred during the boom period. But some of the older farm organizations (such as the National Farmers' Union) also toyed with the idea of playing the OPEC game; and even the staunchly free-enterprise Farm Bureau Federation, which in the past had opposed all government interference, now called for payments to induce farmers to limit plantings.

Responding to these pressures, a bill was passed in the U.S. Senate in March 1978 which would have withdrawn between 30 and 60 million acres from production. The President threatened to veto the bill,

which was,in any event, defeated in the House of Representatives.
But in the effort to forestall the legislation, the Administration,
which had already introduced a modest acreage set-aside program in
August 1977, announced an additional program of acreage diversion
payments designed to raise market prices. While the final results of
the Administration's programs are not yet in, it appears at this writing
that about 24 million acres (11 million acres of wheat and 13 million
acres of feedgrains) have been withdrawn from grain production this
year. This represents a 14 percent reduction from the grain acreage
harvested in 1977.

When the additional acreage diversion measures were announced, the
Department of Agriculture estimated that they would raise market prices
of wheat to about $3.30 per bushel and those of corn to about $2.70,
assuming normal weather.   These prices would thus be 45% and 35%,
respectively, above the loan rates. As of the end of May, actual prices
in Chicago were $3.33 for wheat and $2.67 for corn - a 50% increase from
their low points in August 1977. What grain prices would have been in
the absence of the acreage reductions is, of course, a matter of debate
but it is not unreasonable to assume that they would have been close
to the loan rates.

These price-raising actions represent a significant shift from the
past policy mix, which relied to a greater extent on stock accumulation
and deficiency payments to support farm incomes. Critics have pointed
out that the traditional policy would have been more consistent with
the Administration's objective to wind down inflation and to expand
domestic and foreign markets for U.S. grains and soybeans. The

principal appeal of the present course is that it keeps a lid on the
budgetary costs of the program, by shifting more of the burden from
U.S. taxpayers to domestic and foreign consumers.   The U.S. balance
of payments will also benefit: export proceeds from grains and soybeans
will be higher, at least in the short run, because of the low elasticity
of foreign demand--particularly if it is assumed that other grain-
exporting countries will follow the U.S. price leadership. But in the
long run, a high-price policy may well be counterproductive since it is
likely to stimulate production abroad and erode the U.S. share in the
world market.

THE USDA--NEW POLICY DIRECTIONS

ADDRESS TO THE AMERICAN
COUNCIL ON CONSUMER INTERESTS

by Carol Tucker Foreman

I can't tell you how pleased I am to have the opportunity to address the American Council on Consumer Interests again. I remember very well my last meeting with you at your convention in Atlanta in 1976.

In those days Earl Butz ran the U.S. Department of Agriculture. He stood on the stage of the Department's Auditorium and figuratively dared consumers to express interest or concern about America's food system. Earl Butz is out making speeches instead of making policy. He gets paid now for the kind of cracks that got him fired two years ago. Making speeches pays better than being secretary so I guess that we all benefit by having him in that unofficial role.

His belief that food and the Department of Agriculture belong only to a narrow segment of commercial farming rejected the historical role of the department. When Lincoln created the USDA, he called it "the people's department." Bob Bergland is working to restore integrity of USDA as the people's department.

One way that is in evidence is Secretary Bergland's belief that the nation needs a "nutrition policy" from which we can build a food policy. These must serve the framework for farm policy. There is no way they can be separated.

Through most of history, the human struggle for food has been directed primarily at simply getting enough to eat. This has led to government food policies that have focused mainly on increased production, better means of food preservation, and improved systems for the transportation and distribution of food.

Now, we are at a point where we have achieved a high degree of success in satisfying our domestic needs for adequate production, preservation, and distribution. Yet out of our very successes, new and troubling issues arise.

Today, production in this country is so large and reliable that we are able to feed ourselves and a large portion of the rest of the world and use food sales to help balance trade deficits. Yet this has also meant that we have recurring surpluses and that producers have trouble surviving.

Moreover, although millions of Americans are unable to get enough to eat without assistance, for millions of others nutritional problems are a result of consuming too much food.

We have been so successful in using chemicals to increase production, retard spoilage and preserve foods that we must now be concerned with the health effects of chemicals themselves.

Delivered April 20, 1978. Carol Foreman is Assistant Secretary of Agriculture for Food and Consumer Services.

We have become so dependent upon food processing and upon nationwide food distribution systems that the farm value of production bears little relationship to final costs of food.

And finally, because domestic population growth is leveling off and urbanization has slowed down, the rate of increase in domestic demand for food--which has been growing dramatically for years--may be slowing down.

We need to begin giving the most serious consideration to forging a _new_ food policy--a policy that responds to the dilemmas facing us today in a changing world.

The goal of this new policy should be to make available an adequate supply of safe, nutritious food at stable, reasonable prices--while providing a fair return on investment to farmers, processors and retailers, and decent wages to workers in the industry. The new policy should also be designed to provide for assistance to those at home and abroad who cannot afford the cost of a nutritious diet.

I would like to discuss those elements in some detail. But first, I think it's necessary to observe that this new policy would involve change-- including change in some of our existing programs and policies. It is important that if such changes are made, the resulting burdens should be spread across the population to the greatest extent possible. It is unreasonable to assume that farmers or processors or any other segment of the population should have to carry all the burden of change. At a minimum, change may require some adjustment assistance to those who will have to modify their traditional way of doing business. Further, consumer prices may increase as the costs of changes in processing and retailing are passed on. But, in the long run, the costs of a new system should be more than compensated for by increased efficiency and competition, reduced costs for advertising and some processing, more stable prices, a halt to the precipitous decline of modest-sized farms and perhaps most important, reduced health care costs as nutrition improves at home and abroad.

Now, to the six elements of the new policy.

I. Determination of Nutritional Needs

First, a food policy should be based on a detailed assessment of what the nutritional needs of the people are. To even begin to develop a food policy, we must first know what persons in various age, sex, racial and ethnic groups, lifestyles and geographic locations need nutritionally for optimal growth and performance and continued well being. Determining these needs will require a commitment to increased human nutrition research. A small program of nutrition research has been carried out in the United States since the 1870s but we still do not have adequate answers to some of the most basic questions.

For example, the recommended daily allowances of various nutrients are widely used, but are often of limited value in helping a person select a proper diet suited to particular stages of life and level of physical or mental activity. For some nutrients (such as some trace minerals) so little reliable data exists that no RDA at all has been established although the nutrients may be essential to good health.

We also need research on the relation of diet to disease. It now appears that 6 out of 10 leading causes of death in the United States may be degenera-tive diseases whose onset may to some degree be related to nutritional factors. Some recent studies have linked various nutritional factors to cancer.

At the same time, we need to learn more about the nutritional consequences of our increasing reliance on convenience foods, processed foods, and eating away from home.

To forge an effective food policy, we will need not only to increase our knowledge of nutritional requirements--but also to determine what levels and types of production are necessary to meet these needs. This will require an ability to translate nutritional needs into production terms. We should know, for example, how much wheat and what kinds of wheat should be produced to insure people with adequate levels of B vitamins. It is also important that we know what nutrients are available at consumption after processing. Naturally-occurring vitamins change when wheat is milled. We will need to know if the vitamins can be replaced by fortification. These and similar assessments will have to deal with the combinations required to provide the necessary nutrients in diets as consumed, not just as generated in the laboratory.

II. The U.S. Role in Feeding the World

The second element of a national food policy is the role the U.S. chooses to play in meeting international food and nutrition needs. The federal govern-ment must determine what portion of this will be done through trade, what portion through assistance and how much additional production is necessary to meet those needs.

The 1977 Farm Act calls for a domestic grain reserve system. It also encourages the Secretary of Agriculture to "enter negotiations with other nations to develop an international system of food reserves" for humanitarian relief. Participation in an international emergency food reserve is crucial if the U.S. is to live up to its international obligations. It can also demonstrate that participation in such a system will not ruin domestic farm prices or destroy foreign food markets.

But the complexity of international food issues demands more than a reserve system. Through Public Law 480, amended slightly by the 1977 act, the federal government has for 23 years used U.S. farm production as both a means of developing foreign markets for U.S. goods and as a means of providing food aid. A national food policy must determine how to balance the need of hungry people abroad with the needs of American producers eager to find new markets. We cannot allow over-emphasis on one to undercut the importance of the other. Nor can we permit political consideration to determine where we provide decent assistance.

Maintaining good, stable trade relationships is extremely important. It is clear that a vigorous trade program is essential to keeping stability in our balance of payments. In addition, stable trade relationships protect American farmers--and consumers--from the fluctuations of a speculative market in food exports. We must strive to avoid the circumstances that have led in the past to pressures for embargoes on food exports. The embargoes of soy-beans in 1974 and wheat in 1975 benefited no one. Trading partners and farmers were hurt. No discernible benefits accrued to consumers. Embargoes are basically an admission of policy failure and in an economy like ours, in which food is the keystone, we cannot afford such failures.

are basically an admission of policy failure and in an economy like ours, in which food is the keystone, we cannot afford such failures.

One final point. Although America's capacity for food production is unparalleled in the world, we cannot permit the need to sell American food abroad to destroy the incentive for other less developed nations to become more self-reliant in food production. The U.S. cannot base its entire food economy on exports.

III. Stimulation of Adequate Production

The third element of a basic food policy is to stimulate and sustain production adequate to meet domestic and international nutrition needs, and our country's trade needs.

In one sense, this does not represent a major departure from the policies we have followed for a number of years. Government policies have long encouraged certain kinds of production and marketing and discouraged others through support prices, research and regulation. Government production policies have never benefited all producers equally. Livestock growers, for example, are not covered by support programs. Fruit and vegetable producers are only sporadically covered by federal and state marketing orders. Federal government actions have always helped some areas of agriculture at the expense of others. Support programs leading to higher feed grain prices, for example, hurt livestock producers.

What a new food policy must do is to reassess which areas of agriculture are supported and promoted. In the future, the basis of such decisions must be to meet nutrition and trade needs. This will necessarily involve a reorientation of production patterns.

Naturally, a new food policy that reorients production patterns and support systems will initially be regarded as threatening by some persons. But the new policy does not have to be a threat. Changes can be carefully designed to avoid inequities, to make sure that one region of the country or some group of producers is not victimized by new policy goals, and to remedy inequities.

Indeed, any new policy must be constructed so that over the long run, it will cause less dislocation and be less inequitable than the policies of the past. In previous years federal policies, and the results of federally funded research, have caused ecnmic dislocation of farmers (especially small farmers), of farmworkers, and of some processors and retailers—and usually without any compensation.

There are, of course, a number of factors that would limit reorientation of production patterns. Among these are geographical factors and farmers' knowledge of new and different crops.

One example of the type of action I am talking about, in shaping production policy to meet nutrition and trade needs, is the creation of a domestic wheat and feed grain reserve. The new reserve system established by the 1977 Food and Agriculture Act is aimed at protecting farmers against low prices in years of surplus, and at providing an emergency food supply to meet domestic nutrition needs. The creation of the grain reserve provides a floor for farm production and is a basic step toward stable prices for some of our most essential crops. It also will provide the opportunity for government to

essential crops. It also will provide the opportunity for government to prove it can administer a production program equitably.

Land Price Problems

One fundamental issue of production policy that was not addressed by the 1977 act is the problem of skyrocketing land costs. Record grain prices in 1972 kicked off a boom in land prices that has not relented, despite the dropping grain prices farmers now face.

Nationally, agricultural land prices have doubled, on the average, since 1971. In the Midwest, prices have tripled. In the mid-Atlantic area urban development pressures have pushed up land prices. In the Midwest, speculation based on high farm prices has pushed up costs.

It is estimated that a new farm needs $500,000 to buy a farm and enter production. Few individuals have access to the credit necessary to borrow $0.5 million. This encourages purchase of land by banks, foreign investors and corporations, and it encourages renting rather than farmer ownership of land.

Moreover, if land costs continue to inflate as they have, the nation can expect ever-higher consumer food prices--which would in turn, if past trends remain true, further inflate land costs. In addition, continuously inflating land costs will effectively doom the family farm and seriously deplete competetion among food producers. Such a result is clearly out of line with fostering stable prices.

The federal government should begin an intensive investigation of the reasons for rising land costs and begin to develop policy recommendations to slow the trend. At the same time the department of agriculture must continue to develop more staisfactory formulas for dealing with land costs in support programs.

Finally, a new production policy will have to assure the farmer of adequate supplies of the elements of production. The energy crisis of 1973, and its resulting fuel/fertilizer price spiral, proved how vulnerable our food system, and individual farmers, are to energy shortages. Consideration should be given to the possibility of mandatory allocation of petro-chemicals for farm use. A new production policy might also include energy and soil conservation incentives and incentives for new kinds of energy-saving pest control and fertilization techniques.

IV. Reasonable Food Costs

A fourth element of a new food policy must be to assure the availability of food at reasonable prices.

In past years, full production has sometimes been touted as the answer to reasonable prices. But full production on the farm will not, by itself, guarantee moderate retail price levels. One of the most important elements in determining food prices is what happens to food after it leaves the farm.

Marketing costs have risen so sharply during the past few years that they now comprise 60 percent of the total food bill. Indeed, the Economic Statistics Cooperatives Service observes that the food price inflation of the 1970s has, to a large extent, been attributable to marketing cost increases. Between 1974 and 1976, marketing costs increased about 10 percent annually. According to the ESCS, "Increased marketing costs will again account for most of the rise in consumer food expenditures in 1977."

It is true that some of the marketing cost increase is attributable to higher energy costs and the general inflationary trend. But if we are to have both reasonable levels of farm income and reasonable prices for consumers, we simply must develop mechanisms to discourage unnecessary costs from being built into the food system between the time food leaves the farmer and the time it reaches the consumer.

This means that the government must cease any encouragement of industry practices, and halt the issuances of any government regulations, that add to costs unnecessarily. Government transportation regulations are an obvious area where review and revision could lead to reduced costs. The "back haul" regulations are a case in point.

Other areas that may also lead to unnecessary and inflated costs are inadequate competition, excessive advertising, and excessive packaging.

Inadequate competition is a particularly troublesome area. Recent studies have indicated that economic concentration in food manufacturing and retailing is increasing. According to Russell Parker, former Assistant Director of Economics at the Federal Trade Commission, 20 large grocery chains accounted for 37 percent of total grocery store sales in the United States in 1975. This represents an increase of more than one-third from the 27 percent controlled by the 20 largest chains in 1948. In a study for the Congressional Joint Economic Committee (JED) last year, University of Wisconsin researchers found that the four largest grocery retailers in 194 metropolitan areas held an average of 52 percent of grocery sales. In one fourth of those areas, they held 60 percent or more of sales.

Parker believes this leads to higher prices for many consumers. He asserts that FTC data show that "grocery chaims use hgiher markups or gross margins in high market share areas and have lower markups where they have lower market shares."

The study prepared for the JEC reached similar conclusions. It found "strong evidence that 'monopoly overcharges', i.e., prices above those in competitive markets, are likely in markets that are dominated by one or two firms and/or where sales are highly concentrated among the largest four firms."

The study estimated that total consumer overcharge due to economic concentration in 1974 was $662 million. The researchers concluded that overcharges vary from city to city, depending on the extent of concentration. They found that in 1974, consumers in one city with four-firm competition suffered a $1.6 million overcharge, while in another city with only two firms controlling most of the market consumers experienced an $83 million overcharge.

Concentration is also increasing among food processors. The number of food manufacturers has declined substantially over the past 30 years. In 1947, there were 44,000 food manufacturers. In 1972, there were only 22, 171. This may seem like a large number when compared to domestic automobile or steel manufacturers but several major food lines are highly concentrated.

Four firms control 84 percent of the breakfast cereal market and 95 percent of canned baby foods. Two firms have 58 percent of the soft drink market. There are no meaningful national figures on concentration in the bread baking industry, but on a regional basis, the four top firms in 19 different cities accounted for about 60 percent of consumer bread purchases.

Inadequate competition may explain why soft drink prices, persweetened cereal prices and bread prices rose as sugar and wheat prices went up a few years ago, but have not followed the downward spirals of those raw materials.

Many individual areas of food processing do remain competitive and fairly reflective of changes in the prices of basic commodities, but this is an area where public policy has skirted serious problems. The latest data available on food marketing in many cases is from the 1966 studies of the national commission on food marketing. Ten-year-old studies are of a limited value in making food policy, and a first step in this area should be creation of another commission or a specific mandate from congress to update the food marketing studies. Once the data is available, government should act to assure adequate competition in the food industry.

Of course, when competition on the basis of price declines, competition based on "product differentiation" and making heavy use of advertising, often increases. Competition among airlines is a classic case in point. Airlines now spend enormous sums to tell us that their planes fly in "friendly skies" or feature attractive hostesses who will "fly us" to our destination.

This same pattern is frequently seen in parts of the food industry. The decline of price competition is replaced by an upsurge in product differentiation" competition. In the food area, advertising and packaging are key elements of this growing type of competition. While both advertising and packaging have valid market place roles, expenditures for both have grown beyond reason in some product lines. Both together have become a significant portion of the increasing food marketing bill and need reexamination by manufacturers and policymakers.

Advertising now accounts for about three percent of the food marketing bill. Some of it is price specific but most of it is directed at production differentiation.

Of major concern is the increasingly heavy role of advertising in promoting non-nutritive food items. Government is becoming more concerned with the health implications of food advertising. The FTC has moved to regulate nutritional claims and may act to strictly limit food advertising aimed at children. The FAD commissioner has made clear his view that advertising is an extension of labeling and should be regulated accordingly.

There may be other ways government should encourage food value as measured by price and nutrition. Companies that advertise food on television might be required to gove equal time to nutrition messages. Government could make comparative nutritional price information available to consumers in places where people buy food and/or in the electronic or print media.

Government encouragement of advertising through tax deductibility has been attacked by some consumer organizations and this area is one for examination in public policy formation. Any limits on tax deductibility would, however, have to deal with the problem of special provision for advertising by new competitors entering concentrated markets, and for competitors with a small share of concentrated markets.

Packaging is another important area. Packaging costs now account for 13 per percent of the food marketing bill. Between 1958 and 1974, the consumer products cost represented by packaging doubled for items like dairy products, produce, beverages and candy. The Economic Research Service says that packaging costs are likely to increase 7 percent a year through 1980. The increase will come both from growing costs of materials _and_ from increased use. We don't know how much of these costs are accounted for by unnecessary packaging, nor do we know how much packaging is used solely for product identification purposes or how much packaging is needed for protection in shipping and sales. It is unlikely that government can make reasonable decisions about packaging without that knowledge.

It should also be noted that packaging now accounts for 30-40 percent of total municipal solid waste--and expenditures for solid waste disposal amount to about $4 billion a year. Reasonable public policy should assess whether that is an acceptable cost.

A few final points on food prices and what to do about them should be noted. There are two courses of action that we must resist as possible cost-cutting measures. One is to cut food costs by cutting farmer income even further. The other is to permit the use of questionable substances in foods or to relax health and safety regulations. There are few if any acceptable tradeoffs of safety for savings. A cheap food supply purchased at the expense of health protection is no bargain.

V. Safe and High Quality Food

Given what I've just been saying, it should come as no surprise that the assurance of a safe and high quality food supply is the fifth element of my food policy. Although food safety is virtually unchallenged as an appropriate goal, the means to achieving food safety have been in dispute for over 80 years. The federal effort to assure food safety dates back to 1906, when the original pure food and drug act was passed--in large part because of a grave public concern over the use of chemicals in prepared foods. The acceptability of chemicals in food continues to be a hotly debated issue today.

There are a number of laws on the books--such as the Food and Drug Act, and the Poultry Products Inspection Act--that are firm in their rejection of safe chemicals. A food policy that has as its first concern the nutritional well-being of the public can ill afford to be less strict than present law. Such a food policy must also include vigilant enforcement of these laws.

This may not be enough, however. Government action to promote food safety may need to enter new areas. Present laws deal with food additives and manufacturing processes. Yet evidence now suggests links between high consumption levels of substances such as salt and fat, and such diseases as high blood pressure and a variety of cancers. A food policy concerned with food safety should be able to deal with these problems as well. Perhaps we should become as concerned about the fat in a hot dog as we are about the nitrite.

In any event, whenever government takes action on a food safety issue to protect the health of its citizens--whether the action involved is unsafe chemicals or a substance such as fat--there is a potential for adverse economic impact on some companies and individuals. For example, pending government decisions that could lead to bans on the use of tetracycline in animal feed or the use of sodium nitrite in meat processing may have significant impacts on meat producers and processors.

When government acts to exclude previously approved products, public policy on food safety should include ways to ease the transition. This would require, at a minimum, collection of adequate data on what the real costs to the industry will be. Present data are almost always the industry's "worst case" assessment of the impact. Policy may also have to include mechanisms for easing the financial burden of smaller firms.

I know some will argue that consumer sovereignty in the market place should permit consumers to purchase anything, no matter what its health effects. But in other areas, the federal government does not fall back on that argument as a way out of its responsibilities. The federal government regulates dangerous or toxic chemicals. We attempt to control water and air pollution. Government funds the construction of municipal sanitation systems. Federal programs help protect people from disease via vaccination and innoculation campaigns. Government should play no less responsible role in the food system.

Government policy must also deal with the emerging issue of food quality. Public policy should address more adequately such questions as the construction and composition of processed foods. Industry is engaged in a constant effort to bring new technology to food processing. The results are sometimes ice cream that is not like what mother used to make, or tissue from ground bone in hot dogs. It is unlikely that public policy should exclude the results of new technology from the marketplace but it must find better ways to assure consumers that the quality of new foods--their nutritional value, taste and appearance-- are as good or better than the previous product. We must also find better ways to differentiate between products associated with certain basic materials or processing methods and those made in laboratories or with new ingredients or methods so that customers will understand what they are purchasing.

VI. Domestic Food Assistance

Finally, food policy must also deal with those people who do not have the ability to afford an adequate diet. Present government policy supports food food for such individuals through a variety of programs that approach the problem in various ways. The food stamp program increases food consumption by increasing income and limiting the increase to food purchases. The school breakfast, school lunch and other child nutrition programs provide meals in an institutional setting. The women, infants, children food program (WIC) provides prescription food packages to vulnerable persons at nutritional risk during the most critical phase of human growth and development.

The President has proposed to eliminate the food stamp program in favor of a general cash assistance program. His proposal assumes there will be no appreciable loss of nutrition as a result. Available studies seem to support that assumption. They show that low-income families tend to allocate their money wisely and to get more nutrients per food dollar than the middle income.

In the institutional feed programs--such as school lunch--the issue of food quality is becoming a growing concern. In the past few years, some items of questionable nutritional value--such as fortified grain-fruit products and formulated milk products, were allowed into some of these programs. We have moved to prevent their further use.

Plate waste and meals that fail to meet portion and nutrition requirements are additional problems of the institutional feeding programs.

These programs must be upgraded by placing greater emphasis on serving
healthy, appetizing diets in attractive settings. These programs should be
learning laboratories for good nutrition--teaching by example that food can be
both nutritious and appetizing.

The women, infant, children feeding program has perhaps the greatest
capacity to use good nutrition to improve health and assist in breaking the
cycle of poor childhood development that is often associated with poor nutrition. It provides high quality protein, iron, calcium and vitamins A and C
to pregnant women, nursing mothers and young children. Because WIC operates
through health care programs, it integrates health care, nutrition education
and food assistance. It has been shown to result in substantially increased
visits to prenatal and neonatal health clinics--as well as in the increased
consumption of nutritious foods during a critical growth stage.

Conclusion

The food policy I've described--and the questions it raises--may make
some people uncomfortable. Consumers worry that changes in the food economy
will hurt them by creating higher prices. Farmers are already angry because
more of the returns from retail food sales don't flow to them. They feel that
government intervention in production in the name of health or nutrition will
put them in an even more precarious economic situation. Processors and retailers already complain that their profit margins are too low, and that more
government regulation will cause their financial ruin.

The concern about prices and profits is reasonable. But we cannot ignore
our basic responsibilities to safeguard the nutrition and health of our
citizens. The challenge before us, therefore, is to shape a new food policy
that provides healthful food, and does this at reasonable prices with a reasonable return to those who get the food to our tables. This is a big job, but
it is one of the most important tasks of public and private policy in our time.

A RESURGENCE OF AGRARIAN POPULISM

THE AMERICAN AGRICULTURE MOVEMENT

by C. D. Caldwell

Despite arguments for "logic" from the Washington bureaucracy and for "better judgement" from existing national farm organizations, the American Agriculture Movement (AAM) continues - perhaps not exactly undaunted but still the strongest political protest in recent U.S. agricultural history. Not since the so-called "Farm Holiday Strike" of the 1930s has there been anything to compare with it. Following as it did on the heels of the new farm bill (passed by Congress in September 1977), which in effect set minimum prices for most farm crops, one has to conclude that farmers from the AAM are reacting in part to these prices as they translate to their individual cases. Clearly they are saying the values are simply too low.

What is the AAM? The American Agriculture Movement, because it is a "movement", is difficult to define since it has no official headquarters, records, memberships registration nor constitution. Its membership share only a very broad common objective, often described simply as 100 percent of parity for agricultural prices. They claim to represent one million producers and 90 percent of U.S. agricultural production. While this cannot be confirmed (and is undoubtedly overstated), there is no doubt that they do have a rather large and vocal following. They appear to have a high proportion of relatively young, medium-to-large grain farmers within their ranks. They categorize themselves as being largely class 1 and 2 family farmers which on this scale would indicate they had farm sales in excess of $40,000 per year. They also claim to have representation from 41 states and to have established 2,100 strike offices within those states. There is no question about the fact that they have become a significant political force and thus far they have shown little sign of relenting.

What is the AAM's Approach? The tactics of the AAM have been well reported in the media, including the Canadian press. The main thrust has been geared to drawing public attention to their cause and informing governments of what they call "the facts". Protests have been peaceful in virtually all instances.

They started with a declaration of a "farm strike". This was essentially an ultimatum issued to the Federal Government indicating they would refuse to produce if their demands for higher prices were not met. They then staged a series of tractor cavalcades in Washington, D.C., and various state capitals prior to the close of the Congress in mid-December. They have since held other tractor rallies, including one in Washington in mid-January. They have "blitzed" the Capitol by having a constant stream of members in Washington on a rotational basis talking to Congressmen, Administration officials, including White House representatives, Senators and other agriculture interests. They have kept continuous pressure on their elected officials in both state and

Agriculture Abroad (Canada Department of Agriculture), April 1978, pp. 49-53.
C. D. Caldwell is Counsellor (Agriculture) Washington, D.C.

federal capitals. They have established numerous regional strike offices manned by volunteer farmers. They have raised funds to keep representatives in Washington knocking on people's doors.

Perhaps best known to Canadians was the action to blockade beef imports at various western border points. These activities carried out over three or four weeks effectively stopped livestock shipments to the U.S. The action has since ceased, however, primarily because the AAM members felt they were getting too much adverse publicity which was counterproductive to their cause.

What does the AAM Want?

The AAM wants agricultural commodity prices to be set at 100 percent of parity. Parity is essentially a ratio that compares the prices farmers receive for their commodities with prices they pay for production and living expenses. The comparison is made relative to a base period (1910-1914) when prices received and prices paid supposedly stood in an appropriate relationship to each other. Parity prices therefore are prices that would give a unit of a commodity -- say a bushel of wheat -- the same purchasing power it had in the base period. In the case of wheat, the present parity price has been calculated at $5.04 per bushel.

In addition to "100 percent of parity" prices, they talk in terms of restricting production and imports severely and also of having a farmer-controlled system of sharing the restricted sales at these higher prices. They argue that current prices do not cover their costs, and that consumers have been paying too little for food for too long. Many of their arguments rely on this simple logic and while it appears that they are sincere in their demands, it is equally clear that they would settle for far less.

Their demands are not completely without foundation. For one thing, numbered among the AAM are farmers who made heavy financial commitments during the early 1970s when agricultural prices were very high. These people are particularly vulnerable in the current price slump. Also, in a more general vein, for the U.S. as a whole, while receipts from farm marketings were up last year, so were costs -- and by a higher proportion. Farm assests, on the other hand, went up substantially, reflecting increased land prices which were still adjusting to the higher farm prices of 1973-75. The result was a serious cash flow problem, particularly acute in the grains area.

What is the U.S. Reaction?

Public reaction by and large has been sympathetic to the farmers. The AAM claim they have not received as considered and as extensive a press coverage as they wished and that the press has tended to play down the significance of their movement. On the other hand, the press on the whole has been sympathetic rather than hostile, seemingly recognizing that the AAM members do indeed have legitimate complaints. Not being able to legitimize their representation, the press is naturally guarded in coming out and saying the AAM speaks for American agriculture.

State legislators, as might be expected, have, cautiously at first, but in recent times much more vocally, supported the Movement. Indeed, 15 mid-western state governors, as a group, requested and got special meetings in Washington with the President, the Secretary of Agriculture and other key Washington officials to specifically discuss their concern over the plight of their rural population.

Federal congressional representatives and senators have also reacted in predictable fashion. There has been a spate of what are essentially private member bills introduced into both Houses by representatives who have come under pressure from the AAM. These bills range all the way from legislation that would implement precisely what the farmers are demanding down to simply requesting the Congress to sympathize with the farmers. There are Bills to improve farm markets overseas, to expand credit facilities for exports, to increase acreage set-asides, to control meat and other imports more stringently, to increase target and loan rates for key commodities and the list goes on and on. Most of these bills will never get to the Committee stage of course, but they have the effect of temporarily appeasing some of the farmers. In addition, there have been a number of calls by the Congress for the Administration to use the authority they already have to help alleviate problems in the agricultural sector.

The Administration (where the AAM focus has been principally on the USDA and the White House) has argued that doing what the AAM wants would mean economic disaster in the long run. They point out that 100 percent parity has lost much of its meaning relative to 1978 because of the vastly different circumstances now prevailing. They point to the tremendous burden that would be placed on the Federal Treasury if support levels were raised. They point also to the inflationary implications of doubling farmers' incomes and adding 15 to 20 percent to the consumer's food bill. Finally they argue that foreign markets would be lost and production outside the U.S. would increase to the complete detriment of American agriculture.

The existing farm organizations (e.g. The American Farm Bureau Federation, The Grange, The National Farmers' Union) find themselves in a difficult position with respect to the AAM. They know that the AAM includes many of their own membership whom they do not wish to alienate. On the other hand, they cannot endorse what the AAM stands for or why would they, as an organization, not have demanded similar reform thus obviating the need for a separate organizations. They have denounced the more extreme positions the AAM has taken, including border blockades and outright strike by withholding or plowing under planted acreage, as misinformed judgement and have described 100 percent parity of prices as either too costly and therefore unrealistic or as a goal that should be pursued through the free market.

What Has Been
the Impact of
the AAM?

While impossible to predict the ultimate results of the AAM or the fate of the movement itself, it is interesting to see what impact this movement has had so far. Certainly in terms of consciousness-raising, there are a great many more Americans aware of problems in agriculture today than there were only 100 days ago. On the other hand, the Administration and key members of Congress want to head off the AAM's demands for legislated increases in farm prices because they are convinced it would mean intolerable consumer price increases and begin a renewed round of spiralling inflation. Notwithstanding this conviction on the part of the U.S. Administration, there is evidence that the economic conditions facing agriculture, particularly in the grain sector, are being monitored by government more closely now than prior to the time the AAM activities began.

There have been renewed efforts to convince farmers that the new farm bill will begin to affect prices upward in the months ahead. More emphasis has been placed on the desirability of producer participation in set-asides and reserve programs. Secretary Bergland has increased the payments for grain storage to encourage its movement into reserve and has gone ahead with his 10 percent feed grains set-aside program. He has also announced a number of new programs or program expansions designed to improve the competitiveness of U.S. agricutlural products in foreign markets, including additions to PL 480 and Commodity Credit Corporation (CCC) credit facilities, expansion of trade promotion and cooperator market development offices, and more aggressive pursuit of Multilateral Trade Negotiations (MTN) objectives for trade liberalization in agriculture. In addition, there is a move afoot to increase the loan rate for soybeans and to ease the longer term credit pressure facing many farmers 1/. Secretary Bergland has instructed his Department not to foreclose on producers with outstanding loan accounts with his "Farmer's Home Administration" which loans money to farmers for disaster relief.

While it is not possible to relate any of the above activities directly to the AAM activities, it is possible that the farmers' presence in Washington helped to speed up announcement of the new programs. Certainly it is highly unlikely the Administration or Congress will ever press for measures as far reaching as those proposed by the AAM. However, it is possible that if the AAM protest persists, government will be forced to re-examine their position and could decide to make some adjustment to loan rates on some key commodities. Legislative authority for moderate action on the loan rates exists in the Farm Bill in its present form.

As for the AAM, no one seriously expects their strike action to ever be effectively reflected in actual production cutbacks since history points to a dismal failure on each of numerous previous attempts. They are being looked at less and less as "flash in the pan" reactionaries the longer they persist, but their perseverance in the face of planting time already getting underway in the deep south will really tell the tale. Whatever the immediate outcome from actions of the AAM, in terms of programs and legislation, it may be that we are watching the dawning of a new era in American agriculture. In recent years of high agricultural prices, the commitment of USA producers to the open market and public price formation mechanisms was the norm, at least among grain and oilseed growers. A new breed of U.S. producer, exemplified by the typical AAM member, may be saying that the costs of being the "most efficient" are too great. Certainly there appears to be more interest and less fear of "orderly marketing" concepts in recent times than in previous years.

1/ On March 30, 1978 the Administration did, in fact announce an increase in the loan rate for soybeans, from $3.50 to $4.50 per bushel.

THE AMERICAN AGRICULTURE MOVEMENT--
ITS PROPOSALS, AND SELECTED RESPONSES

by Harold F. Breimyer

In the winter of 1977-78 a new farmers' protest movement burst on the U. S. scene. Parity prices were demanded and a strike threatened. New farm laws were lobbied for. It came to be known as the American Agriculture Movement.

In spite of wide news coverage, the Movement's ideas for farm policy are not well known. The impression was created that AAM leaders thought Congress need only legislate parity prices. Yet when the leaders presented their case to Congress (House Committee on Agriculture) they proposed a tight program of allocating marketing quotas to individual farmers. According to their "Recommendations" the volume of marketings would be limited so as to hold prices parity-high.

The Recommendations are probably the most authentic available statement of AAM proposals. Some are incorporated in a bill, S.2626, recently introduced in the Senate by Senator Hodges of Arkansas among others. Highlights of the Recommendations will be reviewed here.

The Recommendations document was submitted to the Congressional Research Service and to a number of economists, all of whom were asked to examine it and report back. The responses received will be summarized briefly.*

THE AAM'S PREMISES

The AAM statement submitted to Congress begins with these paragraphs:

"The American Agriculture Movement was conceived to preserve the family farm system, the most efficient food producing unit in this nation. We have little time left as more than 25% of farmers and ranchers will be forced either to refinance or to liquidate their operations this year. We have lost equity and enormous sums of money for the last

four years, and we are now on the verge of bankruptcy. Unless something is done, only big money entities, or possibly the government, will be left to produce the food.

"The American Agriculture Movement is not another farm organization. There are no memberships, dues, secretaries, or presidents. We are a group of individual farmers, ranchers, and agribusinessmen, unified together in order to achieve the fair price of 100% parity for all agricultural products."

Highlights of the rest of the statement are:

*The American people pay only 16.8% of their disposable income for food and could afford to pay the 19.9% that would give farmers parity prices.

*Subsidies are not wanted, as farmers are "tired of government dominance, speculation, manipulation, and big money influence . . . ."

*As to markets, "we no longer have a free market system." And, "we can no longer have a free market system."

*Parity prices would "insure a thriving agricultural sector which would revitalize the entire economy."

A NATIONAL AGRICULTURAL BOARD

Heart of the proposals that follow the introductory statement is that a National Board of Agricultural Producers would be established and charged "to devise and approve agricultural production and marketing policy." The Board would have the major assignment of calculating for each year the quantity of farm products needed "for both domestic and foreign trade requirements" and of allocating that national quantity among individual producers.

Producers then would be subject to strict limits, not on their production but on their marketing. "Producers may grow, raise or produce anything and as many units . . . as they desire." But they would be "provided marketing certificates by the National Agricultural Board . . . to assure every producer the opportunity to market a fair share of the market needs." As further explanation, "marketing certif-

---

*The AAM statements and responses to it are published in a Committee Print of the Committee on Agriculture, U. S. House of Representatives, "Evaluations of Proposals Guaranteeing Full Parity for Farmers in the Marketplace," March 1978.

icates for each producer shall be based upon that producer's production history average. Conditions shall be established to
provide marketing quotas for those without
production history . . . ."

The control over marketing is to be
the mainstay of the sought-for 100%-of-
parity prices, which are to prevail "in
lieu of direct and indirect subsidy payments . . . ." But parity prices would be
legislated too. "It will be illegal for
anyone to buy, sell, or trade any agricultural product at less than 100% of parity."
At the same time, to protect the consumer
"a ceiling price of 115% of parity at the
producer level shall be established . . . ."

The National Agricultural Board would
have some latitude in defining parity.
Parity could be set within a range between
the "current revised parity formula" and
the original parity based on 1910-14. Also,
farm products that fail to meet specified
quality standards could be sold at less
than parity.

No farm products could be exported at
less than 100% of parity. None could be
imported at below 110% of parity.

If farmers should produce more than
could be marketed at 100% of parity -- that
is, more than the volume of their marketing
certificates -- they would have to hold the
surplus quantities themselves. The one exception is that Congress would be authorized
to set up a National Strategic Reserve Program. Sales from the reserve could not be
made at less than parity, nor as substitute
for producer sales.

The actions of the Agricultural Board
would be subject to producer approval --
more exactly stated, producer disapproval.
A majority could overturn the Board's program. "If . . . more than a majority" of
producers having a production history who
vote in a referendum "oppose the proposed
rule or regulation, such rule or regulation
shall be withdrawn."

Under the heading of "consumer information" the AAM would require retail
food stores to "post information providing
a comparison between average cost to consumers for food products and the average
farm value of the same product in order to
clearly establish the amount which farmers
receive for their share of the food product."

S. 2626

S. 2626 has been introduced as the
"Consumer and Agricultural Protection Act
of 1978." It is not entirely an AAM bill,
but it has some features that resemble AAM
proposals. The board put in control would
be renamed the National Board of Agricultural Governors. It would represent not
only farmers but a sprinkling of individuals representing consumers, organized
labor, and business.

The National Board would have wide
powers. It could allocate "production or
marketing adjustments" required of farmers.
Compared with the AAM proposals the most
distinctive feature of the bill is that
the price to be set and defended is not
parity price but cost of production price.
Cost of production prices "shall reflect
cost principles and accounting procedures
utilized by business management in industry and trade." The cost calculation is
to include the value of land. Significantly, the land value would not be the current
market price of farmland but a value
corresponding to that used by the Internal
Revenue Service for estate tax purposes.

As is true of the AAM proposals,
referenda are authorized on programs for
each commodity. Producers would have to
vote majority approval before any commodity program could be undertaken. They
could also disapprove a program in force.

ECONOMISTS' RESPONSES

Upon receiving the AAM Recommendations
submitted to it the House Committee on
Agriculture asked the Congressional Research Service to make an evaluation. The
Service in turn invited 19 economists to
offer their judgments.

In general the economists' responses
are negative. Some question the practical-
ity of the AAM proposals. Others relate
to the validity of underlying assumptions.

John Schnittker, for example, doubts
that most farmers would accept certificates. To date, "only producers of
cotton, rice, tobacco, and peanuts" have
indicated a willingness to accept tight
controls. In 1963 wheat producers "turned
decisively against" strict controls, he
points out. Earl Heady notes that the
compulsory feature is essential to the AAM

proposals. Because parity prices would be attractive, "the program could not be successful unless all farms were forced to participate." Dale Butz, Don Paarlberg, D. Gale Johnson, Bob Jones, B. H. Robinson, Marvin Duncan, Luther Tweeten, and John Schnittker chorus that 100%-of-parity prices would cost U. S. agriculture dearly in loss of export markets.

Several economists object to parity as a workable guide for programs.

A fourth kind of objection is different. It suggests that the AAM program would have a backlash effect on the family farm system that it is intended to protect (see opening statement quoted above). Parity prices for farm products would bring a new land boom, giving a bonanza for present landholders but closing the door tighter against new farmers. Luther Tweeten says that the AAM program "could more than triple land price," and "this would have the effect of taking land out of the reach of potential new farm operators . . . . Hence it would mean separation of farm operation from ownership." Finally, "It would mean the eventual end of the family farm." Marvin Duncan and Harold Breimyer use less dramatic words to convey the same idea; and Willard Cochrane writes of speeding up the "cannibalizing" process whereby well financed farmers buy out thinly financed ones.

THE CONGRESSIONAL RESEARCH
SERVICE RESPONSE

The Congressional Research Service report is scarcely more favorable to AAM Recommendations than are the responses of individual economists. It contains much relevant information, however.

"Given parity prices," writes author Leo Mayer, "cash receipts would increase by over $40 billion annually which translates into $15,000 per farm . . . ."

To get parity prices, the acreages of corn, wheat, soybeans and cotton would have to be reduced 66 million from present levels.

The Research Service report, like the 19 economists' replies, shows apprehension about the effect parity prices would have on exports. The United States would become a "residual export supplier of farm products."

The sharpest criticism leveled in the Congressional Research Service report echoes that of Tweeten, Duncan, Breimyer, and Cochrane: the higher prices achieved under

a full-parity program would give most help to farmers who need it least and least to those who need it most.

"There would be a substantial difference," Mayer writes, "between owner-operators and renter-operators. Owner-operators would get the full benefit of higher prices along with the benefits of rising land values which would be very substantial." Land rents would rise very sharply; for renters, "most gains from parity prices would be relatively short-lived . . . ."

But owners' benefits would not be permanent. "Present owners would gain for whatever period they continue to own their land; the next generation of farmers would be no better off and would require a new upsurge of prices . . . ."

Benefits would be distributed "without regard to the economic misfortune of individual farmers or regions." Drouth areas of 1977 were cited as illustration.

But the strongest language is as follows: "Given parity prices, . . . larger farms would receive the largest income increases, although most larger farms are not among those with severely depressed income situations. Raising their incomes would provide them opportunity to purchase more assets from other, less economically strong farm operators. This type of action would tend to drive up prices of land and other assets . . . . Before long, most of the benefits of higher farm incomes would become capitalized into farm asset values, with higher costs for taxes and interest payments."

* * * * * * * * *

Editorial Comment

To use a hoary phrase, both the AAM proposals and the comments on them give "food for thought."

Perhaps one explanation for the spread of publicity given the AAM this past winter is that the Movement was a fresh voice that stimulated new thinking.

But the ideas are not new. The National Farmers Union, for instance, has been calling for full-parity prices for years.

Furthermore, the idea of limiting individual farmers' marketings so that prices can be lifted to a desired level is already in force on crops such as tobacco and peanuts, as Don Paarlberg points out. It has been proposed for other field crops many times.

What the AAM is doing is to put squarely before the farming community a fundamental policy choice: whether to keep farming in its long tradition of independent units that scarcely schedule their production and marketing other than to respond to guesses as to future prices; or to turn to industrial techniques and jointly program production and market deliveries according to what the market will take (at desired prices). The AAM declares that farming must go the latter route.

Present farm programs manifestly fit the former. As such they do little more than take the rough edges off the ups and downs in farmers' prices and incomes. To try to stabilize prices and incomes at anything close to parity level, without enacting programs with sharper teeth, would be too costly.

The AAM, in using marketing controls to get its price goals, deserves credit for its sense of responsibility. The Movement does not call for a drain on the federal Treasury.

The anomaly in the whole situation, missed by every economist who commented, is that the internal structure of agriculture is trending in a direction that, if continued, will make the AAM proposals more sensible than critics reared and schooled in another age now perceive them to be.

Agriculture is being concentrated into fewer farms. Less than a half million now contribute 80% of total output. For each commodity the number is much smaller. As fewer super-farms produce and market more of the total product, the AAM scheme for allocating marketings will become both more attractive and more practical. It might, paradoxically, eventually become less necessary -- the few farms could do what many cannot.

Potential gains from controlled marketings are especially attractive for field crops such as wheat and cotton, which are essentially industrial raw materials. Their prices are divorced from any close relation to consumer prices. On the other hand, the likely effect of price on export sales is a big restraint. This is true even though it is difficult to know how seriously higher prices would reduce exports. The 19 economists quoted above might have been too pessimistic. Much would depend on whether other exporters would fight or follow U. S. pricing.

If agriculture were to adopt industrial techniques as the AAM asks, various of the criticisms leveled by the 19 economists would be irrelevant. An example is the complaint that land prices would be pushed higher. When industrial firms boost selling prices they increase their asset values, and no one objects.

But the deepest meaning that could be read into the AAM is that its leaders might seem to be seeking the kind of agriculture that its proposals would fit. That is, are they promoting, consciously or subconsciously, an agriculture of fewer farms of increasing size? Much of the leadership of the Movement is of large, solidly established farmers even though its members include many smaller and younger farmers who are genuinely in financial trouble. One AAM leader was widely quoted as declaring that smaller farmers were not of the Movement's concern, and are dispensable. The opinions offered by Tweeten, Duncan, Cochrane, and myself, quoted above, may be the most trenchant of all the responses made to AAM proposals.

The AAM may be harbinger for a new kind of U. S. agriculture. Episodes of the past winter might prove to have ushered in a new era in our national agricultural history. At this stage, no one can know.

.... Harold F. Breimyer

* * * * * * * * *

A NOTE ON THE LATEST FARM LEGISLATION

At mid-May President Carter signed a law authorizing a $3.40 target price for wheat and a 48-cent minimum loan for cotton. The wheat target went into effect at once, as did the cotton loan.

The action could be regarded as "turn-about" between wheat and feed grains. Originally, the wheat program was regarded as the more attractive. Then diversion payments were added for corn and other feed grains. Now the wheat target values are raised higher. More important, though, is the sharp difference between program features. In wheat, targets and deficiency payments are relied on; in the 1978 corn program it is land diversion and payment for it.

* * * * * * * *

THE POLITICAL AND ECONOMIC IMPORTANCE
OF U.S. AGRICULTURE TRADE

CHANGING WORLD AGRICULTURAL TRADE

For many years, the United States has been the world's largest producer and exporter of agricultural products. That position is not likely to be seriously threatened in the immediate future, but important changes are occurring in world agricultural trade that have significant implications for U.S. agriculture.

THE BACKGROUND

Exports have become increasingly important to U.S. farm income. The United States exports the production from one of three harvested acres. Over the past 10 years we have exported about two-thirds of our rice production, half our wheat and soybeans, a third of our cotton, and a fourth of our corn.

Farm product exports generate domestic employment, stimulate income and have contributed over $10 billion to the U.S. balance of trade in each of the past four years.

U.S. agricultural exports are equally important to the world's economy. The United States consistently accounts for a much larger portion of world agricultural trade than it does of world agricultural production.

We generally account for more than half the world's trade in coarse grains and soybeans, though we produce less than a third of the world's coarse grains and only 40 percent of world soybeans; two-fifths of cotton and wheat trade, but only a sixth of world production; and 20-30 percent of rice trade, but only 2 percent of world output.

The United States also holds a fourth to a half of all world grain stocks. We are accounting for about 44 percent this year--much more than policymakers believe prudent for the United States to hold.

CHANGING DEMAND PATTERNS

There has been a sharp rise in the volume of U.S. agricultural exports over the past decade. In addition, subtle transitions have occurred in the sources and composition of foreign demand for U.S. farm products.

--An increasing share of our commercial agricultural exports is going to developing nations and to centrally planned nations such as the Soviet Union, Poland, Romania, and Yugoslavia. The centrally planned countries have doubled their share since the 1960's and the developing country proportion has also risen substantially.

Issue Briefing Paper, United States Department of Agriculture. September 27, 1978.

--While the volume of U.S. wheat shipments to developing countries has increased by more than a fourth since the early 1960's, there has been a remarkable shift in the mix of commercial sales and concessional sales. Two-thirds of all our wheat exports to the developing countries during 1961-65 were under food aid programs, compared with one-tenth during 1971-75.

--Food products have continued to account for half of U.S. agricultural exports since the early 1960's, but the composition of the remainder has changed radically. Cotton and tobacco made up a fifth of our exports during 1960-64, as did feedgrains and soybeans. Since then, cotton and tobacco's share have dropped 50 percent, and the feedgrain and soybean share has nearly doubled. Expansion in exports of soybeans and feedgrains accounted for nearly half the growth in U.S. farm exports--from about $5 billion in 1960-64 to nearly $27 billion in 1978.

--U.S. exports to some markets, particularly the Soviet Union and the Peoples' Republic of China (PRC) have grown in importance but have fluctuated tremendously. The Soviet Union bought $18 million worth of farm products from the U.S. in 1970, $12 million in 1971, $954 million in 1973, $410 million in 1975 and $1.1 billion in 1977. China went from $800 million in 1975 to $44,000 in 1976 to $64 million in 1977.

These changes figure substantially in the demand outlook for U.S. farm products and have confronted the United States with severe challenges: To maintain a high volume of exports to our traditional markets; to increase exports to growing markets in less developed and centrally planned areas; and to achieve more stable export growth.

TRADITIONAL MARKETS

The largest among our traditional markets is the European Community. Though it is close to self-sufficiency in food grains, the EC has had to import increasing quantities of feed grains and protein to satisfy its rapidly growing demand for livestock products.

Rising incomes in Japan, as in the European Community, have driven up demand for meat and for feed imports to produce it. Early post-World War II relief shipments of U.S. wheat to Japan influenced consumer preferences and helped create a market that formerly had demanded only rice. In recent years, however, Japanese demand for U.S. feedgrains and soybeans has been growing faster than its demand for wheat.

Another traditional market, India, has grown from a major food-aid recipient during the 1960's to a major commercial importer of U.S. grains in the 1970's. India's normally large demand for U.S. grain, however, has dropped off recently. Favorable monsoons have yielded excellent harvests the past three years allowing India to build up its stocks. India, in fact, became a net exporter of grain last year.

The outlook is mixed for sales to our traditional markets. Though we do not expect substantial gains in volume of exports in the next several years, we should see some gains in value as consumers there demand higher quality foods, especially meat and meat products. Foreign trade will remain vital to Japan and the EC since neither has much potential to expand domestic production to meet the growing demand.

Japanese trade policies have been generally favorable to agricultural imports from the United States. This is likely to continue as Japan attempts to reduce its massive overall trade surplus.

The United States seriously undermined its reliability as a supplier when it embargoed soybean exports in 1973. Japan has since developed additional sources for oilseed and feed supplies.

The EC is less accessible to U.S. exporters because of the Community's Common Agricultural Policy, which is designed to protect the income of their domestic producers. Imports of grains are limited by levies and duties, though soybean imports are not. Maintaining access to EC markets will be a prime concern for U.S. grain and soybean producers for the next several years.

GROWTH MARKETS

The surest potential for growth of U.S. farm exports is in the two fastest growing markets, the Mideast and Eastern Europe.

Developing, oil exporting nations in the Mideast and elsewhere are spending a large share of their rising foreign exchange earnings on food imports--mainly animals, animal products, feedgrains, and oilseeds. Most of these nations have limited productive capacity for agriculture. As long as incomes in oil-exporting areas continue to rise, so will their demand for meat and for U.S. animal and feed products.

The growth in the East European market has been similar to the Mideast's in composition. As in the USSR, governments have felt consumer pressure to improve diets, particularly through increased meat consumption. The inability of Soviets to satisfy their increased feed and livestock demand has forced East European governments to turn westward and provide freer access to U.S. farm commodities. Sales to Eastern Europe should increase, over the short run, at least.

ERRATIC MARKETS

The United States' two sporadic markets--the Soviet Union and the Peoples' Republic of China--loom as major question marks in our farm export future.

The Soviet Union has been our most erratic market. The fluctuation of Soviet purchases has caused wide price variations and has been the single most destabilizing factor on the world grain market this decade.

A five-year bilateral grain agreement, which expires in 1980, is taking some unpredictability out of our grain trade with the Soviets. The Soviets guarantee the United States a minimum six-million ton market every year. In addition, there is a provision that USDA be notified in advance if purchases will exceed eight million tons. As a safety provision, the U.S. also need not honor the minimum-sale amount in the event of a disastrous U.S. crop.

Other provisions of the grain agreement call for increased exchange of information with the Soviets, which should help prevent a repetition of past mistakes in forecasting Soviet harvests on minimal data.

Traditionally, we have had even less data on the PRC.

Last year's crop in the PRC was apparently poor. The Chinese are importing close to 10 million tons of grain from various sources this year, roughly 50 percent more than any year in the past decade. The PRC stopped grain purchases from the United States after some quality problems in 1974, but turned to us this year for about one million tons of wheat after other exporting countries sold out their supplies. We have no bilateral agreement with the Chinese, so their purchases from the United States are likely to continue to be sporadic for some time.

INCREASING COMPETITION

U.S. farm production has almost always been large enough to permit--indeed compel--sizable exports. In fact, carryover stocks of wheat and coarse grains at the beginning of June 1978 were the highest since the early 1960's. This supply situation underscores the importance of another key change in the world agricultural situation in the past several years: Competition for some of our major foreign markets has become tougher and more widespread.

Brazilian soybeans, Malaysian palm oil, Thai corn, and Pakistani cotton are examples of new products that have joined traditional U.S. competitors in world markets.

World demand for food will continue to grow as population and incomes rise. And so will competition.

TRADITIONAL COMPETITORS

Our most important traditional competitors for grain markets are Canada, Australia, Argentina, and South Africa. All four governments directly control agricultural trade through some form of national marketing board, whereas the private enterprise concept prevails in the U.S. With the exception of certain sales to the USSR, the only requirement imposed on our traders is that they notify the government of export sales following the sale. Marketing boards provide price guarantees, generally set a limit on prices paid to farmers and sometimes undercut competitors by subsidizing their own exports when supplies are large.

The world grain supply situation this year illustrates the advantage that government-contributed marketing boards can have. World grain stocks at the beginning of this summer were slightly higher than at the same time last year and the highest in nearly a decade. A breakdown between the U.S. and foreign stocks, however, shows that while foreign stocks dropped about 25 percent, U.S. stocks <u>rose</u> by the same proportion. Some foreign purchasers turned to the U.S. only after less expensive supplies sold through marketing boards were exhausted.

Since U.S. farmers face no price constraints, the freedom they enjoy in the marketplace is tempered by this country's function as residual supplier for world markets, wherein foreign purchasers buy U.S. farm products only after less expensive supplies are exhausted. This makes us the prime adjuster of production and stocks as conditions warrant. Current domestic and international U.S. policies are aimed at spreading the burden of supply adjustment more equitably among nations.

NEW COMPETITORS

Foreign governments are responsible for much of the growing competition. Developing countries see their agriculture as a source of foreign exchange, particularly to pay high petroleum import bills. They exploit comparative advantages in land resources, climate, and labor availability.

The prime example of an awakening agricultural giant is Brazil, which has shifted from a two cash-crop exporter (coffee, sugar) to a multi-crop food exporter. The most dramatic growth has been in soybeans. With some help from Japan which was looking for additional sources of supply, Brazil expanded its soybean output from about one million tons in 1970 to more than 12 million in 1977. Last year Brazil was the world's third largest soybean producer and second biggest exporter. It has been eating into the U.S. share of the EC market.

Brazil is now also exporting corn and cotton and is nearing self-sufficiency in wheat. It used less than half-a-million tons of fertilizer a decade ago, but used 2.6 million in 1977, thanks mainly to government incentive programs. Brazil is one of the few nations with vast untapped resources of arable land. It is likely to step up its competition with the U.S.

The U.S. also faces increasingly tough competition for oilseed markets. Indonesia and Malaysia now exports enough palm oil to compete with U.S. soybean oil. Argentina is exporting increasing amounts of sunflower seed oil.

The transition for most food-deficit developing countries is quite difficult, however. Even in areas where land and climate are suitable for efficient agricultural production, great cultural, economic and political obstacles often remain. Many countries are restricted by traditional land-tenure systems and cultural practices, lack of marketing facilities and cheap-food policies for urban areas.

Looking at the longer term prospects for export competition, two key questions emerge: What is the likelihood of our competitors achieving something close to U.S. grain yields? And, what potential do other exporters have for expanding their cropland?

The answers involve conjecture and vary from country to country. The more developed of our competitors--Canada, Australia, and South Africa-- like the United States, already have the technology and inputs to maximize their yields. The difference is in the climate: Canada is colder, Australia and South Africa more arid.

The big yields in our optimal wheat growing areas, mainly the Central Plains, bring the U.S. average way up. And no country in the world can duplicate our Corn Belt. The combination of consistently good weather over a large area of fertile soil and optimal inputs of hybrid seed, fertilizer and pesticides produces corn yields triple those of some competitor countries.

The three developed-country competitors could increase their grain acreage somewhat over the short term by leaving less land fallow or switching from other crops. However, none has substantial tracts of idle, arable land they could bring into grain production. Barring any great technological breakthrough on yields, then, it is unlikely that Canada, Australia or South Africa will substantially increase their grain output over the next several years.

The situation is different, though, with our three less developed competitors. There is considerably more chance of improvement in yields in Argentina, Brazil, and Thailand, and both our Latin American rivals have fairly large untapped land resources.

With reasonably good weather, Argentina can achieve some of the highest grain yields among U.S. competitors. And this is without much of the technological advances employed in the United States. With wider use of hybrid grain varieties and inputs such as fertilizer, Argentina could approach U.S. yield levels in good years. A key factor here, as in other developing countries, will be the extent to which government policies are geared to encouraging agricultural production and exports.

Besides its potential for considerable yield increases, Brazil probably has the world's highest potential for expanding farm acreage. The agricultural potential of the lush, teeming Brazilian jungle is difficult to assess. Progress has been slow and success will depend on efforts to overcome soil problems that occur after land has been reclaimed. The Brazilian Government apparently is willing to make the large investments required to develop new acreage, which makes Brazil the biggest threat to U.S. grain and soybean export markets over the long run.

Thailand's production potential rests almost entirely on yield improvements. Though the Thais have tripled corn plantings over the past decade, most expansion has been to marginal land. Even that land is nearly depleted. The government is committed to expanding agricultural output and is an aggressive seller--Thailand led the world in rice exports in 1977 and is making inroads in the Japanese and EC feed-grain markets. Japanese support has helped Thailand become a major exporter of corn.

One area to watch is the Sudan. There is potential for commercial agriculture in the Nile Valley but until recently the Sudan lacked capital to exploit it. Arab countries are now investing heavily there, with the hope of making the Sudan the breadbasket for the Mideast in a decade or so.

MEETING THE CHALLENGE

World wheat and coarse grain trade has doubled since the early 1960's, to 168 million tons in 1977/78, and U.S. grain exports have grown two-and-a-half times over the same period.

A continuation of the trend over the past 15-20 years would expand U.S. exports of wheat and coarse grains from 1977/78's 80 million tons to more than 90 million in 5 years. The trend drawn from the past 10 years would spell even sharper export growth.

Foreign demand is growing, but so is competition to meet that demand. There are several factors that will weigh heavily in the United States' success in maintaining its current rate of export growth: domestic and international policies, international trade and commodity agreements, U.S. market development programs, international monetary fluctuations, and U.S. market intelligence efforts.

DOMESTIC POLICIES

Increased interdependence in the world food situation means domestic farm income and price policies have a larger impact internationally than ever. National programs that go too far to help farmers' income in the short run, for example through sharply higher loan and target prices, are likely to make U.S. farm products less competitive on world markets. Though local farm prices would be higher, the longer term effect of reduced export demand would be a lower volume of sales and ultimately little change in farm income.

Domestic income and price policies must be delicately balanced to keep U.S. farmers in business and maintain their competitiveness in world markets. The key to current policy is the farmer-owned grain reserve that offers farmers incentive payments to pull excess supplies off the market. In addition to bolstering domestic prices with minimal government intervention, the reserve enhances U.S. reliability as an export supplier and moderates world price fluctuation.

INTERNATIONAL POLICIES

Closely related to the domestic reserve program is U.S. participation in efforts to establish an international grain reserve. The reserve would modify price variation, which in recent poor crop years have priced some of the lowest income nations out of the world food market. It would also guarantee supplies in event of extreme shortfalls. Unfortunately, talks in the United Nations' International Wheat Council have stalled because of disagreement on price levels and on reserve size and location.

Meanwhile, the U.S. is moving to establish on its own a six million-ton international emergency grain reserve that would be tapped only to provide supplies for critically food-deficit areas.

INTERNATIONAL TRADE AND COMMODITY AGREEMENTS

The United States is participating in forums such as the Multi-lateral Trade Negotiations and the General Agreement on Tariffs and Trade to reduce international barriers to agricultural trade. Progress in the multinational groups has been slow. The participants are committed to trade liberalization but few seem willing to make significant concessions.

The most progress in trade liberalization is being made bilater-ally. The U.S. has entered long-term agreements with Russia and Japan that specify minimum and maximum yearly export levels for the major commodities. We have also set up less formal purchase arrangements with Poland, Israel, Taiwan, and Norway. The bilateral agreements are beneficial in that they guarantee markets in years of oversupply and help stabilize world trade.

The benefits of some international commodity arrangements are less clear-cut. A trend in the developing world toward establishing international marketing groups for commodities such as coffee and sugar could benefit those nations economically in the short run but such agreements retard pro-gress toward trade liberalization overall.

There is talk of a wheat-exporting nations' answer to OPEC. But such an arrangement is untenable morally, or practically, because of avail-ability of other food sources and untapped production potential in many areas.

U.S. MARKET DEVELOPMENT PROGRAMS

The United States spends relatively far less on agricultural mar-ket development than its major competitors. On the basis of percent of farm export earnings, Israel spent 15 times more and Australia 11 times more in 1976. Funding for market development comes mainly from the private sector, and has risen 15 percent in 1978. The Agricultural Trade Act of 1978, now before Congress, would increase government expenditures on export promotion. A less direct support of market development comes from our international technical cooperation programs. The production assistance we give poorest developing countries tends to increase local productivity and income, reduce dependence on food aid and builds demand for commercial imports. Taiwan and South Korea are examples of food aid recipients that grew into major commer-cial markets.

MARKET INTELLIGENCE

To improve U.S. farmers' competitive positions in world markets, USDA is upgrading its mechanism for gathering, analyzing and disseminating market information. The World Food and Agricultural Outlook and Situation Board was created last year to coordinate the department's economic analysis on the world market.

Its goal is to improve the consistency, reliability and objectivity of USDA's outlook and speed the flow of that information to producers and the general public. The board is also seting up a global weather center to enhance the reporting and understanding of weather developments on world crop production.

MARKET DEVELOPMENT INITIATIVES
MARK DRIVE TO BOOST FARM EXPORTS

by Beverly Horsley

With U.S. farm stocks and prices reflecting 3 straight years of record or near-record production, increased attention is being focused on exports as one answer to the problems of low farm prices in this country and a mammoth deficit in overall U.S. trade.

U.S. agricultural exports may total a record volume in fiscal 1978 (October-September), but their dollar value will be somewhat below last year's record $24 billion as a result of reduced unit prices.

U.S. policymakers want to do better, not only this year but in terms of long-term trade growth. Agriculture Secretary Bob Bergland has said that U.S. agricultural trade interests should "spend every waking hour on promoting exports." Congress authorized a $2-million increase for market development in fiscal 1978

from the $13.5 million available to industry cooperators in fiscal 1977. And the U.S. Department of Agriculture (USDA) has put new muscle behind the words by stepping up foreign market development and more than doubling credit available to foreign importers under the Commodity Credit Corporation (CCC) program.

This expanded effort, to be implemented over the next few years, focuses on four new action areas:

• Long-term planning of 5-year marketing programs;

• Opening of FAS trade offices in key country and regional markets;

• Possible establishment of a new intermediate credit program; and

• Expansion of market development activities into new regions.

Long-term planning will be on a country/commodity basis, drawing on existing

expertise both within and outside Government.

According to Kelly Harrison, USDA's General Sales Manager and Foreign Agricultural Service (FAS) Assistant Administrator for Market Development, increased planning of Government-funded market development activities will mean: "Examining all facets of a foreign market—the country's import needs and product standards; social, political, and economic factors that might affect demand and marketing strategies; constraints of the marketing system and how they can be overcome; and available sources of financing."

Better coordination of market promotion work of FAS and the Office of the General Sales Manager will be included in the 5-year framework. For instance, planning will involve an examination of credit available

through the Department of Agriculture—Public Law 480, CCC credit (GSM-5), and the proposed intermediate credit program—to make these tools more readily available for market development.

Trade Offices in Key Cities

The overseas offices will be opened in as many key markets as funding permits. The goal is to have 15-18 such offices eventually, but only a few will be opened within the near future owing to budgetary limitations. Such offices will be supervised by U.S. Agricultural Attachés, but located apart from the embassies to facilitate business transactions. In some cases, they may be outside the capital cities in major commercial centers.

The intermediate credit program probably will offer credit for 5-10 year periods

Foreign Agriculture, February 13, 1978, pp. 2-4, 6-9. Beverly Horsley is Associate Editor, Foreign Agriculture.

potential for U.S. foods in a given market and point out trade restrictions, consumption habits, and marketing practices that will affect such exports.

Despite this multifaceted program, the United States cannot afford to be complacent about its agricultural export trade. "We are not operating in a vacuum," said Dr. Harrison. "A number of other nations need agricultural export earnings just as badly as we do and are employing innovative promotion techniques to sell their products overseas."

Among the competitors: Australia, Brazil, Argentina, South Africa, Israel, and the European Community. These and other leading U.S. competitors together spent more than $146 million on promoting farm products during fiscal 1976, a gain of 3.5 percent above the previous year's level and of 56.9 percent above the previous decade's.

The United States, by comparison, spent $20.7 million on market development during fiscal 1976, against $15.2 million a decade earlier, with most of the increase contributed by U.S. cooperators. And this country's gross outlay for market development amounted to only 0.10 percent of agricultural export earnings in fiscal 1976. By comparison, Israel that year spent 1.54 percent of its export earnings on market development, and Australia, 1.10 percent.

"To meet this competition, we have requested more money for U.S. market development," said Dr. Harrison. "In addition, we must be constantly alert to chang-ing market conditions, imaginative in our promotional programs, aware of foreign buyers' needs and foreign markets' import regulations, concerned always about product quality, and willing to service foreign customers year in and year out."

With the return of agricultural abundance recently following exceedingly short world grain supplies during 1973 and 1974, all leading agricultural exporters have found the competition increasingly tough in foreign markets. The difficulties are evidenced by low world prices for grains and other commodities, reactivation of U.S. setaside programs for wheat and feedgrains, and use of export subsidies and other incentives by some nations seeking to gain a marketing advantage.

A comparable situation in the 1950's led to enactment of the Agricultural Trade and Assistance Act of 1954, or Public Law 480 as it is commonly called.

P.L. 480 called for concessional shipments of U.S. farm products to developing countries under either local currency sales or long-term loans repayable in convertible currencies or dollars. Local currencies have been spent largely within recipient nations.

Since the program's inception, some $26 billion worth of U.S. farm products have been shipped under P.L. 480 to recipient nations. And foreign currencies generated under P.L. 480 have been used in part to help finance overseas market development, contributing to transition of many markets from P.L. 480 imports to large cash pur-chases of U.S. farm products.

Market development began in 1955 with a joint program between FAS and Cotton Council International (CCI)—FAS's first industry cooperator. During the ensuing years, market development efforts such as wheat milling and baking schools and seminars helped bring about the shift from a rice-based diet to wheat and other Western foods in Japan—in fiscal 1977 a $3.9-billion market for U.S. farm products—and sparked similar trends in other Far Eastern nations.

There, as elsewhere, consumers also begin eating more red meat and poultry, prompting livestock producers to adopt the modern feeding techniques necessary to satisfy demand.

U.S. Cooperators Are Active Worldwide

Feeding demonstrations and seminars by the U.S. Feed Grains Council, the American Soybean Association, and the National Renderers Association helped to spark these shifts in France, West Germany, Italy, Spain, and other West European nations; in Japan, Taiwan, South Korea; and—more recently—in Eastern Europe, the USSR, and the Middle East.

Other U.S. cooperator groups, often taking advantage of FAS-sponsored trade shows and point-of-purchase promotions, have familiarized the foreign consumer with everything from blueberries to almonds, popcorn, baby food, avocados, Maine lobster, and wild rice.

At times, the changes in consumption and production —and, more importantly, in government import regulations—have been detrimental to U.S. exports of certain products. But U.S. exporters have been quick to adapt to new conditions.

For instance:

• At the same time that Japan was developing its own poultry industry, market development activities to increase poultry meat consumption were underway. This led to a larger consumer market to accommodate the increased domestic production, as well as increased imports of U.S. poultry products. Today, Japan is one of the largest overseas markets for U.S. poultry meat and egg products.

• With the diminishing of sales opportunities in Western Europe and other traditional markets, the U.S. market development program for cotton shifted its efforts toward the lucrative Far Eastern market, which now accounts for 80 percent of total U.S. cotton exports. Cotton Council International, the FAS cooperator, has directed its attention toward servicing this area and has under consideration a centrally located Far Eastern office to facilitate these activities.

• U.S. citrus fruit exporters cooperating with FAS likewise have focused increasingly on the Far East— and Japan in particular—in response to increased demand there at a time of intensifying competition in West European markets. They also have worked with FAS for removal of Japanese import quotas on citrus.

These ongoing and prospective market development

tors include:

• Plans by the U.S. Meat Export Federation (USMEF), an FAS cooperator since February 1976, to open an office this year in Western Europe and possibly one in the Middle East at some later date. Its first office opened last year in Tokyo.

Thanks in part to aggressive promotion of U.S. red meat by Federation representatives, U.S. exports of livestock and livestock products during fiscal 1977 exceeded imports of such products for the first time in history. Like other cooperators, USMEF also has made an important input into U.S. preparations for the multilateral trade negotiations now underway in Geneva, providing information on how duties, import quotas, variable levies, and other restrictions affect U.S. livestock product exports.

• Stepped-up promotion of soy proteins as food. Last month, the American Soybean Association, the Food Protein Council, and FAS sponsored a Soy Protein Seminar in Singapore, where food uses of soy protein and feed uses of soybean meal were discussed. Similar seminars were held last year in Eastern Europe and the USSR—one of the strong growth areas for U.S. exports of soybeans and meal.

• Reactivation of a market development program for U.S. peanuts following a shortfall in Indian peanut production last year and consequent price increases on the world market. The expanded program will include a 12-month market test in the United Kingdom of American-type peanut butter produced entirely from

U.S. peanuts.

• Launching by the U.S. Feed Grains Council of a modern feedlot demonstration in Poland, with beef feeding trials using various levels of corn and grain sorghum. The potential payoff: Increased sales of U.S. feedgrains to Poland and refinement of a prototype system that can help overcome environmental problems associated with feedlots.

• Expanded export promotion activities by the American Seed Trade Association (ASTA). Exports of U.S. planting seed, up 19 percent last year, continue to expand dramatically in areas such as the Middle East, which has been targeted by ASTA for special promotional efforts. For example, exports to Iran have risen by over 60 percent since promotional activities were begun in that country.

• The recent opening of a new office in Morocco to promote U.S. wheat in North Africa and the Middle East and the planned opening of an office in Singapore to promote U.S. feedgrains in Southeast Asia. (Currently, U.S. grain cooperators alone have some 20 offices located in overseas markets.)

In addition, new offices are planned for U.S. oilseeds and products in the Mideast, cotton in the Far East, and poultry in the Caribbean.

Complementing these undertakings will be activities by FAS, carried out both independently and in cooperation with industry, State, and regional groups.

Some New Initiatives

FAS is considering bringing foreign national employees of U.S. embassies

to the United States to consult with and advise U.S. agricultural firms on ways to comply with the often-strict and ambiguous food and health laws in foreign markets. It is planning a feasibility study into introducing gourmet packets and specialty items at duty-free shops in major international airports and ports of call. And it has scheduled for fiscal 1978 some 18 solo U.S. trade shows, five attaché product displays, two hotel-restaurant-institution shows, two catalog shows, three livestock/feedstuff shows, eight sales team trips to foreign markets, and a host of point-of-purchase (POP) promotions in supermarkets and department stores.

These activities include solo U.S. food exhibits in Italy, Japan, Switzerland, Sweden, West Germany, the United Kingdom, France, Venezuela, and the Philippines; attaché displays of food products in Guatemala and Colombia; livestock/feedstuff shows in France and Italy; and participation in international food shows in the United Kingdom, the Netherlands, and West Germany.

Such shows often generate onsite sales of over $1 million apiece and as much or more than that in follow-up sales of U.S. food and agricultural products. More importantly, they are an invaluable means for U.S. trade representatives—especially those new to a market—to make overseas trade contacts and line up agents and distributors for their products.

Also, sales teams made up of six to eight representatives from U.S. food firms

already have traveled—or will—this fiscal year to Indonesia, Fiji/New Caledonia, Egypt, Norway, the Netherlands Antilles, Trinidad, the Canary Islands, and Iran to seek agents and industry representatives for their food products.

(For a partial listing of 1978 exhibits and teams see *Foreign Agriculture*, Nov. 21, 1977. An updated listing may be obtained from the FAS Export Trade Services Division, U.S. Department of Agriculture, Washington, D.C. 20250.)

FAS encourages regional and State groups to participate in many of these activities. It also supports efforts such as the Reverse Trade Show being mounted this week (Feb. 16-18) in New Orleans by the Southern United States Trade Association (SUSTA)—an export-oriented organization made up of the 15 southern States from Texas to Maryland.

More than 90 U.S. firms will be exhibiting their products at the show to an estimated 150 foreign buyers from more than 40 countries. Such an undertaking permits U.S. firms to test the trade without ever leaving the United States.

Food Studies Assess Demand

In addition, FAS, in cooperation with State Departments of Agriculture, is conducting food studies in Latin America, the Middle East, the Far East, and Africa to assess potential demand for a host of consumer-ready products.

Such studies are the first step in a market development program, as they determine if indeed there is

to countries that are too highly developed to qualify for long-term P.L. 480 funding but not ready yet for 3-year–maximum CCC credit or cash purchases. This program will offer opportunities to finance improved port facilities, reserve storage, and distribution facilities, thereby increasing total demand in a market. It also will be useful in financing imports of U.S. breeding cattle and products for which more than 3 years are needed to get a reasonable return on investment.

In the meantime, credit gaps will be diminished considerably by the more than doubling of CCC credit (GSM-5) available during fiscal 1978—from $750 million originally budgeted to $1.7 billion.

Ready availability of this credit for markets where there is an immediate need is vital. "There are actions that we ought to be taking now," said one top USDA official. "We shouldn't be in a position of having to tell customers to wait for decisions, but instead must get into the commercial mode of doing business."

In addition, a noncommercial risk assurance program on shipments has been developed to make more private financing available for U.S. exports. The program will get underway with a pilot project for cotton this month.

Efforts also will be made to apply foreign currencies earned under the concessional sales program of P.L. 480 toward market development, as well as toward improving internal agricultural distribution in P.L. 480 markets. In the past, both the physical and managerial limitations of such systems have restricted the flow of trade in developing countries, not only cutting into U.S. marketing opportunities but also hindering food distribution in times of emergency.

Expansion of market development into new areas will take U.S. cooperators and FAS trade shows beyond the traditional sphere of operation in Western Europe and Japan into new markets in Asia, Africa, and Latin America.

New Markets Sought

This shift is the natural outgrowth of two decades of rapid U.S. gains in agricultural exports to major developed markets. Such countries have the buying power and consumer demand to sustain their large imports, and must be serviced carefully if the United States is to maintain its competitive position vis-a-vis other agricultural exporters. But they no longer can be considered rapid growth markets, while many U.S. agricultural exporters are already well-established there and not in need of Government market development assistance.

Yet in the recent past, more than 60 percent of U.S. market development funds were spent in Europe and Japan alone.

"We already have relatively good information and marketing networks in the big commercial markets," said Dr. Harrison. "We need to look increasingly at emerging countries, such as the Arab nations and other places where the people are and the potential demand lies."

The Middle East and North Africa, with their tremendous petroleum incomes, are major targets for U.S. exporters of products running the gamut from wheat, feedgrains, rice, and soybeans to frozen poultry, beef, fresh fruits and vegetables, and processed foods.

Heavily populated nations here, such as Iran and Egypt, are rated as the best outlets for grains and other bulk products. Saudi Arabia and other lightly populated but wealthy nations on the Arabian Peninsula have developed into promising new markets for U.S. consumer-ready food products.

The centrally planned countries—particularly the USSR and those in Eastern Europe—recently have been among the fastest growing markets in the world for U.S. farm products. U.S. agricultural exports to these countries rose more than 14-fold between calendar 1970 and 1976 to $3 billion.

Moreover, Eastern Europe and the USSR are seen as areas with much additional potential for growth in the livestock and feed sectors. Virtually all nations here are working to expand their livestock industries and to introduce modern livestock feeding techniques. But many are deficient in the needed feedgrains, most lack high-protein ingredients such as soybean meal, and virtually all need better breeding stock.

Still another region of promise is Southeast Asia. Singapore, with its well-developed port and handling facilities, can serve as a gateway to the region as a whole. The big payoff, however, may come in places such as Indonesia, with its 132 million people, gradually rising incomes, and wealth of raw materials.

India and Pakistan on the South Asian subcontinent have the populations to boost demand greatly with every fractional gain in spending power. Moreover, an improved foreign exchange position in India—alongside recent crop setbacks—already has led to striking import increases in selected products, including U.S. cotton and vegetable oils.

In sub-Sahara Africa, mineral-rich nations such as Nigeria are stepping up agricultural imports. And in South America, Venezuela and Ecuador are rapidly investing increased petroleum incomes on upgrading diets and importing more of the food needed to bring about these changes.

To tap this potential of both new and established markets, the numerous U.S. groups that cooperate with FAS in foreign market development are stepping up activities in the more than 80 countries reached by their programs. These groups include 43 nonprofit agricultural trade organizations carrying out long-term projects, 19 cooperators on periodic projects, and 13 private groups (largely farmer-owned cooperatives).

In addition, FAS works with State Departments of Agriculture and regional State groups in overseas market development. And the industry groups, called "cooperators," work with 1,653 foreign cooperators, as well as with foreign governments and institutions.

Undertakings by coopera-

efforts, in the words of Agriculture Secretary Bergland, "are important now because of the U.S. trade deficit. And they will continue so over the long run because of the growing U.S. role as a food supplier.

"The centerpiece of our agricultural export policy is the development of trading relationships that can endure. World food requirements will probably double in 35 years. If these demands are to be met, we cannot have feast or famine . . . we must do the best job possible."

NEWS RELEASE*

Washington -- Congress has completed passage of a trade expansion act (S. 3447) designed to increase overseas sales of American farm products by authorizing new promotion and credit programs.

"This legislation will help strengthen farm prices by continuing and expanding the movement of grains and other agricultural products to foreign customers. At the same time, it will help the whole national economy because it will reduce the trade deficit which has weakened our dollar," said Chairman Thomas S. Foley, D-Wash., of the House Agriculture Committee.

The bill cleared its final Congressional hurdle Sunday when a House-Senate compromise on the measure was approved on a 356 to 4 roll call vote in the House.

Under the bill, which now goes to the White House for Presidential approval, the Secretary of Agriculture would be directed to open between six and 25 agricultural trade promotion offices in major markets abroad. Also, the diplomatic status of U.S. agricultural attaches in not less than 10 major foreign markets would be raised to the rank of Counsel so they can compete on equal terms with trade representatives of other countries.

In addition, the bill would make several improvements in an existing program under which the Agriculture Department's Commodity Credit Corporation (CCC) provides credit to many foreign buyers of American farm products with commercial-style repayment terms of up to three years.

Countries currently eligible for the three-year credits would also become eligible for "intermediate" credit, with repayments running up to 10 years, for the following purposes: To finance purchases of grain for reserve stockpiling under international commodity agreements or other plans acceptable to the U.S.; to finance purchases of breeding livestock, including freight costs; to finance, where feasible, establishment of facilities for improved handling of imported farm products; and to meet credit competition from other countries, but not to initiate credit wars.

(In the case of grain credits to finance reserves, the Secretary of Agriculture would seek agreements aimed at preventing dumping of reserve stocks. Further, before any individual credit for grain reserves could be approved, the Secretary would have to formally determine the deal would not injure American farmers and would have to give the Senate and House Agriculture Committees 30 days advance notice of the financing.)

*Committee on Agriculture, U.S. House of Representatives, October 16, 1978.

The Agriculture Department, in addition, would be authorized to offer CCC financing for up to three years on sales to the People's Republic of China which is not currently eligible for such credit. In a related action, the bill authorizes CCC credits up to three years to private U.S. exporters who make deferred-payment sales to currently-eligible countries or to China.

The bill would underline the importance Congress wants given to exports by upgrading the post of Assistant Secretary of Agriculture for International Affairs and Commodity Programs to an Under Secretaryship. Also, the measure specifies that Federal cargo prefence law would not apply to the new intermediate credits.

House sponsors of the legislation were Reps. Dawson Mathis, D-Ga., W.R. Poage, D-Tex., and others including Reps. Kika de la Garza, D-Tex., William C. Wampler, R-Va., and Paul Findley, R-Ill.

U.S. FARM EXPORTS REACH RECORD $27.3 BILLION

by Sally Breedlove Byrne

U.S. EXPORT HIGHLIGHTS

• Grain accounted for almost half the growth in fiscal 1978 exports. Wheat exports were up 8.2 million tons over the fiscal 1977 level. Feedgrain exports were up 5 million tons.

• Record export volumes were reached for corn, soybeans, vegetable oils, and protein meal.

• Farm exports to the USSR rebounded from the reduced fiscal 1977 value. Direct shipments and transshipments included 11.1 million tons of corn, 3.4 million tons of wheat, and 805,000 tons of soybeans.

• Farm exports to the PRC totaled $352 million. Major items were cotton, wheat, soybean oil, and soybeans.

• Exports to Japan rose 10 percent in value. Much of the volume growth was in meat, feedgrain, and soybeans.

• Substantial volume gains were made in sunflowerseeds, field and garden seeds, beef, peanuts, fruit juices, live animals, and canned fruit.

The continuing upward surge in the value of U.S. agriculture exports lifted the total for fiscal 1978 (October-September) to a record $27.3 billion, a substantial 14 percent higher than the previous record reached in fiscal 1977.

Other records set during the year's farm-export performance were:

• Fiscal 1978 was the ninth year in a row for record highs in total U.S. agricultural export value.

• U.S. farm exports were valued at $13.4 billion more than import value, adding significant strength to the U.S. balance of trade and thereby strengthening the dollar.

• CCC export credits, which helped generate the huge export gains, reached a total value of $1.6 billion —more than double the year-earlier level. Sales to Poland accounted for nearly a third of the total.

Export volume, led by substantial gains in wheat, feedgrains, and soybeans, rose 20 percent to a record 120 million tons—20 million tons higher than the previous high set in fiscal 1977. Export volumes of cotton, soybean products, and other oilseeds were significantly higher than in the year-earlier period.

Grains and preparations accounted for almost half the increase in value, while oilseeds and products were identified with nearly a third of the gain.

Significant value increases also were chalked up in exports of cotton, fruits, animal products, and tobacco.

By geographic area, U.S.

Foreign Agriculture, November 13, 1978, pp. 3-5. Sally Breedlove Byrne is an economist in USDA's Economics, Statistics, and Cooperative Service.

exports were higher to all regions except the European Community, Canada, and southern Asia. The greatest growth was in exports to the Soviet Union, Latin America, eastern Asia, and the People's Republic of China (PRC).

Exports to developing countries were up 21 per-

cent to $8.9 billion, and exports to the centrally planned countries jumped 85 percent to $3.1 billion. Exports to the developed countries rose 2 percent in value.

U.S. agricultural imports were up 4 percent in fiscal 1978 to $13.9 billion, mainly because of larger ship-

ments of meat, vegetables, fruit, wine, and tobacco. Coffee import volume declined 4 percent, and the import unit value averaged lower. Cocoa, rubber, tea, and spice imports also declined in volume.

he agricultural trade lus widened to $13.4 on in fiscal 1978. The

deficit in total trade moved from $24 billion in fiscal 1977 to $34 billion.

Feedgrain export volume rose 10 percent in fiscal 1978. The USSR accounted for most of the increase, but exports expanded to several other regions including eastern and southeastern Asia, Spain, Japan, and

U.S. Agricultural Exports: Value by Commodity, October-September 1974/75-1977/78

Commodity	1974/75	1975/76	1976/77	1977/78	1976/77-1977/78
	Mil. dol.	Mil. dol.	Mil. dol.	Mil. dol.	Percent change
Animals and animal products					
Dairy products	143	131	170	146	− 14
Fats, oils, and greases	403	406	583	565	− 3
Hides and skins, excl. furskins	291	457	590	614	+ 4
Meats and meat products	382	592	608	687	+ 13
Poultry and poultry products	143	235	302	333	+ 10
Other	304	386	394	466	+ 18
Total animals and products	1,666	2,207	2,647	2,811	+ 6
Grains and preparations					
Feedgrains and products	4,905	6,010	5,391	5,746	+ 7
Rice	941	607	689	833	+ 21
Wheat and major products	5,292	4,787	3,054	4,139	+ 36
Other	124	135	141	148	+ 5
Total grains and preparations	11,262	11,539	9,275	10,866	+ 17
Oilseeds and products					
Cottonseed and soybean oil	601	337	592	746	+ 26
Soybeans	2,989	3,038	4,307	4,749	+ 10
Protein meal	703	843	950	1,176	+ 24
Other	460	474	537	778	+ 45
Total oilseeds and products	4,753	4,692	6,386	7,449	+ 17
Other products and preparations					
Cotton, excluding linters	1,045	910	1,529	1,693	+ 11
Tobacco, unmanufactured	897	929	1,065	1,132	+ 6
Fruits and preparations	675	755	804	976	+ 21
Nuts and preparations	164	182	223	288	+ 29
Vegetables and preparations	534	595	697	658	− 6
Feeds and fodders	299	381	620	575	− 7
Other	559	570	728	850	+ 17
Total products and preparations	4,173	4,321	5,666	6,172	+ 9
Total	21,854	22,759	23,974	27,298	+ 14

U.S. Agricultural Exports: Volume by Commodity, October-September 1974/75-1977/78

Commodity	1974/75	1975/76	1976/77	1977/78	1976/77-1977/78
	1,000 MT	1,000 MT	1,000 MT	1,000 MT	Percent change
Wheat and products	30,404	31,127	25,019	33,219	+ 33
Feedgrains and products	35,361	50,145	50,776	55,747	+ 10
Rice	2,214	1,953	2,231	2,109	− 5
Soybeans	11,486	15,050	15,155	19,698	+ 30
Oilmeal	4,075	4,870	4,263	5,970	+ 40
Vegetable oils	988	965	1,221	1,542	+ 26
Cotton, excluding linters	1,284	733	989	1,317	+ 33
Tobacco	274	273	290	272	− 6
Total	86,086	105,113	99,944	119,874	+ 20

Leading Markets for U.S. Agricultural Exports [1]

Country	1974/75	1975/76	1976/77	1977/78	1976/77-1977/78
	Mil. dol.	Mil. dol.	Mil. dol.	Mil. dol.	Percent change
Japan	3,213	3,408	3,773	4,159	+ 10
Netherlands	1,683	1,742	2,179	2,150	− 1
USSR	596	1,853	1,063	1,797	+ 69
Canada	1,317	1,430	1,570	1,564	0
West Germany	1,535	1,619	1,933	1,460	− 24
Republic of Korea	861	809	919	1,055	+ 15
United Kingdom	608	662	907	938	+ 3
Italy	881	797	836	929	+ 11
Spain	788	658	595	755	+ 27
Taiwan	494	516	612	729	+ 19
Mexico	735	380	608	735	+ 21
Egypt	440	415	563	552	− 2
Poland	280	541	311	523	+ 68
France	413	423	474	504	+ 6

[1] Not adjusted for transshipments.

Latin America. Livestock industries in these areas require larger imports of feed.

U.S. feedgrain exports to the EC[1] dropped 36 percent to 11 million tons in fiscal 1978 because of recovery during 1977 in EC grain and fodder production. Shipments to Eastern Europe declined 3 percent to 4.3 million tons.

Soybean exports jumped 30 percent in volume. The two major factors were the short 1978 Brazilian soybean crop and lower soybean prices, which favored feeding of soybeans over grain. The U.S. soybean export unit value fell from $285 per ton to $241 per ton. The corn export price remained close to $104 per ton.

Soybean export volume expanded to Western and Eastern Europe, Latin America, and Eastern Asia (including Japan). Shipments to Canada fell 18 percent, and shipments to the USSR fell 2 percent.

Protein meal exports increased 40 percent in volume. Shipments were up 83 percent to Canada, 42 percent to the EC, 12 percent to Eastern Europe, and 28 percent to Japan.

Vegetable oil exports expanded 26 percent in volume. Increases were recorded to all major markets except India and Pakistan.

Exports of oilseeds other than soybeans increased 53 percent in value. Peanut exports rose 30 percent in volume.

The largest growth was recorded in exports of sunflowerseeds. Fiscal 1978 exports totaled 906,000 tons, 69 percent of the 1977 U.S. harvest. Fiscal 1977 exports of 403,000 tons comprised 87 percent of the 1976 crop. Major markets were the Netherlands, West Germany, and Portugal.

U.S. **wheat** exports rebounded from the reduced fiscal 1977 volume. Shipments to the EC rose 92 percent because of the EC need for high-quality wheat. Shipments to Latin America increased from 3.7 million tons to 6.7 million because of drought-reduced harvests there. Direct U.S. wheat shipments to the PRC totaled 914,000 tons.

Wheat exports were up 47 percent to North Africa, 37 percent to southern Asia, and 21 percent to western Asia. Shipments also increased to Taiwan, the Philippines, and Indonesia. Exports to Japan declined 6 percent.

Cotton exports continued to grow in fiscal 1978, reaching 5.75 million running bales. Shipments to the developing countries of eastern and southeastern Asia increased 42 percent. Exports to Japan rose 20 percent to 1.1 million bales —still below the 1973/74 record of 1.3 million bales.

U.S. unmanufactured **tobacco** exports declined 6 percent in volume, while the unit value increased from $3.68 per kilogram to $4.15 per kilogram. Shipments to the EC were down 6 percent—a smaller volume to West Germany more than offset larger shipments to the United Kingdom.

Tobacco exports to Japan increased 11 percent in volume. Tobacco exports to the developing countries declined 8 percent, largely because of reduced shipments to Egypt, Thailand, Malaysia, and the Philippines.

Higher prices led to a 6 percent increase in U.S. exports of **animal products.**

Meat and meat product export volume declined 3 percent, mainly because of reduced shipments of pork, and prepared and preserved meat shipments. Fresh and frozen beef exports expanded 31 percent in volume. Meat exports to Japan increased 22 percent to 79,-000 tons. Shipments were down 29 percent to Canada and 7 percent to the EC.

Exports of animal fats and greases declined 7 percent in volume, with reduced shipments to Western Europe, southern Asia, and Japan.

Whole cattle hide exports decreased 6 percent in volume. However, gains were recorded to several leading markets—Mexico, Japan, and Korea.

In fiscal 1978, U.S. exports of fresh and prepared **fruits** increased to $976 million. Exports to Canada— the leading market—increased 11 percent to $341 million. Exports to Japan jumped 36 percent to $176 million. Increases were recorded to all leading markets.

Higher unit values for fresh and dried fruits account for a large part of the value gain, but larger volumes also were achieved for processed fruit.

FARM EXPORTS: SOME CHANGES

by Lauren Soth

Everybody knows that exports of farm products have become increasingly important to this country in the last couple of decades. They are important as a major factor in farmers' incomes and vital as a source of foreign exchange to the nation — especially since the hoisting of oil import prices.

The Department of Agriculture recently issued a report describing "subtle transitions" in the sources and composition of foreign demand for U.S. farm products. The changes don't seem very subtle.

The developing nations are buying an increasing share of America's grain and other food exports. This is not food aid but commercial business. The volume of wheat exports to these poorer countries has increased by more than one-fourth since the early 1960s. In the 1961-'65 period, two-thirds of our wheat exports to these countries were financed under food-aid programs. Between 1971 and 1975, only one-tenth of the comparable wheat shipments were under aid.

Communist countries of Eastern Europe are buying much more grain and soybeans. The Soviet Union and its neighbors in Eastern Europe import twice as large a share of our farm exports as they did in the early 1960s.

The USDA World Food and Agricultural Outlook and Situation Board thinks the surest potential for growth in U.S. farm exports lies in Eastern Europe and in the Middle East. The Communist countries are trying hard to expand production of meat and other livestock products, and they are importing feed grain and soybeans to supplement their own feed supplies. The Middle East countries are getting rich on oil profits, and they are spending a large proportion of their dollar earnings on food imports — livestock, animal products and grains and soybeans.

Although the United States always has been a large exporter of agricultural products, the recent world trends present a new set of policy problems. Congress has recognized this in the trade expansion act passed in the last session. It provides for export credits and other government market development programs. Most of the old prohibitions and curbs on trade with Communist countries have been removed.

The United States faces increasing competition from Brazil, Argentina and other countries. "One area to watch is the Sudan," the USDA report stated. "There is potential for commercial agriculture in the Nile valley, but until recently the Sudan lacked capital to exploit it. Arab countries now are investing heavily there, with the hope of making the Sudan the breadbasket of the Mideast in a decade or so."

The Sudanese government has invited American agricultural experts to visit and help chart a course of development.

So far, American farmers and their organizations have reacted in a sophisticated and farsighted manner to the changed agricultural export situation. They have urged dropping the hindrances to exports, encouraged trade promotion by the government and, for the most part, resisted moves toward protectionism.

But the occasional efforts of commodity groups to fight foreign competition by means of import quotas or other government controls are harmful to the total farm export expansion plan.

Foreign competitors always like to point a finger at the mighty economic power of the United States and complain about trade restrictionism. They may be doing worse things themselves, but the United States is an easy target. For example:

The Australians are complaining about U.S. beef import quotas, and the Europeans are objecting to U.S. import duties on dairy products and processed meats. Common Market officials say the current trade negotiations could collapse because Congress failed to extend the waiver of these duties during trade talks.

The National Farmers Union says this hassle over the "countervailing" duties, which are to be charged against exports deemed to be subsidized, "jeopardizes four years of delicate negotiations to reduce world trade barriers and expand markets for U.S. farm products."

The objectors to U.S. restrictions on beef and dairy products are traditional trading partners. The actual damage of the beef import quotas to Australia and New Zealand probably is not great. The dairy exporters of Denmark and other European countries have a stake in the U.S. market, no doubt, but their objections come with ill grace, considering the variable levies on U.S. exports to Europe.

Yet the fact that the United States is dominant in the world agricultural export business makes U.S. restrictionism look bad. And these bad trade practices can be used effectively against us. It would be better if the United States could find ways of protecting incomes of dairy and beef producers without foreign trade barriers.

American farm organizations and farm politicians have not yet learned how to take an overall, national view on trade without being blinded by special commodity interests. Lawmakers who were promoting the trade expansion act were blasting President Carter at the same time for lifting the beef import quota by 200 million pounds, adding a potential 1½ percent to the U.S. beef supply in a time of rising meat prices.

Des Moines Register, November 8, 1978, p. 10A.

U.S. TRADE RELATIONS
WITH POOR NATIONS:
SUGGESTED REFORMS

Why are so many of the world's people poor and hungry? One answer which has emerged in recent years is that a major culprit is structural inequities in the international economic system. Structural inequities, such as the current pattern of trade relations, effectively prevent the conquest of hunger, poverty, inflation and unemployment and result in a widening gap between the rich and poor.

This answer is increasingly the consensus position of Less Developed Country (LDC) leaders. Convinced of the inequity of the present order, they have, since 1964, called for a "New International Economic Order" (NIEO)[1]. They contend that Third World purchasing power is declining steadily, due to the low and fluctuating prices of the raw materials they export and the increases in the costs of industrial technology, oil, and other items they import. They cite their countries' small and declining share in world manufacturing and trade, and point with bitterness to tariffs, quotas, and other trade barriers which bar their nations' products from ready access to industrialized country markets. They also point to the rapidly escalating debts of many developing countries as further evidence of the malfunction of the present economic order. They see themselves as unequal participants in global political and economic decision-making institutions, such as the UN Security Council, the World Bank and the International Monetary Fund.

Developed nations share perspective

More and more people in the US and other developed nations—including members of the religious community—are coming to share the LDC's perspectives on these issues. Many recent church statements on world hunger and poverty have pointed to structural injustice and inequities as the root causes of poverty and hunger. Stanley Mooneyham, in *What Do You Say To a Hungry World?* thus speaks for many when he says:

> At the heart of the problems of poverty and hunger, injustice and inequity, are human systems which ignore, mistreat and exploit man made in the image of God. If humanity is to be served, if the hungry are to be fed, . . . some of the systems will require drastic adjustments while others will have to be scrapped altogether.

This paper deals with one aspect of the international economic system which needs reform: the present system of world trade.[2] We indicate why trade is so important to poor nations and describe the present structure of trade. We then suggest three reforms and, in conclusion, point to the human meaning of our proposed reforms.

TRADE, POVERTY AND JUSTICE

WHY IS TRADE IMPORTANT TO DEVELOPING COUNTRIES?

Trade is important for at least three reasons:

1. Exports pay for imports. LDCs feel that development can occur more rapidly if they import machinery and other items necessary to increase productivity, rather than wait for such items to be produced locally. These imports can be paid for only with money earned by exporting goods which are available.

2. Many LDCs produce (or could produce) more goods than they themselves need. Access to outside markets would allow them to take advantage of these economies of scale.

3. Export earnings are much larger and more dependable than "foreign aid" and other outside assistance. In 1974, for example, the non-OPEC (Organization of Petroleum Exporting Countries) LDCs earned more than twice as much from their exports ($97 billion) than they received in the form of official development assistance, private investment, loans, and help from private agencies ($40 billion).

WHAT IS THE STRUCTURE OF WORLD TRADE?

Despite its importance to them, LDCs are only marginally involved in world trade. Their share has decreased from 14% in 1960 to less than 12% in 1974. Most international trade occurs within a fairly closed group of developed countries—a wealthy club whose members exchange favors with each other.

Moreover, flows of trade between developed countries and LDCs are usually not "in balance." In 1976, for example, the US had a trade surplus of $1.2 billion with the low income (below $300 GNP per capita) LDCs, which means that we did not buy sufficient amounts of their goods to enable them to pay for what they bought from us. Thus, they unfairly shoulder some of the burden of paying for our trade deficits with other countries, which we incurred primarily because of our large petroleum imports.

Hunger, (Interreligious Taskforce on U.S. Food Policy), Washington, D.C., February 1978.

Fluctuations in the prices of LDC export goods (primarily agricultural and mineral exports) are another problem. Such fluctuations make planning for development extremely difficult, especially for the many countries with exports concentrated in one or two commodities. In the last half of the 1960s, three-fourths of the LDCs earned more than 60% of their foreign exchange from sales of three or fewer primary products.

WHAT CAN BE DONE?

Three reforms would give the LDCs a larger and more equitable share in the benefits resulting from trade: (1) stabilize commodity prices at levels fair to producers and consumers, (2) provide LDCs greater access to developed country markets, and (3) improve US employment policies. The Interreligious Taskforce on US Food Policy believes that all three reforms are needed and merit support.[3]

Stabilize Commodity Prices

The United States should help stabilize commodity prices at fair levels by participating in International Commodity Agreements and supporting the Common Fund basically as proposed by the LDCs. International Commodity Agreements (ICA) stabilize prices by limitations on production for export among producing countries, the establishment of buffer stocks to be built up or sold depending on whether prices are too low or too high, and agreements among producing and consuming countries about the range between which prices will be allowed to fluctuate.

Current discussions focus on creating a Common Fund, which would function as a public international bank providing loans to finance buffer stocks of 10 to 18 commodities of interest to the LDCs. A Common Fund, it is argued, would enable buffer stocks of a variety of products to be maintained with less capital, since the cycles of different commodities would likely be out of phase. The proceeds from sales of one commodity when prices were too high could be used to buy stocks of another whose prices are concurrently too low.

Shift in US position?

Discussions about ICAs and a Common Fund were held in the UN Conference on Trade and Development in Nairobi in mid-1976, and in the Paris Conference on International Economic Cooperation until mid-1977. The US was the leading opponent of the proposals but because of the new spirit of conciliation shown by President Carter and his Administration modest progress has recently been made. At the most recent negotiating meetings held in Geneva in November, the debate was no longer whether or not there should be a Common Fund, but how it should be financed and controlled. However, some feel that this shift in the debate does not represent any real change in US opposition to the Common Fund.

The US and other developed countries are proposing a rather limited arrangement in which the Common Fund would act as a banker for individual ICAs using only the money which they would raise from participants in that particular agreement. In contrast, the LDCs want the Common Fund to raise funds from all UNCTAD countries (about 25% from LDCs, 75% from the rich nations) and provide the money needed for all buffer stocks. They also want the Fund to supply funds to assist in diversification of commodities and for research and market promotion for commodities threatened by synthetics. They further propose a voting system for the Fund which would give them a majority. The lack of progress in negotiations on these issues has delayed the original schedule for completing Common Fund negotiations by February 1978 and the individual ICAs by the end of 1978.

Benefit to developed countries

Developed countries seem willing to join International Commodity Agreements because they realize it will benefit them as well as the developing countries. One study by the Overseas Development Council has shown that if the proposed ICAs had been operating during the period of 1963-1972 the LDCs would have received a total of about $5 billion more for their commodities than they did, plus the benefits of improved stability. The US would have realized about $15 billion in each of several years during the decade in benefits from reduced inflation and unemployment.

It should not be assumed that ICAs and a Common Fund, if established, would represent any major concession of power from the North (rich) to the South (poor). These arrangements are primarily ways whereby producers (primarily LDCs) adapt themselves to the existing market. Because quotas under the ICAs are based on previous market shares, only those countries which were already exporting each commodity will benefit. Countries which would like to diversify production into new commodities are at a disadvantage. Moreover, the benefits to the LDCs will not be large enough by themselves to make a major impact on their rates of economic growth. Thus current proposals will have a beneficial though limited effect on LDCs.

In spite of these limitations, the Taskforce considers the negotiation of ICAs and the broad outlines of the Common Fund proposal of the LDCs significant improvements in the international economic order which merit support and urges the translation of conciliatory speeches into a willingness to negotiate.

Provide LDCs Greater Access to US Markets

The United States should provide LDCs greater access to US markets by lowering trade barriers to LDC manufactured goods. This is the most significant reform needed. Japan had special access to US markets during its years of postwar recovery, and this was an important factor in that country's rapid growth.

An initial step has recently been taken to give preferential access to US and other rich nation markets for certain goods produced by LDCs. Called the Generalized System of Preferences (GSP) and operating in the US since January 1976, the new agreement allows certain non-competitive goods originating within designated LDCs to enter the importing country without any reciprocal concessions by the LDC. In 1976, $3.5 billion worth of goods from non-OPEC LDCs—13% of their total sales to the US but only 3% of total US imports—entered the US under GSP.

Lowering trade barriers necessary

While the GSP represents a modest step forward, the actual benefits to LDCs has thus far been relatively minor because each importing country draws up its own list of goods eligible for GSP and each has various "escape clauses" to protect its import-sensitive industries. Only if remaining barriers are lowered will significant benefits result.

A recent World Bank study indicates that the elimination of all barriers to free trade would increase the annual export earnings of the LDCs by $24 billion by 1985. Most of this increase would go to the middle-income LDCs because they have a larger industrial base and could expand rapidly to take advantage of new opportunities. The low-income LDCs would also benefit from free trade in the long run, but for them foreign assistance will be more important in the immediate future.

Providing greater access to US markets will involve imports competitive with goods now produced in the US. Though justice demands that LDCs be allowed a fair—and therefore much larger—share in global trade in such goods and though US consumers would benefit, opening US markets to competitive goods would require major adjustments. Some patterns of US production would have to shift. For example, the special resources and capabilities of the LDCs suggests that they should concentrate (at least at this time) on such labor-intensive industries as textiles and garments, leather and shoes, glass and pottery. US industries producing such goods are now protected by high rates of import duties or special quota systems. These impediments to greater productivity in the LDCs should be removed. At the same time, US employment policies should be significantly improved.

Improve US Employment Policies

Simultaneously with the provision of greater access to US markets from LDCs, the United States should adopt and vigorously implement a full employment policy and strengthen the Trade Adjustment Assistance Program. The strains of changing patterns of production and employment in the US should not be borne only by the few directly affected. Justice demands that all Americans share the costs as well as reap the benefits of free trade. A US full employment policy is essential to protect US workers.

Trade Adjustment Program must be strengthened

Furthermore, the current Trade Adjustment Assistance Program should be strengthened. While the present program eases eligibility tests for workers and industry adversely affected by imports and raises benefit levels compared to the program in place prior to 1975, a much stronger program is needed to provide economic security for those affected. Unless the program is strengthened, our nation is apt to encounter rapidly increasing "protectionist" sentiment.

The Departments of Labor, Commerce and Agriculture in consultation with labor, industry and farm representatives, the Special Trade Representative, and the Departments of State and Treasury should assess the possible short-term and long-term effects of various trade policy alternatives. Such studies could provide a basis for cooperative planning now for future trade negotiations and adjustments.[4]

THE HUMAN MEANING OF TRADE REFORMS

The adoption of the above trade reforms would have major effects of industrial and agricultural employment in both the developing and developed countries. It would clearly affect tea pickers in Sri Lanka, coffee drinkers in the US and textile workers in both Korea and North Carolina. What is much less clear is the extent to which such trade reforms would benefit poor people in the developing nations. It is possible to make rough calculations of aggregate benefits to specific developing nations from more open world trade or from the Common Fund. It is much harder to make even a good guess at what such policies would mean for the poor majority in their day-to-day struggles. Country "A" might invest additional earnings from the sale of its tea, coffee, or copper in the expansion of primary education, labor-intensive rural industry, and improved health care. Country "B" might use its greater earnings to increase military spending or import luxury goods for a small moneyed elite.

At least two things seem essential if the basic human needs of the poor majority in developing countries are to be met. One is an increase in the economic growth of those countries. No amount of internal reform is sufficient without such growth. As Tanzanian President Julius Nyerere has put it, "However much we reorganize our economic system to serve the interests of the mass of the people, and however much our government tries to weigh the income distribution in favor of the poorest people, we are merely redistributing poverty, and we remain subject to economic decisions and interests outside our control."

Only a relatively few middle or upper-middle income developing countries have been able to diversify their economies, significantly develop both industry and agriculture, and generally gain sufficient economic clout to be able to compete in world markets as near equals of the industrialized countries. The wealthier OPEC countries appear to be a special case because of the deep-seated dependence of industrialized nations on imported oil. Most non-oil exporting developing countries, however, lack such economic power. Countries relying on a few vulnerable commodities or on manufactured goods not in high demand to maintain export earnings are probably at a more or less permanent disadvantage in the world market place—unless they can find some way to reduce significantly their imports on food, oil, and high-cost technology. These nations in particular need the assistance of the rich nations.

Internal equity measures

The other requirement, if basic human needs are to be met, is a commitment by the developing nations to internal equity measures. One of the clearest lessons of the First Development Decade (1960-1970) was that wealth does not necessarily "trickle-down." Economic growth in and of itself provides no guarantee of improved living conditions for needy people. Commitment to equity measures within developing countries is essential. Without such a commitment, even the most far-reaching changes in relationships between nations will fail to affect the poor majority.

In spite of their disadvantaged position in the world economy, many Third World countries, at a variety of stages of political and economic development and with diverse social and economic systems, have achieved relatively high levels of success in meeting basic human needs. Taiwan, Sri Lanka, Vietnam, Costa Rica, and Cuba have all done well in reducing infant mortality and increasing life expectancy and literacy. Internal reforms of various sorts and in varying degrees have been the primary source of improvement in each case. Yet in each instance, external factors, including official development assistance and special trading relationships, have been significant and even critical in the development process.

The need for human needs and international development

It is clear that a new international economic order without a focus on basic human needs is as incomplete as is reliance on programs to help the poor that do not deal with structural inequities.

In today's world, there is no escaping the reality of interdependence. All nations depend, to some extent, on each other for the quality of their existence. This is not to say that interdependence is always "a good thing." Nations, like people, can and often do behave selfishly, spitefully, and stupidly. But trade and aid relationships among nations need not lead to exploitation and inordinate dependence. They can be means of fostering global justice.

The challenge confronting the world's people today is nothing less than that of devising an international economic system, which together with international, regional, and national development strategies, will constitute a global economy geared to meeting for all the world's people basic human needs for food, jobs, clothing, housing and health.

Major contributors to this issue were Howard Jost (Church World Service/Taskforce staff), Tim Atwater (Church World Service/Lutheran World Relief), Dennis Frado (Lutheran Council in USA), and Andy Tyson (United Methodist Church).

U.S. FOOD IMPORTS--
FROM FREE TRADE TO PROTECTIONISM

HOUSE PASSES SUGAR BILL,
ADDS ESCALATOR CLAUSE
CARTER OPPOSES

by Elizabeth Wehr

The House Oct. 6 passed a compromise sugar bill backed by President Carter — but not before tacking on a controversial automatic price increase provision that the president has vowed to veto.

The final vote on the bill was 186-159.

The bill (HR 13750) authorized a new domestic sugar support program that assures producers a price of 15 cents a pound, with semi-annual adjustments upward for the next five years. The upward adjustments would be related to increases in costs of production.

Existing law guarantees sugar producers 14 cents a pound through the 1978 crop year.

The day before the House vote, the Senate Finance Committee reported a similar but more expensive bill (HR 7108 — S Rept 95-1279) that sets the guaranteed price ("price objective") at 17 cents a pound, with a more generous automatic adjustment pegged to changes in the cost-of-living index.

Both House and Senate bills mandate import fees and quotas to keep cheaper imported sugar from driving domestic prices below the price objective.

Both bills also authorize U.S. participation in the International Sugar Agreement (ISA) and include identical minimum wage provisions for sugar workers.

The Finance bill is expected to come to the floor Oct. 9 or 10.

Consumer groups and the Carter administration have fought the automatic adjustment feature (the "escalator") and the 17-cent price, claiming these would add almost $4 billion to consumer food bills in the next five years.

Administration aides have indicated that the president would veto anything but a 15-cents-a-pound price with no automatic increases. The administration prefers to supplement the basic price with direct payments from the Treasury to producers, if production costs rise in the future.

In response to these pressures, the House Ways and Means Committee reworked a proposal reported by the Agriculture Committee, substituting 15 cents for the 16-cent price approved by the farm panel and deleting the controversial adjuster. It was that compromise measure, offered by Rep. Charles A. Vanik, D-Ohio, as a substitute, that was the focus of floor action in the House. *(Ways and Means action, Weekly Report p. 2639)*

House Floor Action

In a free-wheeling debate, members loudly disputed whether direct payments or the automatic adjuster was more inflationary. Some Republican members, led by Paul Findley, R-Ill., argued that no action this year would be the cheapest alternative.

Findley also warned that a far more expensive sugar program would emerge from a House-Senate conference, and perhaps the White House, because of leverage by Senate Finance Committee Chairman Russell B. Long, D-La. Without naming Long, Findley said, "He has in his hip pocket the energy bill, the tax bill, nobody knows what other goodies. I forecast that the president of the United States, being eager to have [these bills], will hardly be in a position to do other than sign this legislation."

Long had added to his leverage by persuading the Finance panel to tack onto the sugar bill an unrelated tariff measure that the president badly wants. *(Story on Long, p. 2737)*

Before voting 186-159 to pass the bill, the House took these actions:

• Agreed by voice vote to the international treaty provisions in the Agriculture Committee bill.

• Agreed by a 194-164 vote to a William A. Steiger, R-Wis., amendment to add the cost-of-production adjuster to the Ways and Means substitute.

• Agreed by a 67-29 standing vote to a Vanik motion to substitute the Ways and Means domestic sugar program for that of the Agriculture bill.

• Rejected by voice vote a Richard Kelly, R-Fla., amendment to eliminate the minimum wage and other provisions designed to protect sugar workers.

• Agreed by voice vote to a Vanik amendment to extend the existing sugar loan program until "market prices strengthened" as a result of the new quota and fee approach.

SUGAR LEGISLATION DIES

Sugar legislation unexpectedly died in the waning hours of the 95th Congress when the House balked at a conference agreement that had been drafted to Carter administration specifications.

The failure left a pending international sugar agreement without ratification, and left domestic producers with an expiring support program.

By a 177-194 vote the House Oct. 15 refused to accept a compromise five-year domestic sugar support program that the Senate had endorsed hours earlier. Before passing the compromise the Senate by a 36-20 vote had decided not to recommit — and thus kill — the bill.

In a weary session that began about 5 a.m. Oct. 15 conferees had bowed to presidential demands that they drop an automatic inflation adjustment to a base per-pound support price for sugar, and that they adopt a relatively low base or "price objective." Both houses had passed legislation establishing a domestic sugar price and authorizing import quotas and fees to keep sugar at that set price. But the president had threatened to veto the legislation as too inflationary.

Conferees finally agreed to the following: a base 15 cents per pound price — the figure adopted by the House — for fiscal year 1979 with a .75 cents supplementary payment for that year only. Thereafter, the price objective would rise 1 percent a year. The Senate bill had set the initial price at 16 cents. *(Senate bill, Weekly Report p. 2922, House action, p. 2788)*

Some sugar producers viewed the conference agreement as just barely adequate — to keep them going until next year, when they will try again for more generous support. Their congressional advocates, led by Sen. Russell B. Long, D-La., pleaded for "aye" votes and the Senate went along.

But many producers, who claim production costs of 16 or 17 cents a pound, were angered by the conference agreement which they said guaranteed their bankruptcy. Corn sweetener interests also objected to the direct payments provision.

These dissatisfactions, plus opposition to an unrelated tariff provision, shaped the negative House vote, according to observers. The conferees had retained a Senate-passed extension of the president's authority to waive countervailing duties, but the import-sensitive textile industry opposed the extension and some members voted against the sugar bill for that reason.

Congressional Quarterly, October 21, 1978, p. 3087.

MEAT IMPORT BILL POSES
DILEMMA FOR CARTER

by William Symonds

President Carter soon will make one of his toughest farm policy decisions: whether to sign a meat import bill that cleared Congress in the final days of the session. To the nation's cattle producers, the bill has become a litmus test of Carter's support for the cattle industry.

Carter must make his decision only days before the Nov. 7 elections. Many cattle-industry experts predict that a veto would unleash a firestorm of political protest exceeding the outburst that followed Carter's decision to boost the beef import quota last June.

Carter administration officials are worried that the measure might fuel beef-price inflation in the future. They are concerned that if the president signs the bill, the administration's battle for a more open world trading system might suffer. The officials point to an Oct. 17 telegram from the Australian prime minister to Carter, in which the prime minister asked Carter — in the strongest terms — to veto the bill, and warned of repercussions if he signed the legislation. Australia is a major foreign supplier of beef to U.S. markets.

Administration officials believe the arguments against the meat import bill outweigh those in its favor. Administration and congressional sources contacted by The Register used such phrases as "highly likely" and "75 percent certain" to describe the chances of a Carter veto.

To understand the importance of the bill to the cattle industry, it is helpful to look back to June 8, when Carter announced that he was increasing the beef import quota for 1978 by 200 million pounds.

The president's decision came when inflation was accelerating, and much of the public's attention was focused on rising food prices. The administration argued that allowing more foreign beef into the country would help hold down beef prices, especially hamburger prices, and could save customers more than $500 million.

The decision was made just as cattle prices were recovering from several unprofitable years. To cattlemen, it looked as if the president was out to deny them a fair profit.

The meat import bill is designed to ensure that cattle producers won't have to experience that again. It

Des Moines Register, October 23, 1978, pp. 8a, 9a.

would make two major changes in current law.

First, it would change the formula under which the quota for imported beef is established. Second, it would severely restrict the authority of the president to tamper with the import quota.

Under current law, which dates back to 1964, the amount of beef that foreigners may ship into the U.S. market varies in line with the amount of beef being produced in the United States. When U.S. production is rising, imports are allowed to rise, but when domestic production is falling, imports are held down.

The minimum amount of beef that may be shipped to the United States is governed by a complex formula, but it generally works out to about 7 percent of U.S. beef production. This minimum is called the base quota.

Once the base quota has been determined, U.S. officials work with the major beef exporting countries to negotiate voluntary agreements governing their shipments of beef. Though the agreements are designed to hold beef imports to the quota level, since 1964, U.S. meat imports have exceeded the base quota levels in 10 years.

If it appears that beef imports will exceed a level equal to 110 percent of the base quota, the 1964 law requires the president to decide whether to impose formal quotas on imported beef (though he may not set quotas lower than the base quota amount), or suspend quotas entirely, allowing beef to flow in unchecked. He may also take actions ranging between these extremes.

Under the 1964 law, the president has broad authority to lift the beef import quota. He may suspend the quota if (1) overriding economic or national security interests require the action, or (2) supplies of beef and veal will not meet domestic demand at reasonable prices. Since 1964, the president has used the authority to suspend the quotas on five occasions, and to raise the quota level twice.

The key problem with the 1964 law is that it is governed by an "upside down formula." When U.S. beef production rises — and beef prices at the supermarket fall — the law lets in more foreign beef, further depressing prices. But when U.S. beef production drops — and prices rise — the law restricts beef imports.

The meat import law thus tends to accentuate the swings in the cattle cycle and beef prices. The law's illogical nature virtually begs for presidential intervention, especially when U.S. beef production is dropping.

The meat import bill that Congress passed is designed to turn the formula governing imports right side up. When U.S. beef production rises, the new formula would force meat imports down. And when U.S. beef production falls, beef imports would be allowed to increase.

By countering the cattle cycle in the United States, the new formula would tend to moderate swings in cattle prices. This would bring more stable beef prices for customers, and a healthier climate for cattle producers.

Disagreement centers on the second portion of the meat import bill. The bill would eliminate the present authority of the president to raise quotas. The bill instead establishes two sets of conditions under which the president could raise or lower the quota amount.

The first would allow the president to raise or lower the quota by as much as 10 percent in the event of rapid shifts in the price of cattle or beef at the supermarket.

This would give the president authority to counter a rapid buildup in the price of cattle by allowing a bit more imported beef into the country. But it is modest authority at best.

John Simpson, a senior official at the U.S. Department of Agriculture, said that the condition demanded under this system has been met once in the past 10 years. Moreover, a 10 percent increase in imports is small.

The second condition under which the president could raise the import quota would be in the event of a declared national emergency or a natural disaster that severely cut beef supplies in the United States.

The meat import bill thus would give the president limited leeway to adjust the meat import quota.

Though the United States imports substantial amounts of beef, few foreigners would be convinced that the U.S. cattle producer needs additional protection from foreign competition. Last year, U.S. exports of livestock, meat and meat products exceeded U.S. imports of beef and other livestock products.

The Carter administration has pushed to open more doors for American farm products at the Multilateral Trade Negotiations in Geneva. Congress recently cleared a bill to increase U.S. efforts to sell farm products abroad.

Any step that would be seen as limiting the access of foreign beef to the U.S. market could hurt the U.S. position at the Geneva talks. As four congressmen noted in a prepared statement, "The success of these [trade] negotiations depends on reciprocity. If we pass this bill, our trading partners are sure to reciprocate with trade restrictions of their own."

MEAT IMPORTS VETO

I have withheld my approval of HR 11545, the Meat Import Act of 1978.

I do so because the bill would severely restrict Presidential authority to increase meat imports and would place a floor or minimum access level for meat imports that I believe is too low. It deprives a President of the only anti-inflationary tool available in this area.

Current law allows the President substantial flexibility to increase meat imports when, in his judgment, domestic supplies are inadequate to meet demand at reasonable prices. I am convinced that this flexibility must be preserved, as a weapon against inflation.

Under this bill, however, authority to increase meat imports would be tied to declaration of a national emergency or natural disaster, or to a restrictive price formula. Under this formula, the farm price of cattle would have to increase faster than the retail meat price by more than ten percent during the first two calendar quarters of a year. Under this formula, quotas could have been relaxed only once in the last ten years.

I also believe that the United State must avoid imposing excessive restrictions on our trading partners who supply us with meat. HR 11545 would impose those restrictions by stipulating a minimum access level for meat imports of 1.2 billion pounds, instead of the 1.3 billion my Administration recommended. I am concerned that the bill's lower level could harm our trade relations with the meat exporting countries and thus impair their long-term reliability as souces of additional meat supplies when our own production is low, particularly at a time when we are negotiating for greater access to foreign markets for both our industrial and agricultural products.

If the Congress had enacted HR 11545 without these objectionable provisions, I would have been pleased to sign it, as my advisers make clear repeatedly. The bill would have amended the Meat Import Act of 1964 to provide a new formula for determining meat import quotas. The new formula would have adjusted meat import quotas up when domestic production of meats subject to the quota went down. Under the 1964 meat import law, quotas are adjusted in the opposite way, so that as domestic production declines, the limits on meat imports are tightened, at exactly the wrong time. This defect has often compelled Presidents to increase or suspend the meat import quota, in order to ensure supplies of meat at reasonable prices. The new counter-cyclical formula would, in most years, automatically make the necessary adjustment in the meat import quota, without involving the President in the normal operation of the meat trade.

This Administration supports such counter-cyclical management of meat imports; in fact, the Department of Agriculture was instrumental in developing the formula which the Congress approved. But for all the advantages of the new formula, it is still an untested mechanical formula which may not respond ideally to all future situations. This is why I find the restrictions on the President's discretion to increase meat imports so objectionable and why my Administration's support for HR 11545 was so clearly conditioned upon removal of those restrictions and on increasing the minimum access level for meat imports to 1.3 billion pounds annually.

I am prepared to work with the Congress next year to pass a counter-cyclical meat import bill which will provide the stability and certainty the cattle industry requires, while preserving the President's existing discretionary authority and setting an acceptable minimum access level for imports.

JIMMY CARTER

The White House,
November 10, 1978

Congressional Quarterly, November 25, 1978, pp. 3359-60.

THE POLITICS AND ECONOMICS OF U.S. DEVELOPMENT ASSISTANCE

DEVELOPING COUNTRY PROSPECTS AND ISSUES

In 1977 the Administration, building on the policies of its predecessors, intensified the efforts of the U.S. to strengthen ties with the developing world and accelerate economic development. Our policies were based on several fundamental considerations:

—The growing U.S. economic stake in the developing countries.

The economic importance of the Third World to the United States has grown enormously. We sell well over a third of our exports to the developing countries, including more manufactures than to Western Europe, Japan and the communist countries combined. LDCs account for almost half of U.S. overseas investment in plant and equipment, and a third of our earnings on foreign investment. Our imports of oil from the LDCs continue to grow, and now constitute half our total needs, and we depend on Third World nations for over two-thirds of imports of several other vital raw materials. Our links in other important economic areas such as transportation and communications also continue to grow.

Taken together, these trends demonstrate how the prosperity of the U.S. and its industrial trading partners are inextricably linked to the economics of the Third World. As President Carter said about North-South economic relations in Caracas:

> "Only by acting together can we expand trade and investment in order to create more jobs, curb inflation, and raise the standard of living of our peoples. . . . The industrial nations cannot by themselves bring about world recovery. Strong growth and expansion in the developing countries are essential. . . ."

—The central importance of Third World nations to our broad foreign policy objectives.

In order to achieve many of our central foreign policy objectives, we must continue to work closely with Third World countries. Areas of cooperation include maintaining peace in regional troublespots such as the Middle East and Southern Africa, curbing the growth of trade in conventional armaments, accelerating the development of the world's energy base, establishing a system of world food security, moderating commodity price fluctuations, reducing the danger of nuclear proliferation,

and enhancing respect for human rights worldwide.

—The increasing emergence of truly global issues.

As we approach the 1980s, we must begin to talk less of developed and developing, North and South, and more of a global community which faces critically important development-related questions. Population pressure is ultimately as threatening to the developed as to the developing countries; the threat of world hunger is a problem for the world, not North or South; the threats to our environment are not divisible into national or regional problems; stable and smoothly functioning commodity markets which reflect fair economic value are in the interests of all; and all countries benefit from free and open monetary and trade systems which allow investments and products to flow where they can be most effectively utilized.

—A desire to approach negotiations with the Third World in a pragmatic, non-ideological fashion.

In recent years the developed and developing nations have been involved in discussions and negoiations on issues central to the functioning of the international economy. These include resource transfers, commodities, debt, technology, investment, and trade. We have taken an increasingly pragmatic approach to these issues, and sought to shift the focus from rhetorical posturing to specific and realistic objectives. We have earnestly sought solutions which benefit all countries—not just North or South—and allow effective participation by all in global economic discussions. The result has been a greatly improved negotiating environment.

—A determination to elevate equity considerations in our development efforts.

Our concern for the promotion of human rights is reflected in, and basic to, our development efforts. Economic rights are an integral part of our overall human rights policy. The clearest manifestation of this link has been the emphasis on meeting basic human needs through our assistance programs. A basic human needs strategy rejects the argument that growth will "trickle down;" in many cases it simply has not. It emphasizes both growth and equity in that it focuses on meeting basic human needs both by providing basic goods and

Development Issues, Third Annual Report to the Congress, Development Coordination Committee (Washington, D.C.: April 1978), pp. 1-4.

services and by increasing incomes of the poor through productive employment.

—A decision that our development assistance levels should increase and that the effectiveness of these programs should be improved.

The President has decided that our foreign assistance performance must be strengthened. He will seek from Congress a larger program for the future, but he has also ordered the Executive Branch to further improve the effectiveness of our foreign assistance programs by rooting out mismanagement and inefficiency where they exist. He has directed ongoing scrutiny to ensure that our programs achieve their assigned objectives. Above all, he expects continued efforts to ensure that our concessional assistance goes to those people who need it most, primarily in the poorest countries but also in other developing countries where particular needs and opportunities exist.

—A determination that development considerations must be factored into all areas of our international economic policy.

Developing nations are increasingly central to our formulation of policies on trade, monetary, and resource issues. We have stepped up the pace and scope of consultations on a variety of international economic issues with key developing nations. We believe strongly that developing countries should participate in the design of international economic arrangements which affect their economic situation and prospects. We will take steps to see that this is achieved, both within our own policy-making process and in international forums.

—Recognition that improved coordination of our assistance programs is absolutely necessary.

Increasing the impact of our development effort requires substantially improved coordination, both within the U.S. Government and internationally. The Executive Branch and the Congress are determined to see that this improvement occurs. The President has not only endorsed the improved coordination objective of the bill introduced by Senator Humphrey; he has also made specific decisions on how he wishes this objective to be achieved and steps are already in motion to carry out these decisions. They will result in a better overall development strategy, and a more effective assistance program. With the more integrated U.S. assistance strategy already established and the more effective coordination of programs now being put into place, the United States will be in a stronger position to discuss its programs with other donor nations and institutions.

This report describes the development problems and issues facing the developing countries in 1977, and indicates the response made by the U.S. to these issues. It covers a broad range of government policies and activities relevant to the development process, many of which have been in transition as the Carter Administration has begun to implement a more positive and forthcoming policy toward the developing world.

This first chapter highlights the major issues and problems, the second chapter examines the central themes of human needs and human rights, and later chapters go into detail on various aspects of U.S. policy and activity.

The prospects of the developing countries are inextricably linked to the state of the global economy; the most important influences on development in 1977 were the continuing effects of increased petroleum prices and lagging growth in the developed countries.

Consequently events which shape the world economy are basic to the solution of the year's critical development issues. These issues are:

—How to assist the poorer developing countries to step up their rate of development from the low levels of the first half of the 1970s, so they can move forward, emphasizing both growth and equity, to improve the lot of the majority of their populations which live close to the subsistence level.

—How to assure that the more advanced developing countries maintain or restore the relatively rapid rate of development that they achieved in the first half of the 70s, so that they can both continue their drive toward developed country status and improve the ability of their poorest people to enjoy the benefits of growth.

U.S. PROSPERITY TIED
TO 'POOR' NATIONS

by David R. Francis

Like it or lump it, the United States and other industrialized nations have become more dependent economically than most people realize on the world's developing nations.

Boston

"It is clear that our most central national interests have become inextricably linked to the future of the developing countries. We are past the time when most international issues were a function of the balance of power between East and West, or turned primarily on events in the industrialized nations alone." — **C. Fred Bergsten, assistant secretary of the Treasury.**

In recent years there has been a dramatic, little recognized change in the economic relationship between the United States and the developing world. The poor countries are no longer just peripheral to the interests of this powerful industrial nation — they are crucial to the welfare of the United States.

Economists often will note that economic affairs in the rich industrial nations are important to the development prospects of the poor countries. When prosperous, the industrial nations are more prone to need and accept a larger volume of the raw materials and simple manufactured goods produced by the development countries; they are more likely to be generous in foreign aid and to open their capital markets to loans by the poor countries.

What is less often perceived is that the prosperity of the industrial nations, including the United States, can now be strongly affected by growth rates in the developing world.

Conditions for achievement

Says John W. Sewell, executive vice-president of the Overseas Development Council in Washington: "The achievement of the domestic economic goals of the developed countries — resumed growth, more jobs, more stable prices — will depend to a much larger degree than heretofore on the growth and prosperity of the developing countries."

John J. Gilligan, administrator of the Agency for International Development, notes that the myth is "still far too prevalent" that the United States is self-sufficient, not dependent on other nations, not dependent on the third world.

Mr. Gilligan and the Treasury's Mr. Bergsten, in talks last month to a conference in Washington on economic development, tried to shake that myth by noting some of the factors tying the poor nations to this rich nation.

1. United States exports to the developing world are now greater than its exports to all of Europe or Japan.

Over the past five years U.S. exports to the developing nations have tripled to almost $30 billion. If this trend continues, they will reach $160 billion only 10 years from now.

Put another way, the nonoil developing countries purchased one quarter of U.S. total merchandise exports in 1977. Including members of the Organization of Petroleum Exporting Countries, the developing world took 40 percent of U.S. exports of manufactured products. Those exports, says Mr. Bergsten, create almost one-million jobs in this country.

Growing dependence

(This trend is part of the growing dependence of the U.S. economy on the rest of the world. The fraction of U.S. gross national product now derived from trade runs about 7 percent, nearly double what it was 20 years ago. Exports today contribute more to GNP than private corporate investment. They are 2.5 times greater than the amount spent on private residential construction. Exports provide one out of every eight manufacturing jobs in the country. One of every three acres of U.S. farm land produces for export.)

2. The U.S. and other industrial nations are becoming increasingly reliant on the developing countries for both their energy supplies and other natural resources.

Annual U.S. payments for oil now amount to $45 billion. Virtually all of that comes from developing countries. Imported oil runs around 50 percent of the nation's total oil supply.

"Five developing countries supply almost 50 percent of world copper," notes Mr. Bergsten. "Two account for more than 50 percent of world tin exports. Two supply almost 75 percent of the world's consumption of natural rubber. Four supply nearly 60 percent of world trade in bauxite. We also import from devel-

Profile of the rich and poor nations
(Data for 1974; values in 1974 U.S. dollars)

Demographic	Rich nations	OPEC*	Poor nations**	World
Population (in billions)	1.1	.1	2.8	4.0
Percentage of total world population	27.5	2.5	70.0	100.0
Birth rate (per thousand)	17	n.a.***	37	31
Death rate (per thousand)	9	n.a.	14	13
Infant mortality (per thousand)	25	n.a.	125	75
Life expectancy (years)	71	n.a.	52	55
Economic				
GNP (gross national product – $ billion)	4,991	165	632	5,788
Percentage of total world GNP	86.2	2.9	10.9	100.0
GNP growth rate (1970-74)	3.6	7.7	5.5	4.5
Per capita income (1974 $)	4,537	1,650	226	1,447
Investment ($ billion)	1,098	31	114	1,243
Per capita investment ($)	100	31	4	31
Investment as a % of GNP	22.0	18.8	18.0	21.5
Exports ($ billion)	808	101	134	1,043
Percentage of total world exports	77.5	9.7	12.8	100.0
Social				
Literate population (in millions)	758	18	746	1,522
Percentage of population	68.9	18.0	26.6	38.0
Malnourished population (in millions)	10	nil	900	910
Percentage of population	0.9	nil	32.1	22.8
Poorest population in millions below $100 per capita	nil	nil	942	942
Percentage of population	nil	nil	33.6	23.6

*Algeria, Iran, Iraq, Kuwait, Libya, Qatar, Saudi Arabia, United Arab Emirates, Venezuela, Ecuador, Gabon, Indonesia, and Nigeria are excluded.
**Includes countries of the third world but excludes OPEC members (except Indonesia and Nigeria).
***n.a – not available.

Source: The Poverty Curtain, Hahbub ul Haq, Columbia University Press, New York

oping countries virtually all of our coffee, cocoa, tea, nuts, spices, vegetable oils, bananas, and fibers."

3. Almost half of all America's direct investment (in plant and equipment) overseas is in the third world. The income from these investments came last year to about $7 billion. That is about 37 percent of U.S. net direct investment earnings worldwide. Those earnings, said Mr. Bergsten, were "an important element of strength for the dollar in the exchange markets."

Words of caution

Mr. Gilligan concludes: "America now, more than ever before, simply cannot afford to allow global problems of hunger, physical degradation, and poverty to block the way of progress in economic and social improvement."

Says Mr. Sewell: "The understanding that there are benefits for the rich countries in accommodating to the proposals of the developing countries for changes in existing international systems is not widespread."

Even Henry A. Kissinger, whose years as secretary of state were devoted largely to East-West, China, and Middle East relations, recognizes the growing importance of the poor countries to the U.S. In a speech last summer, he maintained that the U.S., as the world's strongest economy, would be injured less than others by "an environment of hostility and autarchy" between the rich and poor nations. "But the outbreak of economic warfare between North and South would damage even our own well-being," he said.

Impact of Increase

A report prepared for the United Nations Conference on Trade and Development by economists at the University of Pennsylvania concludes that an increase of 3 percent in the growth rates of the nonoil-producing developing countries could result in a 1 percent boost in the growth rates of the industrial members of the Organization of Economic Cooperation and Development (OECD). Over a five-year period that increase could mean a gain of at least $225 billion in gross national product (the output of goods and services) and a correspondingly large increase in employment.

Such a study is based on econometric models and might be challenged. However, economists pretty well accept the conclusion that the developing countries, by continuing to suck in imports at a high rate, prevented the 1974-75 recession from being even worse than it was in the rich nations. The developing countries' balance-of-payments deficit, argue economists John A. Holsen and Jean L. Waelbroeck in the American Economic Review (May, 1976), sustained demand in the industrial nations "as much as, say, a vigorous [West] Germany demands expansion."

In recent years, Americans have heard many complaints by U.S. manufacturers about the rapid growth in the volume of imported shoes, textiles, and various electronic products from developing countries. They have heard less about the enormous expansion of U.S. exports to the developing countries. From 1970 to 1975, for instance, those exports grew at an annual average rate of more than 19 percent, compared with 15.5 percent for exports to other industrial nations.

'Engine of growth'

Adds Mr. Sewell: "As long as the purchasing power of the developing countries is at least maintained [and preferably expanded], trade between the north and south is likely to increase at a much more rapid rate than trade among the industrial countries."

Mr. Sewell and others argue that the developing countries have become the "engine of growth" for the north. Their import demand sustains growth and increases employment in the industrial countries. Thus there is less need for inflationary internal fiscal or monetary stimulus. Moreover, the imports from the poor countries enhance competition and keep prices from skyrocketing.

In a paper to be published shortly by the Overseas Development Council, Mr. Sewell notes several other reasons why the United States and other industrial nations should be interested in helping the poor countries make rapid progress:

● Industrial nations would benefit from the price stabilization of properly designed commodity agreements.

● Given their huge debts, the continued financial well-being of the developing nations will be an important factor in the stability of the international financial system. This is of "prime importance to the United States and other industrial economies."

● Helping the poor countries increase their food production should prevent inflationary excessive demand for U.S. grains from developing. "Few Americans now understand that what the governments and leaders of those countries decide to do about rural development and the production of food within their own countries will have a measurable impact in the years ahead on the prices that Americans pay for food in the supermarket," says Mr. Sewell.

● The industrial countries should help the poor countries to develop renewable sources of energy, mainly solar, as their chief source of energy. Otherwise, should these countries attempt to follow the petroleum-intensive growth patterns of the rich nations, they would consume by the end of the century almost as much oil as the entire world does today. This would likely accelerate exhaustion of the world's finite supply of oil, increase inflation, and reduce economic growth and development, especially in the poor countries.

● Both rich and poor countries should cooperatively address the world's population problem. Otherwise "the resulting stresses and strains on the globe's political, economic, social, and physical environment are likely to pose a number of almost insurmountable difficulties before the end of the century and beyond." For instance, the U.S. and other industrial nations will face growing pressures from illegal immigration.

Many in both the north and the south are not happy about the growing "interdependence" of their nations. In the south particularly, intellectuals debate the merits of "delinking" wholly or partially from the north. A few countries — Communist China, Burma, Cambodia, for instance — have tried to limit or sever their ties with other nations, especially the rich ones.

But, like it or lump it, most countries are finding that modern communications, technological needs, environmental problems, and economic logic are throwing them together on this more-and-more crowded planet. Mankind is being forced into learning the meaning of true brotherhood.

STATEMENT BY THE PRESIDENT

It is important for this Nation's economic vitality that both the private sector and the Federal government place a higher priority on exports. I am today announcing a series of measures that evidences my Administration's strong commitment to do so.

The large trade deficits the United States has experienced in recent years have weakened the value of the dollar, intensified inflationary pressures in our own economy, and heightened instability in the world economy. These trade deficits have been caused by a number of factors. A major cause has been our excessive reliance on imported oil. We can reduce that reliance through the passage of sound energy legislation this year. Another factor is that the United States economy has been growing at a stronger pace in recent years than the economies of our major trading partners. That has enabled us to purchase relatively more foreign goods while our trading partners have not been able to buy as much of our exports. We will begin to correct this imbalance as our trading partners meet the commitments to economic expansion they made at the Bonn Summit.

The relatively slow growth of American exports has also been an important factor in our trade deficit problem. Over the past 20 years, our exports have grown at only half the rate of other industrial nations and the United States has been losing its share of world markets. Unitl now, both business and government have accorded exports a relatively low priority. These priorities must be changed.

The measures I am announcing today consist of actions this Administration has taken and will take to:

(1) provide increased direct assistance to United States exporters
(2) reduce domestic barriers to exports; and
(3) reduce foreign barriers to our exports and secure a fairer international trading system for all exporters.

These actions are in furtherance of the commitment I made at the Bonn Summit to an improved United States export performance.

DIRECT ASSISTANCE TO UNITED STATES EXPORTERS

1. <u>Export-Import Bank</u>. I have consistently supported a more effective and aggressive Export-Import Bank. During the past two years, my Administration has increased Eximbank's loan authorization fivefold--from $700 million in FY 1977 to $3.6 billion for FY 1979. I intend to ask Congress for an additional $500 million in FY 1980, bringing Eximbank's total loan authorization to $4.1 billion. These authorizations will provide the Bank with the funds necessary to improve its competitiveness, in a manner consistent with our international obligations, through increased flexibility in the areas of interest rates, length of loans, and the percentage of a transaction it can finance. The Bank is also moving to simplify its fee schedules and to make its programs more accessible to smaller exporters and to agricultural exporters.

Office of the White House Press Secretary, September 26, 1978.

2. SBA Loans to Small Exporters. The Small Business Administration will channel up to $100 million of its current authorization for loan guarantees to small business exporters to provide seed money for their entry into foreign markets. Small exporting firms meeting SBA's qualifications will be eligible for loan guarantees totalling up to $500,000 to meet needs for expanded production capacity and to ease cash flow problems involving overseas sales or initial marketing expenses.

3. Export Development Programs. I am directing the Office of Management and Budget to allocate an additional $20 million in annual resources for export development programs of the Departments of Commerce and State to assist United States firms, particularly small and medium-sized businesses, in marketing abroad through:

-- a computerized information system to provide exporters with prompt access to international marketing opportunities abroad and to expose American products to foreign buyers;
-- risk sharing programs to help associations and small companies meet initial export marketing costs; and
-- targeted assistance to firms and industries with high export potential and intensified short-term export campaigns in promising markets.

4. Agricultural Exports. Agricultural exports are a vital component of the U.S. trade balance. Over the past 10 years, the volume of U.S. farm exports has doubled and the dollar value has nearly quadrupled. Trade in agricultural products will contribute a new surplus of almost $13 billion in fiscal year 1978. This strong performance is due in part to this Administration's multifaceted agricultural export policy, which will be strengthened and which includes:

-- An increase of almost $1 billion (up from $750 million in FY 1977 to $1.7 billion in FY 1978) in the level of short-term export credits.
-- An increase of almost 20% in the level of funding support for a highly successful program of cooperation with over 60 agricultural commodity associations in market development.
-- Efforts in the Multilateral Trade Negotiations to link the treatment of agricultural and nonagricultural products.
-- Opening trade offices in key importing nations in order to facilitate the development of these markets.
-- Aggressive pursuit of an international wheat agreement, to ensure our producers a fair share of the expanding world market.
-- Support of legislation to provide intermediate export credit for selective agricultural exports.

5. Tax Measures. I am hopeful that Congress will work with the Administration to promptly resolve the tax problems of Americans employed abroad, many of whom are directly involved in export efforts. Last February, I proposed tax relief for these citizens amounting to about $250 million a year. I think this proposal, which Congress has not approved, deals fairly and, during a time of great budget stringency, responsibly with this problem. I remain ready to work with the Congress to resolve this issue, but I cannot support proposals which run contrary to our strong concerns for budget prudence and tax equity.

My Administration's concern for exports is matched by our obligation to ensure that government-sponsored export incentives constitute an efficient use of the taxpayers' money. The DISC tax provision simply does not meet that basic test. It is a costly (over $1 billion a year) and inefficient incentive for exports. I continue to urge Congress to phase DISC out or at least make it simpler, less costly, and more effective than it is now, and my Administration stands ready to work with Congress toward that goal.

REDUCTION OF DOMESTIC BARRIERS TO EXPORTS

Direct financial and technical assistance to United States firms should encourage them to take advantage of the increasing competitiveness of our goods in international markets. Equally important will be the reduction of government-imposed disincentives and barriers which unnecessarily inhibit our firms from selling abroad. We can and will continue to administer the laws and policies affecting the international business community firmly and fairly, but we can also discharge that responsibility with a greater sensitivity to the importance of exports than has been the case in the past.

1. Export Consequences of Regulations. I am directing the heads of all Executive departments and agencies to take into account and weigh as a factor, the possible adverse effects on our trade balance of their major administrative and regulatory actions that have significant export consequences. They will report back on their progress in identifying and reducing such negative export effects where possible, consistent with other legal and policy obligations. I will make a similar request of the independent regulatory agencies. In addition, the Council of Economic Advisers will consider export consequences as part of the Administration's Regulatory Analysis Program.

There may be areas, such as the export of products which pose serious health and safety risks, where new regulations are warranted. But through the steps outlined above, I intend to inject a greater awareness throughout the government of the effects on exports of administrative and regulatory actions.

2. Export Controls for Foreign Policy Purposes. I am directing the Departments of Commerce, State, Defense, and Agriculture to take export consequences fully into account when considering the use of export controls for foreign policy purposes. Weight will be given to whether the goods in question are also available from countries other than the United States.

3. Foreign Corrupt Practices Act. At my direction, the Justice Department will provide guidance to the business community concerning its enforcement priorities under the recently enacted foreign antibribery statute. This statute should not be viewed as an impediment to the conduct of legitimate business activities abroad. I am hopeful that American business will not forego legitimate export opportunities because of uncertainty about the application of this statute. The guidance provided by the Justice Department should be helpful in that regard.

4. Antitrust Laws. There are instances in which joint ventures and other kinds of cooperative arrangements between American firms are necessary or desirable to improve our export performance. The Justice Department has advised that most such foreign joint ventures would not violate our antitrust laws, and in many instances would actually strengthen competition. This is especially true for one-time joint ventures created to participate in a single

activity, such as a large construction project. In fact, no such joint conduct has been challenged under the antitrust laws in over 20 years.

Nevertheless, many businessmen apparently are uncertain on this point, and this uncertainty can be a disincentive to exports. I have, therefore, instructed the Justice Department, in conjunction with the Commerce Department, to clarify and explain the scope of the antitrust laws in this area, with special emphasis on the kinds of joint ventures that are unlikely to raise antitrust problems.

I have also instructed the Justice Department to give expedited treatment to requests by business firms for guidance on international antitrust issues under the Department's Business Review Program. Finally, I will appoint a business advisory panel to work with the National Commission for the Review of the Antitrust Laws.

5. <u>Environmental Reviews</u>. For a number of years the export community has faced the uncertainty of whether the National Environmental Policy Act (NEPA) requires environmental impact statements for Federal export licenses, permits and approvals.

I will shortly sign an Executive Order which should assist U.S. exports by eliminating the present uncertainties concerning the type of environmental reviews that will be applicable and the Federal actions relating to exports that will be affected. The Order will make the following export-related clarifications:

-- Environmental Impact Statements will not be required for Federal export licenses, permits, approvals, and other export-related actions that have potential environmental effects in foreign countries.
-- Export licenses issued by the Departments of Commerce and Treasury will be exempt from any environmental reviews required by the Executive Order.
-- Abbreviated environmental reviews will be required only with respect to (1) nuclear reactors, (2) financing of products and facilities whose toxic effects create serious public health risks, and (3) certain Federal actions having a significant adverse effect on the environment of non-participating third countries or natural resources of global importance.

Accordingly, this Order will establish environmental requirements for only a minor fraction (well below 5%) of the dollar volume of United States exports. At the same time, it will provide procedures to define and focus on those exports which should receive special scrutiny because of their major environmental impacts abroad. This Executive Order will fairly balance our concern for the environment with our interest in promoting exports.

REDUCTION IN FOREIGN TRADE BARRIERS AND SUBSIDIES

We are also taking important international initiatives to improve U.S. export performance. Trade restrictions imposed by other countries inhibit our ability to export. Tariff and expecially non-tariff barriers restrict our ability to develop new foreign markets and expand existing ones. We are now working to eliminate or reduce these barriers through the Multilateral Trade Negotiations in Geneva.

United States export performance is also adversely affected by the excessive financial credits and subsidies which some of our trading partners offer to their own exporters. One of our major objectives in the MTN is to negotiate an international code restricting the use of government subsidies for exports. In addition, I am directing the Secretary of the Treasury to undertake immediate consultations with our trading partners to expand the scope and tighten the terms of the existing International Arrangement on Export Credits.

I hope that our major trading partners will see the importance of reaching more widespread agreements on the use of export finance, to avoid a costly competition which is economically unsound and ultimately self-defeating for all of us. These international agreements are essential to assure that American exporters do not face unfair competition, and this Administration intends to work vigorously to secure them.

CONCLUSION

While these initiatives will assist private business in increasing exports, our export problem has been building for many years and we cannot expect dramatic improvement overnight. Increasing our exports will take time, and require a sustained effort. Announcement of my Administration's export policy is not the end of our task, but rather the beginning. To ensure that this issue continues to receive priority attention, I am asking Secretary Kreps, in coordination with officials from other concerned government agencies, to direct the continuation of efforts to improve our export potential and performance.

I will shortly sign an Executive Order to reconstitute a more broadly-based President's Export Council to bring a continuous flow of fresh ideas into our government policy-making process. I expect this Council to report to me annually through the Secretary of Commerce.

Increasing U.S. exports is a major challenge--for business, for labor, and for government. Better export performance by the United States would spur growth in the economy. It would create jobs. It would strengthen the dollar and fight inflation.

There are no short-term, easy solutions. But the actions I am announcing today reflect my Administration's determination to give the United States trade deficit the high-level, sustained attention it deserves. They are the first step in a long-term effort to strengthen this Nation's export position in world trade.

WHY FOREIGN ASSISTANCE?

1. <u>Background</u>: US foreign assistance programs began in 1947 with
the successful Marshall Plan for the economic reconstruction
of Europe. In the 1950s, foreign aid was considered mainly as
a short-term national security measure to strengthen allies,
including some less developed countries (LDCs), against Communist invasion or takeover. In the 1960s, we continued to use
aid to support countries against internal subversion, but we also
emphasized development as an end in itself. It became apparent,
however, that some LDCs were not undergoing the same development
process that had occurred in the industrialized countries. In
recognition of these different economic patterns, Congress passed
a new Foreign Assistance Act in 1973. The act initiated the
current phase of the aid program, which focuses on meeting the
basic human needs -- food, shelter, health, education -- of the
poor majority in the LDCs. Support for family planning programs
is also an increasingly important part of our assistance. This
is not an international welfare program but an effort to help the
poor help themselves. Steady economic and social progress in the
LDCs is important to world peace and prosperity and to US security
and economic well-being.

2. <u>Present situation</u>: Today there are:

   - 1.2 billion people without access to potable water;
   - 700 million, including 100 million children, without enough to
     eat (more than 15 million children die each year from malnutri-
     tion and disease);
   - 550 million who cannot read or write; and
   - 220 million without adequate shelter.

   Many LDCs have average per capita incomes of less than $150 per
   year. Not only are they very poor; in many cases, their living
   standards have not risen because population increase has canceled
   out economic growth. They need financial and technical assistance
   on easy and affordable terms.

3. <u>US security and well-being</u>: Our humanitarian concerns are well
   known, but we also have major security and economic interests in
   the LDCs. Increasingly, the effective management of our economy
   will depend on mutually beneficial economic relations with them.

   - <u>Raw materials</u>. Although amply endowed with natural resources,
     we are not self-sufficient in raw materials, and our dependence
     on the LDCs is growing. For example, we depend on them for 100%
     of our natural rubber, 99% of our bauxite, 98% of our manganese
     ore, 97% of our cobalt, 86% of our tin, and 42% of our oil.

<u>Gist</u>, November 1978. <u>Gist</u> is a reference aid on U.S. foreign relations put out
by the Bureau of Public Affairs, Department of State.

- <u>Markets</u>. We rely on the LDCs for markets for many of the finished goods their raw materials make possible. They are also important markets for our agricultural products, taking 50% of our wheat exports, 60% of our cotton exports, and 70% of our rice exports. The non-oil LDCs alone take one-fourth of all US exports; including oil producers, they take 36%.
- <u>Employment</u>. To the degree that foreign aid can improve the economic vitality of the LDCs, it will not only develop markets for our goods but also create jobs for our unemployed. US exports to the LDCs now account for an estimated 2 million American jobs.
- <u>Debt</u>. Since 1973, the LDCs' international debt has almost tripled, from $55 billion to $155 billion. Their financial well-being is vital to the stability of the international financial system.
- <u>Food</u>. In recent years, worldwide food deficits and soaring food prices have contributed to global political instability and adversely affected the lives of Americans. We must try to equip the LDCs with the skills and resources to grow more food. By 1985, expected world food needs will exceed the developed countries' capacity to produce, transport, and distribute food.
- <u>Population</u>. By the year 2000, about 80% of the world's projected population of 6 billion will be living in the LDCs. Unless their problems are effectively addressed -- and food supplies and population brought into balance -- their daily lot will be misery and despair, and no nation, including the US, will be secure.

4. <u>Achievements</u>: Although it is impossible to separate foreign aid from other factors that promote development, aid has been central to such achievements in the last 25 years as the following:

- Many LDCs have advanced more rapidly than either they or the developed countries had grown in any other period. Some have achieved such high rates of economic growth that we have ended our grant aid.
- Average life expectancy has increased from 35 years to 50 years; some communicable diseases, such as smallpox, have been virtually eliminated.
- Birth rates have fallen significantly in many countries, including South Korea, Taiwan, Indonesia, and Colombia.
- The number of primary school children in the LDCs has tripled, while the number of secondary students has increased six times.

5. <u>US aid program</u>: The US aid program is small. Today we rank only 13th among industrialized donor countries in the proportion of our resources devoted to aid, spending about one-fourth of 1% of our GNP -- 1% of the Federal budget -- on foreign aid. In FY 1979, the Carter Administration is spending $3.4 billion for bilateral development assistance; $1.6 billion for international financial institutions; $260 million for international organizations and programs; and $1.4 billion for Public Law 480 food aid.

FINAL CONGRESSIONAL ACTION
ON FY 79 DEVELOPMENT ASSISTANCE FUNDING

The House and Senate completed action on the Foreign Assistance and Related Programs Appropriations Bill for Fiscal Year 1979 (HR 12931) by approving, during the final hectic days of the 95th session, the Conference Committee Report which reconciles some 100 differences between the House and Senate bills.

The resulting legislation, which became Public Law 95-481 with the President's signature on October 18, 1978, represents a significant victory for the Carter Administration in at least two major respects. First, drastic cuts in foreign aid funding levels were warded off even though Congress faces elections in November and has been acutely sensitive to the growing public clamor for curbs on public spending. Second, the legislation emerged free of troublesome political and economic constraints on the use of US contributions to multilateral development agencies. Skillful and intensive efforts by key congressional supporters of foreign aid of both parties, by the Administration, and by non-governmental organizations including the religious community contributed importantly to this positive outcome.

Funding Levels

The legislation provides $7.3 billion for foreign assistance, a substantial increase over last year's levels and a compromise between the $7.4 billion Senate and $7.2 billion House figures. Included is $1.2 billion for bilateral functional development assistance administered by AID, $260 million for international organizations and programs, and $2.5 billion for multilateral financial institutions. The measure also provides $1.8 billion for US participation in the supplementary financing facility of the International Monetary Fund and $2.7 billion for security supporting and military assistance. Economic development assistance of various sorts in the amount of about $4.5 billion accounts for less than two-thirds of the total "foreign aid" package and about half of the total amount appropriated in this measure. The $4.5 billion for development aid approved in FY 79 contrasts with $3.6 billion in FY 78.

The Administration's request for economic assistance was reduced $1.2 billion by the Congress, $1 billion of it involving US contributions to multilateral banks. While the cut affected all international banks, the International Bank for Reconstruction and Development (IBRD) and its soft loan loan window, the International Development Association (IDA), bore the brunt of the burden. IBRD was cut $400 million, IDA $292 million. Appropriations for the international banks are still roughly one-third higher than for Fiscal Year 1978--in IDA's case, more than 50 percent higher. However, in the absence of full funding for IDA, the US will be $292 million in arrears in its IDA commitment. No other contributor is in default.

Funds appropriated for bilateral aid in areas such as food production, nutrition, health and family planning, while $130 million below the Administration's request, remain about 20 percent higher than last year. Appropriations for international

Food Policy Notes (Interreligious Taskforce on U.S. Food Policy), Washington, D.C., October 27, 1978.

organizations and programs were $22 million less than requested but about 8 percent above 1978, an increase which hardly offsets the rate of inflation. Reductions in appropriations requested for security and military assistance were, as usual, considerably more modest.

Restrictions

As recommended by the Taskforce, the legislation accepts the Senate position deleting restrictions on US contributions to international financial institutions for use in Vietnam and Cuba. This eliminates the potential problem of policy language rendering US contributions to such bodies legally unacceptable. Also included is House language requiring US governors of International Financial Institutions (IFIs) to propose and seek the adoption of amendments to the banks' articles of agreement that would establish human rights standards to be used in consideration of all loan applications.

No restrictions were placed on the use of US funds for loans to countries producing commodities which might compete with US commodities. The legislation calls instead for international consultations to develop standards to govern the allocation of development assistance for the production and export of such commodities (an approach the Taskforce opposed).

The legislation establishes fixed ceilings on the share of future US contributions to international financial institutions. Such ceilings could mean sizable cutbacks in the US share of future IDA replenishments as well as in US contributions to the Fund for Special Operations of the Inter-American Development Bank. The Taskforce favors equitable burden-sharing with other contributors but questioned the wisdom of setting fixed percentages without regard to the particular circumstances.

Other Provisions

--The legislation restores $15 million of the $30 million House cut in the $90 million US contribution to the Sahel development program recommended by the Administration.

--It provides substantially higher funding levels for Migration and Refugee Assistance than requested by the Administration, including $1.5 million for Cambodian refugees in Vietnam. The use of US funds in Vietnam for Cambodian refugees could set the stage for the eventual granting of much-needed US aid to Vietnam in its own right, although that eventuality was opposed by Senator Dole (R-KS) who joined with Senator Kennedy (D-MA) to propose the Cambodian refugee item.

--The legislation continues existing prohibitions against bilateral aid to Angola and Mozambique.

--Although the legislation generally avoids country-specific sanctions regarding US military aid, the Philippines were singled out for a $2.5 million reduction because of the human rights practices of the Marcos regime.

In a distressing year-end development, Congress approved the State Department appropriations bill's prohibition of international organization expenditure of any assessed contributions from the US for providing technical assistance. Funds were reduced by $27,176,000 accordingly. (Assessed contributions are paid by the US on a proportionate basis to certain UN agencies; voluntary contributions are made without reference to a fixed US share.) This provision calls into question the acceptability of US FY 79 contributions to such organizations as the World Health Organization, the Food and Agriculture Organization, and UNESCO which provide technical assistance. UN agencies such as the UN Development Program and UNICEF, which receive US voluntary contributions are unaffected. Removal of the prohibition will be sought early next year. In the meantime, the status of US support for certain UN agencies remains unclear.

Preliminary Assessment

As noted earlier, the results of this year's congressional appropriations discussions, while somewhat disappointing in regard to funding levels (particularly that of IDA), are, on balance, considerably more positive than many had feared and a substantial improvement over last year's outcomes. A variety of factors help explain the results:

--An energetic and thoughtful group of Members of Congress of both parties provided concerted leadership throughout the appropriations process. On the House side, special leadership came from Representatives Obey (D-WI), McHugh (D-NY), Wilson (D-TX), Stokes (D-OH), Conte (R-MA). Others not on the Appropriations Subcommittee who were helpful on issues of concern to the Taskforce included Foley (D-WA), Harkin (D-IA), Pease (D-OH), Montgomery (D-MS), Hyde (R-IL) and Simon (D-IL). Leadership in the Senate Appropriations Subcommittee came from Democrats Inouye (HI) and Leahy (VT) and Republicans Schweicker (PA), Brooke (MA), Mathias (MO), and Hatfield (OR), with support at key points from Senators Kennedy (D-MA), Church (D-ID), and Case (D-NJ). The Democratic and Republican party leadership in both Houses was helpful. Without active Republican support the outcome would have been far less favorable. The active involvement of many Members of the various authorizing committees was also important, as was that of the staffs of Members and of the committees.

--The President, the Vice President, Cabinet Secretaries and other ranking Administration officials played a more active and better orchestrated role in this year's appropriations process. Their presentations stressed US self-interest as well as humanitarian concerns.

--The troublesome political issues of last year (e.g., antagonism to certain countries and to competitive commodities) had moderated somewhat, although they remained potentially explosive. The decision to seek to state human rights concerns in general rather than country-specific terms avoided a recurring unpopularity contest among would-be recipients of US aid.

--Various private groups made thoughtful and numerous representations of their support for the development aid portions of the bill. The President himself met with religious leaders (See NOTE 78-24) who communicated their views directly and indirectly to Members of Congress. The United Nations Association, New Directions, and other civic, labor, and business groups also made their views known. However, communications from national organizations to

Members of Congress were generally not reinforced by expressions of views from districts and states.

--There was a general sense that development assistance agencies (particularly AID) are doing a better job now than earlier. However, serious questions about the effectiveness of aid agencies in reaching the poor remain--and will be a major point of discussion next year.

DEFYING CONVENTIONAL WISDOM

by William J. Lanouette

It was supposed to be a disaster. A rout. A sitting duck for right-wing rage. A chance for congressional rectitude after Proposition 13. After all, the saying goes, "Foreign aid has no constituency." And this is an election year, no time to be spending money overseas; no time to be bankrolling international bankers. Conventional wisdom, in and out of Congress, was nearly unanimous in its verdict—this year's foreign aid bill would be torn to shreds.

Conventional wisdom was dead wrong.

Indeed, the Carter Administration's handling of this year's foreign aid bill could serve as a textbook case to illustrate the techniques and results of effective lobbying. "The Administration did one helluva lot better job than I thought possible," said Rep. David R. Obey, D-Wis., an active foreign aid supporter. "Quite simply, they were able to sit down, nose-to-nose, to explain the facts of life on the expected amendments. . . . Then, halfway through the debate, congressional pride asserted itself and a majority of Members decided they were not going to cave in to a bunch of demagogic amendments."

This year's success was a direct result of last year's failure. When the foreign aid bill was before Congress last year, President Carter invited 120 Members to the White House in a personal attempt to salvage the measure. "He saw the disarray and confusion of our lobbying effort," one Administration lobbyist recalled, "and he vowed it wouldn't happen again. He told his staff to start planning early."

Last December, Colby King, deputy assistant Treasury secretary for legislative affairs, prepared a postmortem on the fiscal 1978 aid bill's international finance and banking sections. In January, he was drafting strategy memos on how to deal with three targets in the House: the Budget Committee, the Appropriations Committee and Members who are not on either panel. By February, lobbying strategy was cleared with liaison officers in the White House, the State Department and the Agency for International Development (AID).

"We found out that a large number of Members were unfamiliar with the international financial institutions," King said. "So we targeted about 200 Members, divided up the House, and went to see them." Treasury Secretary W. Michael Blumenthal and assistant secretary for international affairs C. Fred Bergsten personally called on Budget Committee members before the vote on the first budget resolution. Treasury officials who deal with the World Bank began visiting other House Members in their offices.

"Just before the Easter recess," King recalled, "we started to contact a large number of Members. You can't educate them when they're walking to the floor to vote. You've got to sit down, in a calm and relaxed atmosphere, before the issues and the votes and the constituents are on top of them."

At the White House, Robert Beckel, a special assistant for congressional liaison, acted as interagency coordinator. "We formed a 'legislative interagency group'—called it a 'lig'— to work on the aid bill," said Jean Lewis, assistant AID administrator for legislative affairs. "We'd meet weekly, sometimes daily when things really got going." Henry Owen, special representative of the President for economic summits, sat in on some of these sessions. It was his idea to enlist former Secretary of State Henry A. Kissinger in the lobbying effort, and to prepare a joint letter to be signed by eight former Treasury Secretaries.

Lewis also prepared a thick issues book that contained analyses of probable amendments and arguments and strategies for their defeat. Outside groups, such as the League of Women Voters of the U.S. and the Chamber of Commerce of the United States, mounted lobbying efforts of their own. Religious leaders met with the President, then went to work on wavering Members of Congress. Packets of background material were mailed to newspapers around the country. Lists were circulated to House Members, showing them how much foreign aid money is actually spent in their districts. Administration lobbyists made the point that foreign aid creates new overseas markets for American goods and services. AFL-CIO president George Meany wrote to House Members and Senators arguing for aid to the drought-stricken Sahel region of Africa and urging Congress to defeat country and commodity restrictions on aid.

National Journal, October 14, 1978, p. 1654.

"There was much more central coordination this year than last," said Douglas J. Bennet Jr., assistant secretary of State for congressional relations. "Beckel did a superb job of managing the whole effort. Obey formed an effective group in the Appropriations subcommittee. [Sen. Daniel K.] Inouye [D-Hawaii] did an impeccable job of managing the bill in the Senate. And I think that Members are much more sensitive than ever before about the impact that the international economy has in their own districts."AID administrator John J. Gilligan is also credited with an effective lobbying effort.

Obey organized squads of House Members who favored foreign aid, assigning them to prepare refutations of possible floor amendments. But as efficient as the lobbying seems, there still were plenty of tense moments. In committee, $1.1 billion was cut from the $10.4 billion requested by the Carter Administration. When the Appropriations subcommittee chairman, Rep. Clarence D. Long, D-Md., failed to win even deeper cuts in the subcommittee, he ignored the panel's majority and took his campaign to the House floor. But there, too, cuts were held to a minimum.

"Members themselves want to say they cut the bill," Lewis said, and the floor managers gave them all a chance by considering line items separately rather than voting across-the-board cuts. As a result, everybody got four or five chances to slash away, but this was always held to tight limits."

In the Senate, new restrictive amendments were added to the bill and some House amendments and cuts were rejected; and the House-Senate conference committee compromised by working out a $9.1 billion bill. After the conference, AID critic Long was heard to remark, "This is the first time I realized the raw power of the foreign aid lobby."

Not a bad recommendation for a program that "has no constituency." □

THE NATIONAL AND INTERNATIONAL POLITICS OF FOOD AID

FOOD AID: BEYOND DEPLORING

by Mark Schomer

Food aid has become an issue of controversy among those who seek the common goal of an end to hunger. Nearly all agree that something should be done. But should food aid be reformed or abolished? Some argue that the U.S. Food for Peace program (under Public Law 480) should be phased out. They claim that it has often been harmful to poor countries. Others, however, contend that the program can be a useful resource for development, and would like to see it reformed and expanded. Two important facts argue for working on reform:

1. A broad consensus has emerged in recent years that in the long run the food needs of the world's poor must be met primarily by their own agricultural efforts. Increasingly, food self-reliance is being proclaimed as a desirable goal—but many nations are a long way from achieving it. Official sources predict a sharp rise in the grain deficits of poor countries during the next decade, in spite of efforts to increase local production. In the short run, these deficits will have to be met either by costly commercial imports, which many countries cannot afford, or by food aid.

2. Food aid has been one of the most popular aid programs approved by Congress, and will probably remain so despite growing criticism. Whatever its defects, food aid is likely to continue.

Many food aid critics base their views on an affirmation of human dignity growing out of religious convictions or traditional U.S. values. These values point towards a more just and sustainable world, which is in the nation's long-range interest. Congress should respond to the critics by enacting fundamental changes in PL 480 legislation, with self-reliance in food as the program's objective. However, reforming food aid should be seen as only one of many steps needed to address the growing gap between the world's rich and poor people.

How Food Became Aid

Historically, U.S. food aid grew out of a need to dispose of huge agricultural surpluses. These surpluses occurred at a time when U.S. foreign policy sought above all to contain communism in an emerging and non-aligned "Third World". The 1954 Agricultural Trade Development and Assistance Act (Public Law 480) states in its subtitle that it is "An Act to increase the consumption of U.S. agricultural commodities, to improve the foreign relations of the United States, and for other purposes." The Act recognizes that, due to its fertile plains and high level of agricultural technology, the United States has a "comparative advantage" in food production which can be harnessed to serve a variety of national interests (see box, p.1). Combating hunger and promoting development overseas did not become explicit purposes until 1966, and have always had to compete with the traditional trade expansion and foreign policy purposes of the act, though at times these aims have been compatible.

Because food aid has been used to provide many benefits to the United States, it has been easier to secure Congressional support for PL 480 exports than for other foreign aid programs. Food aid has also been far easier to support than the changes in international trade and finance sought by the

> The Agricultural Trade Development and Assistance Act of 1954 (Public Law 480), as amended, is designed, in its own words: "to expand international trade; to develop and expand export markets for U.S. agricultural commodities; to use the abundant agricultural productivity of the United States to combat hunger and malnutrition and to encourage economic development in the developing countries, with particular emphasis on assistance to those countries that are determined to improve their own agricultural production; and to promote in other ways the foreign policy of the United States."

poor nations in their call for a "New International Economic Order."

Whatever the motives, food aid has become a big business. Over $27 billion worth of agricultural products have been shipped abroad under PL 480 since 1955. Last year 6.1 million tons of agricultural commodities worth over $2.1 billion were exported. Although PL 480 represents only 5% of current U.S. agricultural exports, it has a significant, and controversial, impact on many poor countries.

Criticisms

Critics often argue that the availability of donated or subsidized food aid from abroad can itself be an obstacle to self-reliance:

1. **The needy do not get much.** In 1977, 79% of PL 480 foods were provided to governments under Title I (concessional sales), generally for resale on

commercial markets where only those who have money can buy. The main beneficiaries of Title I have been governments, which receive income immediately from local sales and can reimburse the U.S. government over 40 years at 3% annual interest.

2. **Small farmers are undermined.** When massive food donations were sent to Guatemala after the 1976 earthquake, small farmers in the affected region saw market prices for their locally-produced corn drop significantly, while laborers who would normally help harvest corn spent long hours standing in relief lines.

3. **Rural areas are neglected.** In a number of countries, food aid has allowed governments to neglect rural development while building urban constituencies. Most U.S. food aid to Bangladesh, for instance, has been resold to urban middle classes at subsidized rates and has not reached the severely malnourished in rural areas.

4. **Political abuse.** In 1974, congressional cutbacks in other forms of aid to South Vietnam and Cambodia were circumvented by the administration's award of $461.5 million in Title I loans.

This represented 78% of the world-wide total for that year, despite acute famines in Africa and Asia. Although congressional restrictions on political abuse of food aid were subsequently imposed, ways have still been found to favor political allies within these limits.

5. **Unreliable supplies.** After the Soviet Union bought unprecedented amounts of U.S. grain in 1972, supplies were reduced and prices soared. Food aid consequently dropped from 9.9 million tons to 3.3 million tons in 1974. Millions of people starved in countries which could not afford to buy grain, or which had become dependent on food aid.

6. **Inappropriate resource.** Food itself is an awkward resource with which to promote development. It is produced seasonally and its irregularity makes it subject to market speculation and abuses. It is perishable, and has to be provided to recipients before it spoils, even if required self-help programs are poorly designed. And because it meets a vital need of consumers, food aid can easily create dependency.

7. **Debt.** Most food aid is bought on credit and thus increases the indebtedness that is already a burden for many poor countries.

Food for Development?
On the other hand, there have been cases in which food aid has been used creatively despite its limitations. In Southern India the Kottar Social Service Society successfully used Title II food aid (grants) to promote a variety of community development activities ranging from fishing and pottery cooperatives to health education, soil and water conservation, and resettlement schemes. In the eastern jungles of Peru unemployed petroleum workers organized a new agricultural colony and cultivated 120 hectares of land. Food aid enabled them to survive until their first rice harvest provided adequate income to repay their debts.

Such cases show that properly used food aid can promote development. Food aid could help achieve such desirable ends more frequently if the basic reforms advocated below were put into effect.

Recommended Food Aid Reforms

A thorough redrafting of PL 480 along the following lines, together with careful monitoring of how it is implemented, is needed to make U.S. food aid promote self-reliance:

1. *The primary purpose of PL 480 should be to stimulate equitable economic development and combat hunger and malnutrition abroad.* Any other economic or political benefits to the United States should be incidental, and not driving forces behind the program. PL 480 should be fully integrated into an over-all U.S. development assistance policy which supports efforts of the world's poor to become more self-reliant.

a) **Administration.** PL 480 should become more independent of the U.S. State Department (where political considerations prevail) and of the Department of Agriculture (where marketing considerations prevail). Administration of PL 480 should be located within a new cabinet-level International Development Cooperation Administration (IDCA), to be considered in 1979. As part of IDCA, food aid would be reviewed in Congress primarily by the foreign affairs committees rather than the agriculture committees, whose primary responsibilities are domestic agricultural production and distribution.

b) **Promotion.** U.S. agriculture export promotion (at present done largely through Title I of PL 480) should be handled through new or existing programs independent of PL 480. Such programs should provide assurances that they will not undermine development. For example, any concessional sales to food-deficit countries should not be on terms that allow countries to evade PL 480 requirements on human rights and self-help development.

2. *To be eligible for food aid, countries should meet strict criteria regarding need and development performance.*

a) **Need.** Current law requires that at least 75% of PL 480 food sales under Title I go to the poorest countries (those with a per capita GNP of $520 or less). While this restriction corrects earlier abuses by limiting to 25% the amount of food aid which the administration could give to less needy but politically favored allies, it defines need only on the basis of a relatively high per capita GNP (which is the gross national product of a country divided by its total population). Over 2 billion people live in the more than 70 countries which have a per capita GNP of $520 or less. Moreover, per capita GNP does not specifically take into account food availability or income distribution patterns which determine who can obtain food. A better indicator of food need is the Food and

Agriculture Organization's list of "Food Priority Countries," to which the bulk of U.S. food aid should be provided.

b) **Performance.** Once legitimate need is established, assurance should be given that food will reach the needy in ways that increase their self-reliance, and that the proceeds from any food which is sold by recipient governments will support sound development programs which benefit primarily the poor. Governments (as well as voluntary agencies receiving U.S. food aid) should therefore demonstrate that they are:

—committed to domestic policies which reduce deprivation and rich/poor disparities while enhancing human rights;
—promoting rural development which increases local food production, small-farmer income, and rural employment;
—implementing a national food and development plan into which food aid can be integrated without undermining local food production and employment; and
—willing and able to monitor their progress and correct any errors or abuses.

Any conditions for receiving aid in present PL 480 legislation which contradict the above should be abolished, while conditions based mainly on U.S. domestic interests should be clearly separated and given secondary priority.

c) **Political aid.** Countries which have formerly received large quantities of U.S. food aid for general budgetary support or for political purposes should also be subject to the above need and performance criteria, and should stop receiving food aid if they do not qualify.

3. *Concessional PL 480 food sales (Title I) should be gradually eliminated or converted to development grants.*

Countries which can afford to pay for food should buy it commercially or under other U.S. government-sponsored programs. Countries that really need food aid should receive it free on condition that they use both the food and the savings to promote development which benefits the poor and reduces the need for further aid. A precedent for this was set in 1977 with the enactment of Title III of PL 480. This "Food for Development" provision allows the poorest recipient countries to keep repayments due on debts from Title I food purchases, and use these funds to support multi-year development programs. It is not expected to apply to more than 15% of all Title I sales by 1980, and only two countries (Bangladesh and Bolivia) have signed Title III agreements so far. If experience shows that Title III agreements can be carried out successfully, they should become the principal form of government-to-government non-emergency food aid, and should cover all past PL 480 debts. This would greatly expand resources available for develop-

ment, while reducing pressure to use exports of PL 480 to improve the U.S. balance-of-payments.

4. *Stable and emergency food supplies should be guaranteed.* The U.S. should guarantee food aid for development as well as humanitarian purposes. Multi-year development projects undertaken by recipient countries under Title III require assurances of continued supply. Guaranteed supplies should be backed by an international emergency food reserve. When crop shortfalls or natural and man-made disasters result in exceptionally severe food shortages, a portion of this reserve should be available immediately to the affected country, over and above normally programmed needs for food aid.

Budgets and reserves for food aid should increase in relation to growing world needs, but should not be so large that they create artificial needs. No obligation should be made to ship minimum yearly tonnages of food if this would undermine development. With abundant harvests in recent years, the time may be politically opportune to expand guaranteed PL 480 supplies and build needed emergency reserves. However, poor countries should not count on receiving U.S. food aid indefinitely. In the long-run, non-emergency food aid should be phased out as food-deficit countries develop their own agricultural resources. With self-reliant development as its objective, a reformed food aid program would seek its own elimination.

NEW DIRECTIONS FOR
U.S. FOOD ASSISTANCE

Executive Summary

The Task Force was appointed in response to the Congressional mandate in the 1977 Food and Agriculture Act which called for a review to include, but not be limited to, organizational arrangements for the administration of Public Law 480, allocation criteria and procedures, quality control including handling and storage through the first stage of distribution in the recipient country, and regulations of businesses and organizations to which services are contracted under Public Law 480.

. . . . . .

In fulfilling its role, the Task Force found it necessary to examine the world food situation as it is today, the increasing acceptance world-wide of a responsibility to make dramatic inroads on hunger and malnutrition, and the implications of evolving United States policy toward meeting world food needs.

Several inescapable conclusions followed this examination:

-- Unmet world food needs are enormous. The number of hungry and malnourished individuals in the world is estimated to range between 400 million and 1.2 billion people.
-- A permanent solution can come only from increased production within the food deficit developing countries and an increased capability to participate in world agricultural trade.
-- Food aid programs can contribute significantly in the meantime to help feed the malnourished, to improve food security, and to contribute to the necessary increases in food production and trade capacity.
-- Concerted international action is called for. While food aid targets require reassessment, there is an even greater need for mechanisms to assure that these levels are met on a consistent basis. Current food aid deliveries are less than they were during the 1960s and early 1970s and even the internationally accepted 10 million ton target falls far short of meeting the growing needs.
-- The United States has a past record--265 million tons of food valued at $26 billion since the inception of P.L. 480 in 1954--unmatched by any other nation in history. Others are increasing their efforts markedly, but the leadership role remains with the United States. As the world's major producer and exporter of food, the United States has a key role for the forseeable future.

The 1977 amendments to P.L. 480 are a reflection of the values and intentions of the American people. These amendments contribute to the continuing evolution of U.S. food assistance from an early emphasis on surplus disposal to a program that is more consistent with feeding the hungry and promoting economic development to meet basic human needs. The Task Force, recognizing the unique role food aid can play in promoting international peace, prosperity, and social justice, endorses this trend. This shift in emphasis poses a new

Report of the Special Task Force on the Operation of Public Law 480 to the Secretary of Agriculture, May 1978.

challenge for the administration of the program.

The Report

The report describes the evolution of U.S. policy since the inception of the P.L. 480 program, then considers global food aid needs and the current prospects for improving food security, recipient country considerations, U.S. domestic economic and political considerations, program development and administration, and program operations.

By the nature of the assignment, the main function of the Task Force was to seek out and illuminate the ways in which food assistance efforts might be improved. The criticisms should in no way be construed as a condemnation of U.S. food assistance efforts. Nevertheless a number of factors, including a limited responsiveness to world hunger needs during periods of world wide shortages, vulnerability to domestic prices, administrative obstacles within the program, and the use of food aid for foreign policy objectives unrelated to long term development efforts have at times compromised the program's effectiveness. In the light of the new directions and the emphasis reflected in this report, the Task Force believes that improvements are necessary and achievable.

The Task Force has attempted to identify problem areas, propose changes in operational and administrative procedures, suggest some legislative changes, and provide a basis for further assessments. A number of recommendations have been made which can be acted upon expeditiously. The Task Force will continue in operation and will meet as needed to study, evaluate and report on the evolution of the new P.L. 480 regulations arising from changes in the 1977 legislation. These additional findings will be added to the report by October 1978.

Recommendations Consistent with the New Directions

The Task Force recommends that priority in U.S. bilateral food aid be given to combating hunger and malnutrition, promoting economic development, and assisting developing countries (particularly the lowest income countries) that experience severe shortfalls in food production or temporary balance of payments problems.

The Task Force recognizes that United States foreign policy objectives must continue to be given appropriate consideration in P.L. 480 decision making as food aid inevitably involves foreign policy considerations. Nevertheless, food assistance policy should firmly establish a consistent program commitment to feed the hungry and malnourished through direct distribution of food and to use P.L. 480 more effectively to promote economic development. While such a policy could be implemented within the present legislated objectives for the P.L. 480 program, it implies a shift in priorities among these objectives. In order that such a shift not reduce our ability to promote U.S. foreign policy, other assistance programs may need to be enhanced. The Task Force believes that food assistance used for humanitarian and development objectives is consistent with the long term goals of United States foreign policy, and reflects the values held by the American people.

The Task Force believes further that there is essential compatibility between humanitarian and development objectives and market development. Feeding hungry people enables them to function more effectively when productive employment opportunities are available. As economic development occurs, the ability of indigenous people to purchase food increases. This in turn leads to the sustained expansion of markets for agricultural products and other goods and services. Experience indicates that the greatest effect on the development of markets has come from economic development in the recipient countries.

At the present time, there is a strong commitment by the United States to the global food aid grain target of 10 million tons established by the World Food Conference in 1974. In view of the magnitude and persistence of world food needs, the Task Force recommends that the adequacy of the 10 million tons be reexamined, but that before commitments are made to higher levels of food aid, donors should demonstrate that the global 10 million ton target is achievable on a sustained basis.

The Task Force recommends that the United States commit itself to increasing substantially the level of food aid to poor countries provided that it can be demonstrated that these countries individually can use a greater volume of food assistance wisely and efficiently. The United States should be prepared to supply roughly half of the 10 million ton target plus an additional amount set aside for emergency needs resulting from crop failures and temporary balance of payments problems.

Substantially increased levels of food aid will be required for multi-year programs to support economic development and nutrition intervention goals if food aid is to make a meaningful contribution to meeting recipient country needs. The Task Force recommends that detailed country assessments be carried out in order to determine appropriate levels of food aid and the rate at which food aid can be effectively increased to meet nutritional and developmental needs. These assessments should be used to develop a broad policy framework to guide U.S. relations on food and agricultural matters. Consideration should be given to concessional and commercial trade as well as scientific and technical collaboration and the extent to which food aid can support basic human needs objectives.

Reasonable increases in the levels of U.S. food assistance, even a doubling, would not result in substantial cost increases to the American taxpayer or greatly increased food prices for consumers as long as the domestic supply does not tighten appreciably. With market prices below target price levels, increased P.L. 480 shipments would strengthen farm prices. Strengthened farm prices would reduce governmental deficiency payments and thereby offset in part the increase in P.L. 480 costs. If market prices were above target levels, there would be no deficiency payments made, hence no decrease in deficiency payments to offset P.L. 480 costs as shipments increased. The presence of both the farmer-held reserve and the United States emergency wheat reserve would serve to moderate price movements and allow the United States to continue to meet its quantitative food aid commitments. Food assistance needs should be taken into account when planning programs for domestic production and stock levels.

Future considerations of food aid levels should recognize a distinction between stable and variable components of food aid. From the recipient's standpoint, economic development and nutritional intervention programs require a stable inflow of food aid. The efficient allocation of scarce development resources and rational planning at the national level requires continuity of support.

Variable needs for food aid include meeting disaster/emergency needs; domestic production shortfalls due to erratic weather patterns and crop diseases; and temporary balance of payments problems. These unpredictable demands for food assistance compete with the limited food resources being made available and run the risk of undermining food availability for the stable needs. The availability of food aid for variable needs contributes to the long term developmental objectives of the recipient. Supply assurances by the donor, therefore, are critical.

For donor countries, a commitment must be made to meet stable needs for nutrition intervention, development programs, and emergencies which arise every year, though occurring in different places. In addition, the donor must also be capable of responding to variable needs which result from production shortfalls due to weather fluctuations and other acts of nature, and short term balance of payments problems in times of world wide shortages and high prices.

The stable needs of recipient countries require a commitment by food aid donors to multi-year programming of food aid. The Task Force recommends that the United States make a commitment to year-to-year continuity in food aid programs. These multi-year commitments should support economic development and nutrition intervention programs. Consistent with this commitment, the Task Force further recommends that the assurances of supply (in Section 401 of P.L. 480) be broadened beyond "urgent humanitarian purposes" to include development uses of food aid.

Many low income developing countries face intermittent food insecurity and are unable to stabilize per capita food consumption with their own resources. Food insecurity is particularly disruptive to efficient resource allocation in their economies and magnifies the problem of hunger and malnutrition. Bilateral and multilateral arrangements, as well as in-country programs which provide food assistance on a counter-cyclical basis, are needed to increase food security. The Task Force recommends, therefore, that the United States continue its efforts to establish an international food reserve system to moderate world price swings and to develop a new Food Aid Convention which would contain provisions for additional food aid, over and above the 10 million ton target, to be allocated to low income countries in times of special need.

So that the United States can meet its international commitments for food aid and any additional commitments required under a new International Wheat Agreement, the Task Force recommends the immediate passage of legislation to create a U.S. International Emergency Wheat Reserve. This reserve, along with the farmer-owned reserves, will further help to establish the United States as a reliable supplier, and thus contribute to world food security.

The establishment of international food security measures does not preclude the development of programs within developing countries to improve food security (including the use of food aid to build reserves). The Task Force recommends that increased multilateral and bilateral assistance be made available to develop and improve storage, transportation, and marketing facilities and to improve food security in other ways. Assistance for developing grain reserve programs in individual developing countries should be considered, particularly if an international reserve system is not initiated. The Agency for International Development (AID) should give priority attention in its development programming to ways in which increased food security can be promoted within the developing countries.

CHANGING CONDITIONS IN EGYPT ENSURE ROLE AS MAJOR U.S. FARM MARKET

by John B. Parker, Jr.

Egypt, already a major market for U.S. farm products, undoubtedly will continue in this role as its import-export policies, initiated in recent years, begin to take full effect, and consumers, benefiting from a stronger economy, start to spend more of their incomes for imported foods. Social changes also are causing a rise in food imports.

Egypt is the leading Arab market for U.S. agricultural products and also is this country's top Mideastern market for a sizable list of commodities, including wheat and wheat flour, corn, tallow, tobacco, soybean meal, and frozen poultry.

Egypt was the 11th most important market for U.S. farm products in 1977—up from 15th place in 1976. This move put Egypt ahead of India, France, Belgium, and Poland, countries that had preceded Egypt in 1976.

In 1978, Egypt is expected to stay in the same relative position as an importer of U.S. farm products.

Taking a record $540 million worth of U.S. agricultural exports in 1977, 19 percent more than the record of $453.6 million set in 1976, Egypt is expected to reach a new high of $650 million in 1978. This compares with only $43.6 million as recently as 1972. Larger sales of cotton, grains, cottonseed oil, and tobacco provided most of the U.S. gain between 1976 and 1977, and may account for a large share of the 1978 rise.

Egypt's imports of agricultural commodities from all sources are likely to reach $2 billion in 1978—up from $1.8 billion in 1977 and $1.5 billion in 1975. The U.S. share of Egypt's 1978 agricultural imports is expected to rise from about 30 percent in 1977 to nearly 33 percent. The U.S. share of all imports is expected to be 20 percent of the total.

Reduced competition from Australia and Latin America will help make possible this 3 percent gain, although larger European Community (EC) deliveries of wheat flour and dairy products are likely. U.S. exports of cereals and wheat flour to Egypt in the current year might reach 3 million tons.

In the past, U.S. Government programs have financed a sizable share of U.S. food exports to Egypt, but it is likely the future will see a larger share of these purchases being made through commercial channels.

Egypt's dependence on imported farm products is extraordinarily strong. Over 90 percent of the bread baked in Cairo and Alexandria in 1977 was made of imported flour or of flour ground from imported wheat. Between 1971 and 1976, almost 40 percent of the grain consumed in Egypt was imported, along with half of its vegetable oil, and all of its tobacco,

tea, coffee, rubber, and jute.

Before 1973, Egypt's policymakers put obstacles in the way of Egyptian tradesmen trying to import some commodities such as cotton and rice—both of which are grown in Egypt. Other barriers to trade were restrictive laws and complex foreign exchange regulations that hampered private transactions. But at present, a more relaxed policy allows sizable imports of processed foods and other farm products for the tourist trade, as well as large purchases of bulk commodities.

Foreign exchange earned by Egyptians in other countries can now be used to import food products into Egypt. Previously a series of regulations hampered such purchases.

This change in policy has sparked a boom in the export of new U.S. farm products to Egypt ranging from apples to almonds. The Ministry of Supply continues to control imports of basic foods and the Ministry of Industry controls those of raw materials for manufacture.

In addition to these policy changes, increased amounts of foreign exchange available from OPEC (Organization of Petroleum Exporting Countries) and other sources have helped Egypt increase its food imports.

Over 1 million Egyptians now work in OPEC countries and send back to Egypt over $600 million annually. This capital inflow is the result of changes in Egypt's banking policies that provide incentive to send money home.

OPEC itself has made loans and grants to Egypt in recent years totaling $2 billion annually. Loans also have been made to Egypt to finance imports and development projects through the Gulf Organization for Development of Egypt (GODE) from funds provided by Kuwait, Saudi Arabia, Qatar, and the United Arab Emirates. Iran has a separate program to assist Egypt's development, which provides over $300 million annually.

With the reopening of the Suez Canal, the inauguration of petroleum flows through the recently constructed Sumed pipeline, and the strong influx of tourists, larger amounts of foreign exchange have become available. In 1978, all of these factors are expected to remain strong, while exports of petroleum are expected to increase as wells in the Sinai Desert, and along the Gulf of Suez raise their output.

Egyptian exports of petroleum and products have risen from $134 million in 1975 to $381 million in 1976 and to $721 million in 1977. The value of these exports is expected to climb to about $1 billion in 1978. By volume, Egypt's petroleum output reached 21 million tons during 1977, and is expected to reach about 26 million tons in 1978.

The movement to the city by Egyptian farmers and loss of cropland to urban uses means a loss in production that must be compensated for from some other source—and importing seems to be the best way to make up the deficit. Farmers remaining on the land prefer to raise high-value crops for the domestic market that bring immediate cash returns, rather than those ordained by the Government for which payment is sometimes delayed.

For example, growers want the large and immediate profits from producing vegetables for nearby city dwellers rather than the deferred payments for growing wheat or corn, produced under the Government's allocation system.

The urban population is seen rising from 17 million in 1978 to about 20 million by 1980 as part of an overall 2-percent annual growth to 42 million for all of Egypt. To house this increase, developments are springing up near Cairo, along the Mediterranean, and in the Suez Canal area.

Some 14,000 hectares of farmland were converted to urban and industry uses each year between 1974 and 1977. But since the financial gain by industry was greater than the loss

to the agricultural sector, there are those who say it was a change for the better.

Yields for most of Egypt's crops are high, yet total production can be increased very little because all farmland is now in use. Furthermore, it takes many years and large sums of money to convert sterile desertland to productive farmland. The inhabited area of Egypt is about the size of Maryland, but Egypt's desert regions are about 35 times the size of Maryland. So the desert is there to be converted into farmland, but the wealth to make the conversion is lacking.

Maintaining relatively low, subsidized food prices for urban consumers has top priority with the Egyptian Government. Financing for this program comes from monies received from tobacco import duties and cotton exports. Under this scheme, which cost more than $1.2 billion annually during each of the past 3 years, bread can be bought for about 5 U.S. cents per kilogram at retail shops and from street vendors.

The cost to the retail customer is less than a third that paid by the Ministry of Supply to buy the wheat and/or flour and to finance distribution. The program helps provide over 2,700 calories a day per person, but is largely based on foreign grains.

Egypt's imports of wheat and flour combined (in wheat equivalent) were 4.35 million tons in 1977/78 (July-June), up from about 3.88 million tons in 1976/77. They are expected to reach 4.6 million tons in 1978/79.

Much of the 1978/79 increase is likely to come from the United States.

Although faced with strong competition from Australia (1.25 million tons of wheat shipped to Egypt in 1977/78), Canada, (550,-000 tons) and Argentina (50,000 tons), the United States exported 1.5 million tons in 1976/77 and 1.4 million in 1977/78. However, lower prices brought the value of U.S. shipments down from $169 million in 1976 to $133 million in 1977.

In 1977, wheat and wheat flour combined accounted for 24.6 percent by value of all U.S. agricultural exports to Egypt, down from 39 percent in 1974. Even with this drop, Egypt still stood fourth last year as a world market for U.S. wheat and wheat flour, after the Soviet Union, Japan, and South Korea.

Total wheat flour imports reached 706,000 tons in 1977/78, and might reach 800,000 tons in 1978/79.

Commercial purchases accounted for over $200 million of U.S. agricultural exports to Egypt in 1976 and again in 1977. Most of the 1977 transactions were P.L. 480, Title I, purchases of wheat and wheat flour. In addition, the Agency for International Development (AID) financed purchases of commodities that rose in value from $35.8 million in 1976 to about $100 million in 1977.

Egypt's corn crop remained steady at 2.7 million tons in 1976 and 1977, but U.S. exports of corn to Egypt rose from 557,000 tons in 1976/77 to 655,000 tons in 1977/78.

In 1978/79, U.S. corn exports to Egypt are expected to surpass 700,000 tons.

Egypt's programs to foster rapid growth of industrial output depend on imports of U.S. cotton, tallow, tobacco, and other farm products.

Planners in Cairo have since 1977 pushed a plan to import U.S. short-staple cotton and to export Egypt's costly extra-long staple cotton to bring in foreign exchange.

The contribution to the gross national product (GNP) from 1 hectare of cotton is in the vicinity of $2,500 annually, about five times the value of wheat or corn grown on the same land. As a result, it would appear to be profitable to shift some land from wheat and corn—grown for domestic consumption—to cotton—an export crop—

and pulses and vegetables.

The plan did not work during the first year, however, since severe insect damage reduced yields of cotton in 1977, particularly on farms lying to the south of Cairo.

Cotton area was increased by 14 percent in 1977, and production rose from 1.82 million bales to 1.83 million in 1977, a year in which Egypt bought about 110,000 bales of U.S. cotton valued at $46 million. Purchases of U.S. cotton in 1978 totaled 59,000 bales through August; further sales depend on availability of financing.

Rapid expansion in Egypt's output of textiles, soap, cigarettes, and other items has created greater demand for U.S. farm products.

Egypt's soap industry

gets most of its tallow from the United States. Although demand for Egyptian soap is soaring on both the domestic and export markets, U.S. exports of tallow to Egypt declined from 127,500 tons in 1976 to 113,400 tons in 1977. However, value rose from $51 million to $54 million. A strong rise in sales of U.S. tallow to Egypt is expected in 1978.

Egyptians prefer cigarette brands containing a high percentage of U.S. flue-cured and burley tobacco. As a result, imports of cigarettes from the United States and Europe rose sharply to about 2 billion pieces in 1977. Total cigarette output in Egypt rose from 22 billion pieces in 1976 to 25 billion in 1977, but imports and domestic production combined are insufficient to meet the

demand.

U.S. tobacco exports to Egypt jumped from 5,044 tons in 1976 to a record 12,119 tons in 1977, and value soared from $17.6 million to $43.8 million. Larger imports of U.S. tobacco to some extent substitued for smaller purchases from Eastern Europe, India, Iraq, and southern Africa. Egypt's total imports of leaf tobacco increased from about 26,000 tons in 1976 to nearly 29,000 tons in 1977.

U.S. exports of tobacco to Egypt should show another increase in 1978, but financing of such purchases must still be worked out. In view of the importance of tobacco import duties in financing Egypt's subsidized food program, large cash purchases

BUILDING A U.S. FOOD RESERVE

STATEMENT TO JOINT HEARINGS
BEFORE THE COMMITTEES ON
INTERNATIONAL RELATIONS AND AGRICULTURE,
U.S. HOUSE OF REPRESENTATIVES

by Rev. Paul Kittlaus

Reverend KITTLAUS. Good morning, Mr. Chairman.

My name is Paul Kittlaus. As part of my function as director of the Washington office of the United Church of Christ, I serve as the vice chairperson of the Interreligious Taskforce on U.S. Food Policy.

We have been privileged before to present testimony to both these committees.

I have with me Mr. Tim Atwater, who is employed by Lutheran World Relief and Church World Service, and who works with the Interreligious Taskforce. He did much of the preparatory work for this testimony.

The Taskforce, on behalf of whom I testify today, welcomes the opportunity to present testimony in this joint hearing. The Taskforce is a team of Washington-based staff of national religious bodies whose work is supported by over 20 Protestant denominations and national Roman Catholic, Jewish, and ecumenical agencies.

Our very existence reflects the widespread concern in the American religious community for the twin problems of global hunger and poverty, and the widespread conviction that one way in which we in the religious community are obligated by our religious faith to seek justice for the needy is through addressing public policy issues.

Reserves deserve a prominent place in U.S. food and agriculture policy. In testimony on the 1977 Food and Agriculture Act, we noted before the House Agriculture Committee that grain reserves are not, and can never be, a panacea for all the world's food and food-related problems.

Increased agricultural production in the developing countries, more development aid, more just trade arrangements, more equitable distribution of resources among nations, and especially greater purchasing power for the world's poor majority will continue to be urgently needed even after international reserves become a reality.

Such steps need to be vigorously pursued even as discussions on establishing reserves take place.

Food reserves, after all, are not an end in themselves, but one of several essential means to the end of improved nutrition for all.

Having said this, we went on to underscore the very real importance of maintaining adequate food supplies, both for meeting emergency needs and for moderating extreme fluctuations of price and supply.

In the absence of consciously held and carefully managed reserves, the drastic drawdown of U.S. stocks in 1972–74 brought skyrocketing prices, panic buying, and radically reduced levels of U.S. food aid.

Some genuine progress toward world food security has been made in the years since the crisis which led to the calling in 1974 of the

U.S. Congress, House, Committees on International Relations and Agriculture, International Emergency Wheat Reserve: Hearings on H.R. 9045, H.R. 11439, and H.R. 6014, 95th Cong., 2d sess., 13 and 21 June 1978, pp. 35–41. Rev. Kittlaus is Vice Chairperson, Interreligious Taskforce on U.S. Food Policy.

World Food Conference. At the international level, 72 countries have now subscribed to the U.N. Food and Agriculture Organization's Undertaking on World Food Security, pledging themselves to the building of their own national reserve stocks in an internationally agreed manner. Current negotiations toward a more formal reserve stocking arrangement within the context of an international wheat agreement are said to be proceeding with a new sense of earnestness, although serious difficulties remain.

At the urging of governments in several international forums, the World Food Program has developed an international reserve for emergencies, with a stock target level of 500,000 tons. The United States has made an initial contribution of 125,000 tons to this small but worthwhile venture and is considering the appropriate level for its replenishment.

There is also considerable international interest in reviewing and strengthening the current Food Aid Convention. The United States has increased its pledge significantly from the current 1.89 million metric tons to 4.47 million metric tons, with an additional 20 percent to become available in years of particular need.

The fourth U.N. World Food Council meets this week in Mexico City to address the issue of world hunger and malnutrition. We understand from one of our members who is serving as an adviser to the U.S. delegation that in preparatory meetings last week many delegates concurred with the generally gloomy picture presented by U.N. authorities.

There has been, consensus runs, "* * * a general lack of progress in the fight against hunger and malnutrition" in the last several years. Despite increased production in many areas, the number of severely undernourished people is greater now than earlier in the decade: 455 million.

Particular concern is being expressed for the Sahel, Laos, Vietnam, Indonesia, Afghanistan, Lebanon, and Nepal. The food imports of MSA's are expected to be more this year than in earlier years, with food aid needs also higher.

In this context, deliberations of this joint hearing are of crucial international importance. Action to report out and pass legislation to create an international emergency reserve is urgently needed and will be widely welcomed by the international community, particularly by those in poor developing countries.

On the national scene, the farmer-owned grain reserve which Congress enacted last year represents significant forward movement on the world food security agenda. Recent steps taken by the administration to raise storage payments, advance the entry date for the 1977 crop feed grains and partially forgive interest charges have further improved the effectiveness of the farmer-owned reserve. Over 340 million bushels—9.3 million metric tons—of wheat, as well as more than 134 million bushels—3.1 million metric tons—of feedgrains have now been placed in the extended loan/reseal program.

The task force has from its earliest discussion in the Senate Agriculture Committee last year strongly supported the idea of a farmer-owned reserve. We are now advocating further steps to increase participation in the reseal program, including higher loan levels for wheat and feedgrains and somewhat higher release prices.

Unfortunately, the Congress failed to include enabling legislation for emergency food reserves as part of last year's Omnibus Farm and Food Act. The legislation signed by the President last September did, however, encourage—rather than explicitly authorize—the President to enter into negotiations to establish an international emergecy reserve.

On August 29, 1977, the administration announced it would seek specific congressional approval for "a special International Emergency Food Reserve of up to 6 million tons." Lamentably, the actual transmittal of draft legislation to the Hill was delayed until March, apparently due to prolonged interagency discussions within the executive branch.

Meanwhile, a number of Members of the House and the Senate have introduced bills of their own to establish reserves for emergencies. In the House, Agriculture Committee Chairman Thomas Foley and International Relations Committee Chairman Clement Zablocki have introduced by request the administration's proposal—H.R. 12087. Congressman Matthew McHugh introduced a reserves bill—H.R. 9045; identical bills have now been cosponsored by 87 Members. Congressman Edward Beard introduced his reserves bill—H.R. 6014—over a year ago. Congressman Benjamin Gilman's bill—H.R. 11439—was introduced in March.

In the Senate, Agriculture Committee Chairman Herman Talmadge has introduced the administration's bill by request—S. 2869. Senator Henry Bellmon has introduced a reserves bill of his own—S. 3133—and had cosponsored with the late Senator Hubert Humphrey the reserves provision which was included in the Senate version of last year's farm bill—S. 2278. Senator Richard Lugar has also sponsored emergency reserves legislation—S. 2641.

Against this background of growing interest in world food security in general and an international emergency reserve in particular, I would like now to comment on the various legislative options and urge prompt action by the Congress to enact such a reserve without further delay for, despite forward movement along the lines indicated above, world food security remains an elusive hope for many of the world's people, particularly the poor majority.

Let us turn now to a comparative analysis of existing legislative proposals regarding international emergency reserves, analyzing each in terms of the major objectives which, in our view, such a reserve should serve.

The purposes of an international emergency reserve should, we feel, be at least twofold: providing humanitarian relief and offsetting unforeseen crop shortfalls in developing countries. The Zablocki-Foley bill specifies these two purposes and adds a third, to fulfill expected U.S. reserve stock obligations under the Wheat Trade Convention, WTC.

The McHugh bill spells out only the first two of these purposes, although it clearly advocates creation of U.S. reserves simultaneously with the carrying out of negotiations for an international system of reserves for emergencies.

The Gilman bill also allows for the use of reserves to meet U.S. commitments under an international reserves agreement, without naming the Wheat Trade Convention.

The Beard bill does not address the issue of an international reserves system.

The task force supports the negotiation of international agreement on reserves, both for price stabilization and emergency purposes. This should not be taken as carte blanche endorsement of an eventual WTC agreement. We would encourage Congress to provide the administration with explicit authority to hold stocks pursuant to such a WTC agreement. The necessity for Senate ratification of an actual WTC agreement guarantees further congressional review of the specific terms.

In addition to endorsing the purposes of the Zablocki-Foley bill, we feel the bill would be strengthened by adding policy language along the lines of the McHugh bill: "The Congress * * * finds and declares that the health, well-being and lives of people throughout the world are endangered by the absence of consistent and coordinated efforts among the governments of those people to establish and maintain food reserves as a safeguard against food emergency situations and severe crop shortfalls."

Assured continuity of supply for U.S. food aid is central to any U.S. grain reserve designed to meet international emergencies. Such continuity is essential if U.S. food aid is to serve productive development and nutrition purposes.

Assured continuity of supply seems likely to be best guaranteed by the Zablocki-Foley bill, which in section 6b waives the operative sentence of section 401 of Public Law 480. Section 8 also excludes commodities in the reserve from the total domestic supply for the purposes of section 401 and from any limitations which might be imposed on U.S. exports.

None of the other House or Senate bills afford such an explicit waiver of section 401. The McHugh bill, however, requires prompt replenishment in equivalent amounts following each use of reserve stocks. While it may not be necessary to maintain the reserves at a constant level, the McHugh bill would clearly assure continuously adequate supplies of food aid.

The Gilman bill allows for the release of stocks in times of short supply but limits procurement of reserve stocks at such times.

The Beard bill allows for the release of food from reserves only to meet food emergencies which result from "a natural disaster." A separate section of the Beard bill allows foreign governments to purchase and store food in the United States on commercial terms, with the assurance that such stocks will be exempt from export embargoes. While of interest, this provision relates to a set of issues somewhat distinct from those most directly related to discussion of reserves for emergencies.

While any of the House bills would offer increased protection for Public Law 480 and would add to world food security, the Foley-Zablocki and the McHugh bills seem to us to offer the most in these respects.

Regarding tonnage levels, legislative proposals range from about 2.8 million tons to 7.5 million tons to 6 million tons plus whatever additional amounts might be needed to meet U.S. obligations under a Wheat Trade Convention. The task force favors the latter range as set forth in the Zablocki-Foley bill. Reserves of such magnitude should be sufficient to meet short-run emergency needs and would not represent an undue cost burden.

The size of the proposed international emergency reserve is roughly comparable to the size of the projected reduction in wheat carryover stocks had the flexible parity approach of H.R. 6782 been adopted. Placing about the same amount of wheat under reserve would benefit both farmers—USDA estimates that wheat prices would rise by 15 to 20 cents per bushel with a 6-million-metric-ton procurement—and the cause of world food security.

The relation between reserve stocks and Public Law 480 flows may require clarification. Our interpretation of the Foley-Zablocki, McHugh and Gilman proposals is that such reserves under normal conditions would serve to backstop rather than supplant regularly programed Public Law 480 commodities. The reserves would assure that food aid for humanitarian and developmental purposes could be maintained at, or close to, normal programed levels when supplies were low and acquisition costs were high.

In most years, such reserves would not be tapped for Public Law 480 uses. In situations of either widespread or localized food scarcity, food might be drawn down and speedily programed through Public Law 480 to provide additional tonnage on a countercyclical basis or to avoid otherwise likely reductions in normal Public Law 480 levels. For the most part, however, allocations made from reserve stocks would be additional to normal Public Law 480 tonnages.

We are concerned with statements made by the administration

during Senate hearings to the effect that they would like the authority to operate the proposed emergency food reserve outside of the framework of Public Law 480 on occasion. Human rights provisions in Public Law 480 were specifically mentioned by the administration as a major reason for desiring such authority.

Our viewpoint is that properly understood, human rights' constraints in Public Law 480 are minimal and should not be bypassed. First, rights' provisions apply only to title I and thus should not be applicable in the vast majority of emergency situations. Second, the law allows food aid—and other forms of economic assistance—to go forward even when a government is deemed a consistent human-rights violator if food or revenue from the sale of food will benefit needy people.

Most importantly, having the option of being able to make end-runs around normal Public Law 480 channels could prove to be a too-strong temptation for any administration. Abuse of reserve supplies earmarked for humanitarian purposes, whether for shortrun political purposes or to relieve burdensome agricultural surpluses, could provoke widespread cynicism and do irreparable damage to the cause of world food security.

As for stocking, restocking and release arrangements, we favor the earliest possible stocking of emergency reserves, coupled with prompt replenishment following use of stocks. Each of the bills specifies acquisition through Commodity Credit Corporation—CCC—takeovers and purchases in the market. We have a slight preference for the McHugh approach, which specifies that purchases would make up the balance of whatever is unavailable through CCC takeovers. We are pleased to note in passing the expressed intention of the administration to place into reserve 6 million metric tons of wheat—220 million bushels—"before the beginning of the 1978 crop year."

The McHugh bill calls for prompt replenishment whenever use is made of reserve stocks. As noted previously, this might result in maintaining supplies at more rigid levels than necessary; however, it seems to us much wiser to err on the high side, rather than the low side, given that human lives are likely to be at stake at some point.

The Zablocki-Foley bill authorizes replenishment when purchases "will not unduly disrupt the market"—an authority which may or may not be adequately broad.

The Gilman bill limits replenishment in times of short supply, as defined by section 401 of Public Law 480. It is not clear under what conditions the Beard bill would allow replenishment.

Each of the bills before you authorizes release of food for humanitarian relief and disaster or emergency situations. The Zablocki-Foley and the McHugh bills seem to state most clearly the specific circumstances and conditions warranting release.

In sum, we encourage these committees to report out favorably and speedily legislation to create an international emergency reserve. In our view, the Foley-Zablocki and the McHugh bills merit particular attention. We favor stipulating that the reserve include at least 6 million metric tons for the purposes of humanitarian relief and offsetting crop shortfalls so as to protect this amount against depletion in the fulfillment of any eventual market stabilization obligations under the Wheat Trade Convention.

As E. A. Jaenke has observed, "The world's poor, malnourished and starving bear a tremendous human cost when food supplies get as low as they did in 1974 and 1975. Many paid this cost with their very lives. In order * * * to respond with compassion to people caught in food shortage emergencies, droughts, floods or earthquakes, food must be available immediately and in considerable quantity."

It is because of our concern for the world's poor that we make these recommendations.

STATEMENT TO JOINT HEARINGS
BEFORE THE COMMITTEES ON
INTERNATIONAL RELATIONS AND AGRICULTURE,
U.S. HOUSE OF REPRESENTATIVES

by Winston Wilson

Mr. WILSON. Thank you, Mr. Foley.

Chairman Foley and members of both committees, I am Winston Wilson, wheat producer from Quanah, Tex., and vice president of the National Association of Wheat Growers. Accompanying me today is Carl Schwensen of our Washington, D.C., staff.

The National Association of Wheat Growers is pleased to have this opportunity to present its views on legislation which would establish a system of Government-owned international emegency wheat reserve for the purposes of food aid and meeting any U.S. commitment to a world reserve system that might result from international wheat agreement negotiations which are once again underway.

The NAWG opposes this legislation. We feel that it is unwise at this time for the U.S. Government to unilaterally establish a separate wheat reserve to meet a nonexistent international commitment and we see no clear or apparent need for our Government to buy and warehouse wheatstocks as a reserve for Public Law 480 and other foreign assistance.

The NAWG strongly believes that all nations have a food security responsibility and that the United States should encourage the development of a truly international system and avoid premature steps which would signal that we are once again willing to carry the world's inventory at direct cost to our producers and our Government.

Efforts now to establish a separate U.S. international reserve are premature and we believe that enactment of legislation such as that being considered here today would significantly weaken efforts to gain the participation of wheat importing and exporting nations in an equitable world system.

Instead of the unilateral undertaking advanced by this legislation, the NAWG favors the development of an international program of shared food security responsibility established by negotiated national reserve commitments under an agreed upon international plan. Such a system should strictly avoid the creation of price-depressing buffer stocks and insure that the burden of adjustment to supply fluctuations is shared among both importing and exporting nations.

The United States is presently operating a very successful producer-held grain reserve program which, by law, calls for the accumulation of between 300 million and 700 million bushels of wheat. The program, which operates through an extended loan mechanism, was sought and supported by the NAWG. Program improvements, also sought by the NAWG, have generated a strong level of participation and current enrollments exceed USDA's target and total more than 340 million bushels of 1976 and 1977 crop wheat.

This grain is in producer hands and it is directly available to the market at the option of the producer once the established trigger

U.S. Congress, House, Committees on International Relations and Agriculture, International Emergency Wheat Reserve: Hearings on H.R. 9045, H.R. 11439, and H.R. 6014, 95th Cong., 2d session., 13 and 21 June 1978, pp. 90-94. Mr. Wilson is Vice President of the National Association of Wheat Growers.

level is reached—140 percent of the current loan rates. An increase in the 1978 wheat loan level and immediate reserve eligibility for this year's crop would further strengthen the program and these steps have been recommended by the NAWG.

This is a sound program which reserves grain at the producer level for future domestic and foreign commercial and concessional demand. Producers are responsible for storage and quality maintenance, and incentives are provided to make the program operable. The market-oriented nature of this program must be protected and any reserve stock obligation which the United States may later accept should be a reserve of last resort and must not be released until the producer reserve has been liquidated.

At this point I would like to depart a little bit from my prepared text.

From our standpoint, one of the real problems connected with the proposed legislation is that there are very few restrictions placed upon the release of this reserve. This has been mentioned previously.

Under the current language in the bill, the President is empowered to release this grain for sale or donation during any period of tight supplies.

We are concerned that domestic political pressure will build for the release of the reserve at any time that prices increase substantially, with or without a genuine international food emergency.

Since U.S. wheat prices are for the most part determined by world demand and world prices, there is a definite danger, we feel, that untimely release of this reserve would adversely affect our domestic prices.

The United States and other govenments have actively discussed the development of a new agreement to replace the 1971 International Wheat Agreement ever since that treaty was concluded and particularly since the fall of 1977. Six weeks of negotiations held earlier this year in Geneva failed to produce a new agreement and likewise failed to resolve major differences in country positions.

Interim talks have taken place in subsequent months but major divisions still exist over the fundamental character of the agreement, the definition and size of a proposed international reserve, stock accumulation and release mechanisms, price bands, importer and exporter obligations and a continuing list of related elements.

Consequently, we do not feel that it is safe to assume that the conclusion of a new treaty acceptable to U.S. producers is imminent and we remain apprehensive regarding the final outcome of the negotiations. United States action now to unilaterally establish its own international stockpile is unwarranted and it would impair the goal of gaining the participation of other nations in an acceptable world security plan.

We are not persuaded by the U.S. Agricultural Department's argument that congressional authority to establish what might later become our commitment to an overall world reserve scheme is needed promptly to demonstrate our good faith to other nations. On the contrary, the U.S. Government has demonstrated its willingness to take the lead in world food security at the World Food Conference, before the International Wheat Council, at treaty negotiations earlier this year and currently at interim committee sessions of the IWA negotiating conference.

The fact that this legislation has been introduced on behalf of the administration further attests to our Government's willingness to deliver on commitments which might later be made.

Frankly, we feel that the United States would be jumping the gun in enacting this legislation now and to do so would seem to diminish rather than enhance our bargaining position with other nations.

There is another argument which has been advanced by USDA

which merits comment. Department officials have stated that recently enacted legislation eliminated the financial reserve for Public Law 480 assistance by limiting the borrowing authority of the Commodity Credit Corporation to comply with congressional budget policy; therefore, it is argued that a physical reserve is now needed to back up our foreign aid commitments.

As we see it, if the Agriculture Department believes that a mistake was made by Congress in altering CCC borrowing authority, then it should seek restoration of such authority instead of attempting to establish its own grain stockpile. Also the ability of Congress to meet increased foreign assistance requirements through supplemental appropriations should not be ignored.

Finally, the current and foreseeable U.S. supply situation further substantiates the absence of any immediate need for further U.S. reserve actions. The United States began the 1978–79 wheat marketing year on June 1 with approximately 1.2 billion bushels of wheat on hand. This is the largest beginning stock level in 16 years and 72 percent more than we had in 1973. If the modest 1978 wheat set-aside program is successful and past domestic and export disappearance levels are maintained, we can still expect beginning stocks next June to approximate this year's large level.

Thus, large U.S. supplies, the uncertain outcome of International Wheat Treaty negotiations, the success of the U.S. producer-held grain reserve initiative and the need to encourage other nations to share equitably in the establishment of a world food security system cause the NAWG to recommend against enactment of the legislation being considered here today.

In short, I think I can sum up our position as being that if the current negotiations are successful, and we do have a good International Wheat Agreement, and there is a need for supplies to back up our commitment in this agreement, then we would be willing to encourage legislation to make this possible.

Until that agreement is in hand, we are not in favor of establishing a new wheat reserve because we do feel that the 300 million bushel plus farmer held reserve is sufficient for emergency needs at this point.

We appreciate this opportunity to present our views and would be happy to answer any questions you might have.

Chairman FOLEY. Thank you, Mr. Wilson. We appreciate your testimony.

NEWS RELEASE

Washington--The House Agriculture Committee today agreed to substitute a tightened "last resort" three million ton International Emergency Wheat Reserve proposal by Chairman Thomas S. Foley, D-Wash., for a broader six million ton administration proposal.

The Committee is scheduled to meet for a final vote on the wheat reserve program next Tuesday.

Foley said his version of the program would significantly improve world food security by providing a stockpile of 110 million bushels of wheat, ready for quick dispatch to help meet emergency food needs in developing countries when all other world supplies are exhausted.

At the same time, Foley said, building the reserve now "could help strengthen prices for American farmers by taking stocks off the commercial market at a time when supplies are more than ample."

The Committee rejected a second substitute plan which would have given the government spending authority for wheat purchases to meet international emergencies during periods of tight grain supply.

Foley said his bill, in order to protect farmers agains sales of the reserve stocks at low prices, would allow the grain to be released by the President for emergency-stricken developing countries only through the Food for Peace program--and, even then, only if regular Food for Peace purchases from the open market would cut U.S. stocks below levels needed for domestic use, adequate carryover, and anticipated cash exports.

Foley noted that his substitute has been endorsed by the board of directors of the National Association of Wheat Growers, and pointed out that restrictions on release of reserve grain under his bill are more restrictive than those proposed by the administration.

The reserve stock of three million tons, or 110 million bushels, would be purchased from farmers or earmarked from wheat acquired by the Agriculture Department under its regular price support program. The wheat would be held for use only in meeting emergency food needs in developing countries. It could not be used, as the administration proposed, for meeting International Wheat Agreement reserve obligations.

Committee on Agriculture, U.S. House of Representatives, August 11, 1978.

YOU CAN'T EAT MONEY

by Brennon Jones

Religious groups urge the Administration to assist famine-struck nations with additional food aid, but are turned down because of the impact such purchases would have on domestic prices. U.S. consumers boycott in protest of sky-rocketing prices. And U.S. farmers lobby against embargoes and export restrictions that are imposed because of tight grain supplies.

This sounds like fiction, but it all happened during the 1972-74 food crisis. And the chances of a recurrence are strengthened if a bill presently moving through Congress is adopted.

The bill, entitled the International Emergency Food Fund, authorizes the President to spend up to $500 million during periods of international food emergencies for purchases of U.S. food aid for humanitarian relief. Introduced by Senator Dole, the bill was reported out of the Senate Agriculture Committee on August 16 in preference to legislation that would establish grain reserves for such emergencies.

When the World Food Conference met in Rome in 1974, a key part of the global strategy that emerged for avoiding food crises in the future was establishment of an international grain reserve system. The Carter Administration endorses the concept, and has advocated U.S. international emergency reserves. Both the House Agriculture and International Relations Committees passed legislation in mid-August that would establish such reserve stocks. The justification for emergency grain reserves is clear: such stocks insure that food aid levels do not shrink at precisely the time when they are most needed--during famines. Without reserves, food aid is bought at the current market price, and in times of scarcity the price soars. So the same aid dollar buys considerably less grain. Thus U.S. food aid shipments dropped from 9.9 million tons in 1972 to 3.3 million in 1974.

The building of such reserves is clearly in the interest of U.S. producers, because grain for stocking them is purchased on the market--an insight that has not escaped the National Association of Wheat Growers who have endorsed a wheat reserve of 3 million metric tons. The Congressional Budget Office (CBO) estimates that should a 6 million metric ton wheat reserve be established (the size the Carter Administration supports and the House International Relations Committee bill would provide) U.S. wheat prices could initially rise by as much as 51¢ per bushel with a season average increase of up to 34¢. Such increases would result in a reduction in government outlays for price support payments to farmers of $235 million in fiscal year 1979 alone. And stocking the reserve would allow for a removal of wheat supplies from the U.S. market roughly comparable to the amount of wheat that would have been taken out of production had Senator Dole's own "flexible parity" emergency farm bill been adopted this past spring--but without jeopardizing world food security.

Members of both the House Agriculture and International Relations Commit-

Bread for the World, September 1978, pp. 3-4. Brennon Jones is an Issue Analyst with Bread for the World.

tees clearly favored the international emergency reserves over the "International Food Fund." By votes of 27-16 in the Agriculture Committee, and 12 to 2 in the International Relations Committee, each rejected amendments to substitute the "fund" in place of grain reserve bills. The arguments against the fund are based on these considerations:

(1) Unlike a grain reserve, a fund insures only that money--not food--is available. Ample grain supplies are on hand for the near future, but a combination of poor weather, rapid population growth, and increased consumption due to rising affluence could quickly put us back into a period of scarcity. According to the International Food Policy Research Institute, by 1985 (just 6½ years from now) the annual food deficit of the developing nations alone will increase from this year's level of 36 million metric tons to at least 95 million.

(2) A food fund has price impact at exactly the wrong time. Purchases would be made in the market only during times of limited grain supplies and high prices, when a President would be most reluctant to make such purchases for fear they would radically increase domestic food prices and spur inflation. And should the fund be used, the U.S. consumer bears the brunt of the price impact--a situation which could set the stage for embargoes and export restrictions that ultimately disrupt commercial sales and hurt U.S. Producers.

(3) Having a food fund does not insure its use. The fund is similar to the existing authority the President already has through the Commodity Credit Corporation (CCC). During the 1974 food crisis, when supplies were tight and prices high, the Ford Administration had approximately $10 billion in unused CCC authorizations that it could have used to purchase grain on the market for emergency relief purposes. But because of the potential price impact, the choice was made not to respond immediately. Ironically, Senator Dole, as one of the leaders of the congressional delegation to the 1974 World Food Conference, urged a one million ton increase in U.S. humanitarian food aid at that time--an appeal that was denied for months for fear of the domestic price impact. For similar political and economic reasons a President is likely in the future to choose not to enter the market with an emergency food fund, when food is critically needed.

(4) Cost is an additional factor that works against the food fund approach. There are potential cost advantages in that a fund earns interest when not in use, while a grain reserve entails annual charges, including those for storage and quality control. However, the price at which grain is acquired is the key determinant. A grain reserve is acquired when market prices are depressed, or at least not excessively high. But a food fund would be tapped only in critical situations when supplies are tight and prices escalating--as in the 1972-74 period when wheat prices initially doubled, then ultimately tripled. A mere doubling of current wheat prices would be $5.60. Even if the Administration were to purchase for the reserve at the current price of $2.80 per bushel (a price they have indicated they are unlikely to purchase much above) and held the stocks for six years, the initial purchase cost, plus annual carrying charges, would still be cheaper than the $5.60 minimum price at which a food fund would conceivably be tapped.

Food fund or grain reserve? Now its up to House and Senate floor action in September to decide which approach they want to take. Before they do, they might reflect on House Agriculture Committee Chairman Foley's comment during the committee's consideration of the International Emergency Food Fund: "People can not eat dollars. Even less can they eat CCC credits."

ORGANIZING FOR DECISION-MAKING
WITHIN THE U.S. EXECUTIVE

MEMORANDUM FOR THE HEADS OF
EXECUTIVE DEPARTMENTS AND AGENCIES

This Administration is determined to develop food and agricultural policies which help the people who need help most, both in the United States and abroad. By encouraging efficient agricultural production, especially on the family farm, we can ensure reasonable incomes for producers and fair prices for consumers. An efficient productive system will also help us meet the demands of foreign markets. Our policy should give our producers the greatest possible access to foreign markets, while helping poor nations improve their own ability to produce and distribute food.

The Secretary of Agriculture has primary responsibility in the Executive Branch for developing policies and actions in food and agriculture. In order to exercise this responsibility, the Secretary of Agriculture must weigh and balance interests represented in other parts of the Executive Branch. Accordingly, I am directing the Secretary of Agriculture to form a Working Group on Food and Agricultural Policy. This Working Group will be chaired by the Secretary's designee and will be composed of representatives at the level of assistant secretary from these organizations:

Department of State
Department of the Treasury
Department of Agriculture
Office of the Special Representative for Trade Negotiations
Agency for International Development
Council of Economic Advisors
Office of Management and Budget
National Security Council

The Secretary of Agriculture may invite representatives of other organizations in the Executive Branch to serve in the Working Group.

In consultation with the Secretary of Agriculture and the White House Domestic Policy Staff, the Working Group will develop an agenda for policy considerations on domestic and international food and agriculture. The Secretary of Agriculture, in consultation with the Domestic Policy Staff, will inform me of policies adopted and actions taken and will refer to me policy options on issues requiring Presidential decision.

A subcommittee of this Working Group will serve as the vehicle for developing an Administration policy on world hunger. This Subcommittee will report its findings and recommendations directly to me and to the Secretary of Agriculture.

To insure coordination, I am asking the Domestic Policy Staff to inform other organizations in the Executive Branch of policy issues to be addressed and decisions made on domestic and international food and agriculture.

The Department of Agriculture and the Domestic Policy Staff will provide staff for the Working Group on Food and Agricultural Policy.

Jimmy Carter

Office of the White House Press Secretary, September 30, 1977.

PRESIDENTIAL COMMISSION
MEMBERS NAMED

The President's Commission on World Hunger, created by the President on September 5, 1978, held a preliminary meeting October 5. President Carter met with the group to launch its work and to stress his own personal concern that ways be found to deal more effectively with world hunger. The Commission is charged with making a preliminary report to the President by mid-1979 and completing its work by June 30, 1980.

The Presidential Commission is an outgrowth of congressional resolutions passed by both Houses late last year (cf. Note 77-20). Its membership of 18 persons includes 14 persons from the private sector appointed by the President and 4 Members of Congress (one from each party from each House). They are as follows: Sol Linowitz (Chair), Washington attorney and co-negotiator of the Panama Canal Treaties; Jean Mayer (Vice-Chair), president of Tufts University and an expert on nutrition; Stephen Muller (Vice-Chair), president of Johns Hopkins University and Johns Hopkins Hospital; Norman E. Borlaug, of Minnesota, director of Wheat, Barley and Triticale Research and Production Programs at the International Center for Maize and Wheat Improvement in Mexico; David W. Brooks, of Atlanta, chairman of the Policy Committee of Goldkist, Inc.; Harry Chapin, the recording artist, also founder of World Hunger Year; John Denver, the recording artist, also producer of a film, "I Want to Live," about the problem of world hunger; Walter P. Falcon, director of the Food Research Institute and professor of economics at Stanford University; Bess Myerson, newspaper columnist and former commissioner of consumer affairs for New York City; Howard A. Schneider, director of the Institute of Nutrition and professor of biochemistry and nutrition at the University of North Carolina; Adele Smith Simmons, president of Hampshire College in Amherst, Massachusetts; Raymond C. Singletary, Jr. of Blakely, Georgia, president of the Blakely Peanut Company and past president of the Georgia Association of Soil Conservation Districts and Southeastern Peanut Association; Eugene L. Stockwell, of Ridgewood, New Jersey, associate general secretary for overseas ministries of the National Council of the Churches of Christ in the U.S.A.; Clifton R. Wharton, Jr., chancellor of the State University of New York, and a specialist in economic development. From the Congress are Senators Patrick Leahy (D-VT) and Bob Dole (R-KS) and Representatives Richard Nolan (D-MN) and Benjamin Gilman (R-NY). The two remaining vacancies on the Commission are expected to be filled later in the year, probably by outgoing Senator Muriel Humphrey and Thomas Wyman, President of the Green Giant Food Corporation.

The Executive Order creating the Commission charges it with developing factual data as to the causes of world hunger and malnutrition and with making recommendations to reduce their prevalence. The Commission is authorized to "encourage public participation by holding hearings, issuing reports, and coordinating, sponsoring, or overseeing projects, studies, and other activities related to the understanding of the problems of world hunger and malnutrition." Congress has authorized $1.5 million and appropriated $1.3 million for Fiscal Year 1979 (October 1, 1978-September 30, 1979).

Food Policy Notes (Interreligious Taskforce on U.S. Food Policy), October 13, 1978, 2 pp.

The Commission's October 5 session was an informal one, providing members a chance to get acquainted with each other and to hear from the President. Formal meetings, which will be open to the public, are expected every 6-8 weeks, interspersed with meetings of subcommittees which are now in the process of being set up. The Executive Order provides that private citizens who are not members of the Commission may serve on the subcommittees. The first formal meeting may come late this month or early next month.

There is considerable speculation as to how effective the Commission will be. There are a number of hopeful signs. The President has a personal interest in the subject and has pledged serious consideration to the group's recommendations. Congressional interest in and membership on the Commission holds promise for building support on Capitol Hill for remedial steps which need to be taken. The Commission has attracted a widely respected Chairman and Vice-Chairmen and members with substantive experience in the field. The hunger issue is timely and will remain so during the life of the Commission. The interest of the Commission in spending considerable time during its second year in working to implement its recommendations and its tentative plans to hold hearings outside of Washington point to a welcome "activist" approach to its tasks.

On the less hopeful side, presidential commissions have by and large had a limited effect on US policy. A series of recent reports and studies of US hunger and development policy, including that of the World Hunger Working Group chaired by Dr. Peter Bourne, remain for the most part unimplemented. (The portfolio of Dr. Bourne as an international basic human needs advocate in the White House has not survived his departure intact; the Commission's point of contact with the White House is to be the National Security Council.) The make-up of the Commission lacks a certain breadth in areas such as labor, farm, civic, student, and Catholic/Jewish interests, and the other responsibilities of the Commission members may limit the time they are able to devote to the Commission's work. The actual creation and staffing of the Commission has moved rather slowly, with less than 21 months remaining in which to complete its work.

The Commission will be housed at 734 Jackson Place, N.W., Washington, DC 20006. Daniel Shaughnessy, formerly Deputy Director of the Food for Peace Program at AID, has been appointed as Deputy Executive Director of the Commission. When fully staffed, the Commission is expected to have about 15 direct staff, with additional persons serving as consultants.

Commission members at the first meeting were given copies of the Report of the World Hunger Working Group headed by Dr. Peter Bourne, entitled: World Hunger and Malnutrition: Improving the US Response. (One of the Bourne group's recommendations was that such a Commission be created.) Copies of the Report are available from the Presidential Hunger Commission at the above address.

The Taskforce will monitor the work of the Commission on an ongoing basis and will issue NOTEs from time to time on its activities.

IMPLEMENTING THE U.S. GRAIN STANDARDS ACT, AS AMENDED IN 1976

NEW STANDARDS BRING QUALITY IMPROVEMENT IN U.S. GRAIN TRADE

United States grain inspection procedures recently have undergone an exhaustive overhaul in an effort to improve the monitoring of standards of U.S. grain destined for foreign markets.

Weaknesses in the U.S. Grain Standards Act have been corrected. A new U.S. Department of Agriculture agency, the Federal Grain Inspection Service (FGIS), has been formed to enforce the stiffened Act and improve grain handling generally. And innovations that may benefit both U.S. exporter and foreign buyer are being made as a result of new applied research and overseas monitoring programs.

Grain (including soybeans), of course, ranks as far and away the most important component of U.S. farm trade, last year accounting for nearly two-thirds of the $24 billion worth of all U.S. agricultural exports.

The U.S. Grain Standards Act, passed in 1916 and revised for the first time in 1968, originally provided for official inspection agencies —including private groups, boards of trade, grain exchanges, or State Governments. These were designated by the U.S. Government to perform the original inspection responsibilities under Federal supervision.

Promulgated to overcome chaos in the grain trade at the turn of the century, the Act did bring uniformity to grain inspection. According to the 1977 FGIS annual report to Congress, prior to 1916 there had been "30 States and trade organizations inspecting grain for quality at 64 inspection points in the United States, often with widely different standards, terminology, and regulations."

On the other hand, the Grain Standards Act contained sufficient ambiguity and diversity of responsibility to allow fraudulent practices to develop. And even the extensive revamping of the Act in 1968—with its stiffened licensing requirements and additional testing services—failed to eliminate the potential for abuse.

Before 1976, for instance, there was no standardized federally supervised weighing of grain. Partly because of this lack of supervision, problems developed regarding grain quality, weighing of grain, certification of ships as being clean to receive grain, and insect infestation. In addition, verification of foreign complaints—although not impossible — was sometimes difficult.

As a result of these and other shortcomings, Congress pushed through major amendments to the Grain Inspection Act, effective November 20, 1976, and in 1977 made further amendments — mainly as followup to the 1976 provision.

Congress also mandated formation of FGIS in November 1976 to oversee implementation of the Act and initiate studies and procedures aimed at improving grain handling.

The amended Act basically provides for direct Federal inspection and weighing of export grain and tougher penalties for abuses.

The Act further requires additional rules for compliance. Grain exporters must register with FGIS each year and receive a certificate of registration.

In addition, FGIS has a program of recordkeeping at the terminal elevators. This shows what happens to the grain, what kind of grain—and how much—comes into an elevator, what happens in the handling, and what goes out. Such inventory control will aid in assuring that all parties in the trade receive full credit for grain they ship or handle.

A key element of this recordkeeping is a new national program of weighing. All grain that moves into an export elevator must be officially weighed by FGIS, or State officials who have been delegated by FGIS to perform this function, or elevator employees under supervision of these authorized personnel.

Similarly, grain moving out of an export elevator must be examined by licensed inspectors. Samples taken during such inspections are held on file for 30 days on sublots as documentation of inspectors' results.

Spot checks are used to see that these procedures are enforced.

Immediately prior to the 1976 amendments, 15 private agencies were doing export inspections, in addition to 10 State groups. The last of these private inspectors was phased out as of February 27, 1978, and now inspection is done exclusively by FGIS and nine States. Those States include California, Washington, Minnesota, Wisconsin, Alabama, Mississippi, Virginia, Florida, and South Carolina.

In most cases, inspection of grain destined for export is mandatory for the 10 products listed under the Grain Standards Act—soybeans, wheat, corn, barley, oats, rye, grain sorghum, flaxseed, and triticale (a cross between wheat and rye).

The only exceptions to this inspection requirement are grain shipments not sold by grade and accompanied by copies of the related sales contract.

Inspection of grain moving in intrastate trade, on the other hand, remains optional, and licensed nongovernmental agencies still can perform these inspections.

Optional inspection also is performed for a host of related products under authority of the Agricultural Marketing Act of 1946. These products include dried beans, peas, and lentils; hay; straw; and processed grain products—cornmeal, flour, grits, bulgur, and others.

Adding muscle to the amended U.S. Grain Standards Act are the increased penalties for violations. These fall into three areas —administrative, civil, and criminal.

Penalties Set

On the administrative side, every licensed inspector originally had a right to a long, involved formal hearing, even if he had been convicted of violating the Act. Now, persons found in violation of the Act can be suspended immediately with a right to a hearing within 7 days.

On the civil side, there was no penalty before. Now, persons found in violation of the criminal part of the Act can be fined up to $75,000.

On the criminal side, the penalty has been changed

from a misdemeanor to a felony, and the fines and prison possibilities are much greater than before.

Probably the most severe penalty, however—it is difficult to sell and export grain without official grades —is FGIS's option of refusing inspection of grain for persons found in violation of the Act.

In addition to its inspection services, FGIS is conducting two studies required under the 1976 Grain Standards Act.

One involves examining the present standards and their effectiveness.

The other study—being conducted by FGIS together with the General Accounting Office and the USDA Office of Investigation—is focusing on inspection and weighing activities in the U.S. interior, where procedures so far have not changed materially.

FGIS also is carrying out several action programs to improve the handling of U.S. grain generally. These include monitoring of overseas complaints and shipments, an applied research program, protein testing and other special export services, and a safety program aimed at overcoming hazards of the grain trade.

So that buyer and seller problems could be more readily investigated, a Foreign Complaints Monitoring Unit was established in September 1977. One of the unit's first assignments was to review the 20 foreign complaints about grain quality—including insect infestation, odor, foreign material, and protein content —received between No-

vember 20, 1976, and September 30, 1977.

Those complaints were handled on a case-by-case basis, with teams sent to some of the countries concerned. Only a small percentage of them proved to be valid.

Currently, about six teams go out each year, largely to markets where complaints have been filed. However, the ultimate goal is to send more teams and include some routine inspections in markets where complaints have not been registered.

As part of the program, FGIS staff members meet with foreign teams when they come to the United States to inspect U.S. facilities.

In some instances, FGIS officials spend a number of days with them explaining the U.S. marketing system, how it functions, and how grain inspection and weighing procedures work. The teams leave with a greater knowledge of the U.S. system and better appreciation of what is being done to ensure accurate inspection of grain.

One problem that arises in the export of U.S. grain is deterioration during shipment. A study by the University of Illinois, for instance, found a significant increase in broken corn and foreign materials (BCFM) during a test shipment of corn and soybean from Toledo, Ohio, to Rotterdam. From an average of 3.7 percent BCFM at the Toledo elevator, the percentage rose to 7.6 percent by the time the corn had been transferred to barges in Rotterdam, and BCFM in

the top-off of that shipment rose 3.6 percent to 15.2 percent.

Such changes are not the responsibility of U.S. shippers under the standard "certificate final" arrangement, which states that the basis for a grain sale is the quality or quantity of grain at the time of loading.

But it does contribute to confusion on the part of foreign buyers about the quality of the products they receive.

According to FGIS officials, other problems arise due to differences between grain standards and inspection systems of the United States and foreign markets.

Tolerances Vary

"Some countries have tougher tolerances for moisture and insect infestation than we do," according to one source. "Tied into that is the matter of insect kill. One program now underway with the Soviets is looking into means of effectively killing infestation without resorting to dangerous and time-consuming procedures used in the past."

In this experiment with grain shipments to the Soviet Union, a new procedure was applied to tankers for the first time. The team involved in the test recently returned to the United States, and its final report will be evaluated soon.

Prompt action on foreign complaints is a key requirement. "If we receive a valid foreign complaint, we must act on it and report to the Congress within 30 days from the time we have completed action," said David

H. Galliart, Deputy Administrator for Program Operations, FGIS. "In addition, we must submit to Congress quarterly and yearly summaries of these complaints and the FGIS followup."

He explained that a foreign buyer with a legitimate complaint can contact the U.S. agricultural attaché to his country. The attaché then will send a detailed description of the problem to personnel in Washington. If it involves inspection of grain, the complaint goes to FGIS, which will:

• Check records of the shipment to see how it was graded;

• Check the samples taken during inspection to see if a mistake was made;

• Meet with field office supervisors and the personnel who actually performed the inspection; and

• Test the accuracy of equipment used.

If no problem is found, the complaint is considered invalid; if the complaint is legitimate, the buyer and seller are contacted and given all the facts that have been developed.

To facilitate these efforts to improve grain handling FGIS has instituted an applied research program that now has about six projects underway. These include improved tests to:

• Detect any signs of sprout damage in white wheat.

• Check insect infestation before it even has emerged from the corn kernel; it is hoped that a promising new machine will detect carbon dioxide levels generated by even one insect.

• Use infrared radiation to kill insects.

In addition, a new protein test that can be done in a matter of minutes—compared with several hours previously—has allowed inclusion of protein testing under the U.S. Grain Standards Act. This means that protein results may be indicated on the same certificate showing grade for U.S. Hard Red Winter and Hard Red Spring wheats.

Test Time Cut

Instituted May 1, 1978, the program utilizes near-infrared equipment that can perform a single test in about 5 minutes, compared with 2 hours required for the traditional Kjeldahl method. It thus makes possible the testing of each sublot (40,000-bushel portion of the typical 1-million-bushel shipload), whereas previously only a single test per lot was done, resulting in complaints of nonuniformity of protein content.

The new process eventually will be used for other types of wheat and to measure the oil content of soybeans. It also may be used to determine protein content of barley and oats.

Since February 1, 1978, another voluntary test has been offered for aflatoxin—one of the mycotoxins that inhibit growth in certain animals and act as a carcinogen in humans. Tests showing more than 20 parts per billion of aflatoxin are considered positive; those with less, negative.

Either buyer or exporter can request the test. So far, however, only one country is requiring it.

THE PARTICIPATORY ROLE OF THE CITIZEN

HOW TO INFLUENCE YOUR MEMBERS OF CONGRESS

Hundreds of millions of malnourished or starving people in foreign lands have no representation in the US Congress, although they are deeply affected by the policy it establishes. They are voteless and voiceless in our political process. Tens of millions of poor and malnourished individuals within our national borders can and sometimes do vote; yet, their influence on Capitol Hill is but a whisper compared to their need.

Bills passed by Congress are, to a large degree, the result of the influence brought to bear on the Members of Congress who voted aye or nay. Public policy which directs the allocation of US funds and food to the poor and hungry at home and overseas is, to a significant extent, the product of political persuasion.

Many Protestants, Catholics, and Jews understand their faith as a call to work for justice and bread on behalf of the poor and oppressed. As a result, an increasing number of individuals from the religious community are working together to shape US food policy by influencing Members of Congress who make that policy.

In addition, most major faith groups have Washington-based staff who spend at least part of their time monitoring and advocating legislation before the Congress. These staff members have responsibility for development of policy recommendations and reliable background information for your use. A partnership can be formed between these staff and you as you, in response to the call of faith, develop contact with your own Members of Congress. The Washington office of your denomination or faith group can also serve as an important contact as you need information or strategy suggestions or as you report back your success stories and failures.

This HUNGER offers suggestions for the very important work which needs to be done in congressional districts. The suggestions are geared to groups small in number, funds, and resources—who are near drowning in briefings, newsletters, and calls for action! They are offered in the conviction that a much more just and humane US food policy is possible—but only if those of us who are concerned with hunger and oppression become more effective at influencing our elected representatives.

The religious community in this country may not have the political clout of the American Medical Association or the United Auto Workers. Many lobbying groups act from a sense of self interest. The religious community advocates on behalf of the poor and dispossessed. Our theology—not our own betterment—defines our task. Hundreds of millions of hungry people need advocates in the policy making process. We need to be as effective as possible.

While some Members of Congress hardly seem "movable" on the key food policy issues, the majority are genuinely open to the views of their constituents. You can influence them by writing effective letters, making effective visits, and generating public support for your point of view.

How to Write an Effective Letter

Year in and year out, there are few methods of communicating with Members of Congress more effective than a letter which reflects both an understanding of the issue involved and the personal viewpoint of the writer toward that issue.

Here are some tips, suggested by the Friends Committee on National Legislation, on how to write such a letter:

1. Be brief and address only one issue. Come to the point quickly, clearly, and concisely.

2. Make the letter your own. "Form" letters and petitions do not receive the same attention given to a well informed, individually written letter.

3. Ask a question. Questions often generate more attention in the congressional office.

4. Begin with a commendation for a vote or speech where possible. Support a courageous stand and encourage continued leadership.

5. Make your letter timely. (See following section on "Times to Act.")

6. Write more than once a year. Don't become a pest; but recognize that your goal is a long-term influence on food policy, not just passage of one particular bill.

Address Senators:	Address Representatives:
The Honorable _____	The Honorable _____
U.S. Senate	U.S. House of Rep.
Washington, DC 20510	Washington, DC 20515
Dear Senator _____ :	Dear (Mr., Mrs., Miss, Ms.):

Sometimes circumstances may mandate a more immediate form of communication—such as a phone call, telegram, or mailgram. Here, too, your message should

Hunger (Interreligious Taskforce on U.S. Food Policy), September 1978, 4 pp.

be brief and to the point, yet thoughtful.

• The phone number for the Capitol switchboard is: (202) 224-3121.

• For $2.00, you can send a 15-word Public Opinion Telegram. Call your local Western Union office.

How to Choose the Right Time to Act

Timeliness is the essence of effective political action. The "right time" to contact your Senator or Representative depends on (1) his or her committee assignments, and (2) a particular bill's status in the legislative process.

You can learn your Senators' and Representative's committee assignments by calling their local office, or by referring to a resource such as the "Register Citizen Opinion" (available for 30¢ from: United Methodist Service Department, 100 Maryland Avenue, N.E., Washington, D.C. 20002). To determine the status of a bill, check the most recent IMPACT/ACTION Alerts or call us toll-free at (800) 424-7292.

Timeliness is also important in your local organizing efforts. The hard work you do initially to mobilize and maintain the interest of a local group may be jeopardized by having activities executed too early or too late. On the other hand, an initial, well-timed success can be a big boost for further participation and involvement.

TIMES TO ACT

Citizen influence on the legislative process is most significant at these points:

FOR ALL MEMBERS OF CONGRESS:

• **Just after a bill has been introduced.** Members who introduce bills try to gain support for them by the addition of names as co-sponsors. This adds weight to the chances that a bill will get a hearing.

• **Just before a bill comes to the floor for a vote.** If your own Member of Congress does not serve on a committee with jurisdiction over the bill, communication at this time informs him or her of the impending vote, as well as your opinion of the bill.

FOR MEMBERS ON COMMITTEES AND SUB-COMMITTEES WITH JURISDICTION OVER A PARTICULAR BILL:

• **During the hearings** which are set up by that committee to gather testimony for and against the legislation.

• **During "mark-up,"** at which time Members determine actual wording for the bill. Many Members of Congress cite the volume of mail they have received from constituents at this point.

Committees and subcommittees are the creative heart of our law-making process—bills generally receive the most attention at the committee level. The value of constituent communications to Members of Congress at the committee level cannot be over-emphasized.

How to Visit Your Member

Talking with a Member of Congress in a face-to-face interview is a very effective way to influence him or her. Individuals and small groups can schedule appointments with the Member either in the home District office or in the Washington office. Here are some suggestions:

1. Write in advance for an appointment. Indicate when you would like to see the Member, but give alternate dates. (See preceding section on "How to Write an Effective Letter" for appropriate addresses and phone numbers.)

2. Telephone the Member's office to confirm the appointment.

3. Plan the interview. As a rule, no more than two or three subjects should be discussed. *Be prepared with background information and know something of the Member's voting record.* (Contact our toll-free line if you need help in gathering this information.) Also, become familiar with the personal side of the Member's life. Look for common ground in your membership (church, clubs), alma mater, profession, military service, or interests.

4. Be on time for the appointment. Be positive, constructive, friendly, brief. Begin with areas of agreement. Commend the Member for stands he or she has taken of which you approve.

5. State your views clearly and concisely. Tell of personal experiences you have had which illustrate your points. Members of Congress are interested in what people back home are thinking. Tell them if your church, organization, or club has taken a stand on the issue under discussion.

6. Suggest that he or she do something specific, like voting for or against a pending bill, sponsoring a bill, agreeing to persuade a colleague to vote in a certain way, or meeting with some particular group when he or she returns home.

7. If possible, leave the Senator or Representative some printed material which summarizes at least some of the points you want to make. This might be your own statement, a statement of an organization, or a reprint of a newspaper or magazine article. Brevity is important: lengthy statements are often filed unread.

8. If the Senator or Representative is not available, *talk to his or her aide.* Aides are often very knowledgeable and quite influential in helping form the Member's views.

9. Follow up your visit with a letter, expressing thanks for the visit and reaffirming your view.

How to Build Public Support for Your View

Here's a "success story." A small group in a Midwestern community developed and implemented the following strategy during the 1977 legislative battle over food stamps.

In this particular district, both the Representative and the constituency leaned toward the position that elimination of the purchase requirement would open up the system to widespread abuse. The common arguments they cited had been discussed and opposed clearly in IMPACT publications on food stamps. Education of both the Representative and the constituents was in order. The beauty of the strategy the group used was that it was designed in one well-planned meeting and implemented through a few simple steps.

For the planning meeting the leader had assembled all available study material. Sections of the background material which addressed the objections of the Representative had been underlined. The group's goal was two-fold: to create a climate for discussion within the community and to impress the Representative that some of his constituents did not share his fears. Six members of the group committed themselves to deal with a separate objection in a letter to the editor. They used the statistics and arguments of an IMPACT/ACTION and added points that applied to their own city. The group agreed on a one-week period for sending these letters to the paper. The newspaper catered principally to local issues.

The group further agreed on three follow-up actions, and everyone took an exact assignment.

1. Each member looked for a letter to the editor. The day it was published each asked at least two friends to clip the letter and send it to the Representative. Many people who do not feel equipped to write a personal letter on the subject respond to this kind of simple request. Messages were suggested to accompany these: "I found this to be very interesting and would like your opinion."

2. One person volunteered to call the local radio station the day after the letter to the editor appeared. That station ran a talk show where people called in opinions on any subject. Before calling the station, she alerted other members of the group through a phone chain set up at the initial meeting. She told the station that she had seen the letter in the paper, read it over the phone, and wondered if others would care to comment on the issue. The same people who had written other letters were prepared to call in and add their points to the discussion—or to wait until others had called with objections. The group had alerted others in the community of the plan and so expanded the original number involved in the project.

The calling resulted in a three day debate on the talk show. This was unusual and, because media people need to cater to the interests of the public, the leader of the original group was invited to appear as a guest on the morning show of the affiliated television station.

3. A little later, three members of the group called the Representative to make an appointment to talk about food stamp reform. They cited the letter to the editor and the subsequent discussion on the radio and TV. The office was aware of the widespread interest in food stamp legislation—and the Representative agreed to meet with the group the next time he was in the district!

The entire action took only a few weeks to execute, and it quickly involved many members of the community who had no previous interest in the issue. Once the debate was established as being a matter of public concern, the local newspaper did a feature on food stamp legislation.

ELECTION YEAR OPPORTUNITIES

An election year campaign provides unique opportunities to raise the hunger issue to public visibility and to express your views to candidates. Because hunger is no longer on the front pages, this continuing human problem is apt to be ignored in this year's election campaigns unless you seize your opportunities. Below are a few suggestions. For more information, see Bread for the World's "Election Kit" (available to non-members for $1 from: Bread for the World, 207 East 16th Street, New York, NY 10003).

How to raise the hunger issue in an election campaign:

1. Use the local media. Write a letter to the editor. Such a letter not only registers your concerns with the candidates (who are carefully watching for a reading of the district or state) but also generates interest and discussion among other concerned citizens. (Note: A letter to the editor is more apt to be published if it responds to a recent article or event.) Calling a radio talk show to discuss a food-related issue can serve the same function. Likewise, television stations often schedule an "editorial" segment, with citizen response, as part of the local news broadcast.

2. Identify local needs. For example, investigate through your state or county health department how many persons are *eligible* for the Women, Infants, and Children's Supplemental Feeding Program (WIC) as compared to how many *participate*. Share your findings with the community through the local paper.

3. Write each congressional candidate of your concern for a national food policy, and specify your particular area of interest (e.g., grain reserves). Ask for his or her position.

4. Meet with the social action committee of your church or synagogue and discuss the implications of this election for the hungry at home and abroad. Ask the committee to publish information in bulletin inserts or congregational newsletters.

How to set up a meeting with candidates:

Many candidates are delighted to meet with groups of voters *if* those meetings are well planned. See if your local council of churches, clergy association, or interfaith group will jointly sponsor a meeting with candidates. If you secure a go-ahead, here are several pointers to bear in mind as you make contact with a candidate's staff:

1. Explore the possibilities of media coverage before you contact the candidate's staff. Radio, TV, and newspaper coverage not only expand the candidate's visibility, they also help generate more public concern about the

food policy issues discussed.

2. Be exact in your request for a candidate's time. Start and finish on time. Respect for the candidate's time is not only gracious, it establishes your track record of reliability.

3. State as closely as possible the number of persons who will attend. Many candidates and elected officials will meet with six people if that is the initial request. If you have estimated 300 will attend and six show up, the candidate is rightfully disappointed.

4. Consider who might be influential in the discussion. Personal acquaintances, professional colleagues, labor leaders, persons directly affected by domestic food and agriculture programs (such as food stamp recipients or farmers), and religious leaders from your district or state may be among these.

5. Plan follow-up at the same time you plan the event.

6. Remember the thank you letter after the meeting.

How to determine a candidate's position on food policy issues.

Here are several ways to learn a candidate's concern about poor and hungry people and his or her positions on key food policies:

• Ask specific questions of the candidate at political forums. All candidates are as against hunger as they are for motherhood. Don't let candidates escape with generalities. This is particularly important if the candidate has not previously served in public office.

• Study the candidate's voting record. Persons who are serving in Congress have already taken public stands on food policy issues. Last year's food policy voting record, printed as an insert in HUNGER No. 12, can be ordered from IMPACT. For a report on how your Members voted in 1978 on hunger-related legislation, contact the Member's state or district office or your library.

• Keep a record of campaign promises so that you can remind the Member during the congressional term.

This paper is but an initial effort to note in a single document some of the tips and pointers advocates have learned for influencing elected officials. These suggestions are by no means conclusive. Your own experience may indicate the need for revisions in these guidelines. We would like to know what has been a useful tactic or a successful strategy in your work. If you have information or experiences to share, please write to IMPACT or your faith group office.

Major contributors to this issue were Sr. Madeleva Roarke of NETWORK, Tom Hunsdorfer of the United Methodist Church, and Janet Vandevender of the Taskforce staff.

IV. *Who Will Feed Tomorrow's Hungry?*

INTRODUCTORY COMMENTS

The world food problem does stubbornly persist, of that there seems to be almost no doubt. According to the calculations of the Interreligious Taskforce on U.S. Food Policy, "roughly one billion people (a fourth of humankind) continue to live in absolute poverty. More than 700 million people in developing countries do not have enough to eat. . ."[1] One could argue over the degree of reliability of the data, but the figures seem to be those that are accepted, in general, by those who are the presumed experts in matters concerning world food conditions.

Political problems soon come to the forefront, however. As noted earlier, there is a lengthy continuum of ideologies and interests when it comes to asking and answering the questions: (1) how did this come about, and (2) what should be done about it? The breadth and depth of these differences are so extensive that one could easily despair.[2] However, there is a broad international consensus that the major effort, although it should only be one among several, should be directed at increasing food production in the developing nations. As the excerpts from Ruttan's paper explain, there are reasons for optimism when one examines the prospects for agricultural growth in the poverty nations. His analysis certainly points toward an optimism of hope: "In most developing countries the productivity potential remains largely unex-

188

189

ploited." The seminal question, posed rather too tritely, has come to be:
"But is there the political will to develop this potential?"

The essay by John Gilligan, then the Administrator of AID, presents one
view as to what should be done at the micro-level--that is, the individual/
family level of society. His case for a substantially greater role for women
in the rural areas in the Third World is very persuasive. Change is taking
place, more rapidly in some of the regions of the world than others, but in
his judgment the tempo is far too slow.

At the macro-level--that is, the large-scale, integrated, public policies
enacted by nation-states and resolved within international agencies--the OECD
article summarizes the opinions of the ministers of agriculture in the OECD
member-states. From their perspective, the world food problem is three-fold:
instability of markets, the inadequacy of food and development in the poverty
nations, and the lack of (and need for) an international, and often a national,
food strategy.

Vernon Ruttan and Lincoln Gordon have two rather different sets of recommendations as to the matter of strategies. Ruttan reviews the six basic models
of growth and change in agriculture in the last three centuries. He agrees
that the challenges are severe and the complexities are profound, but his
analysis has a fairly optimistic tone.

Lincoln Gordon's review of "alternative long-range development strategies"
is far more encompassing than Ruttan's, and perhaps rather more somber and
cautious. Gordon sees the need for innovation and experimentation in macro-
and micro- policy areas, but he also has some doubts and uncertainties. His
"recommended strategy" is rather typically American--pragmatic, eclectic,
humane, incremental, rational.

They would probably agree with the proposition that "numerous decisions will be made by U.S. policy-makers in 1979 which will significantly affect whether the number of children who go to bed hungry in 1985--and in the years between now and then--increases or diminishes."[3] And these decisions will necessarily become political because several questions must be asked and answers agreed to: for what purposes, through which means, at what costs, for whose benefit, with what likelihood of success, and who will pay?

NOTES
1. Food Policy Notes (78-36), December 21, 1978, p. 1.
2. Chapter II in the first readings book (same title and publisher, but for the years 1972-1976) contains several examples from the broad range of what might be termed: world food ideologies.
3. Food Policy Notes, op. cit.

WOMEN AND THEIR IMPORTANCE
TO THE THIRD WORLD

by John J. Gilligan

In the year that I have been administrator of the agency for International Development, two facts have become more and more apparent to me. The first is that the economic and social development of two-thirds of humanity may well depend on women—far more than it will depend on men. And second is that the success of women in expediting the development of Third World countries will very significantly affect our own future security and well-being.

Let me supply some of the background that has led me to those conclusions:

• In the next 25 years, the world's population will increase from 4 billion to 6 billion people. Most of that increase will be in developing countries: By the year 2000, 87 percent of the world's population will be living in the less developed countries—the "LDCs."

• By the year 2000 there will be a food deficit of 100 million tons in the Third World. That deficit can be made up only if the developing countries increase their agricultural production 3 to 5 times.

• Most of the people of the LDCs are unhealthy. . . . Major components of disease are inadequate nutrition and sanitation. 100 million children under the age of five are always hungry. Fifteen million children die each year from a combination of infection and malnutrition.

• There are 800 million illiterates in the world; nearly two-thirds of them are women. The number of illiterate men rose by 8 million between 1960 and 1970. The number of illiterate women increased by 40 million, bringing the total number of women unable to read or write to half a billion.

Once upon a time the people of this country might have supposed that, grim as life was in the Third World, the problems were theirs, not ours. But if that belief was ever true, it is so no longer. What happens in that half of the world now has impact directly on our lives and on our future. . . .

As a result of record population growth in the last two decades, people in many countries are entering the job market faster than the economy can absorb them. Unemployment in many of the LDCs runs from 25 to 45 percent. This trend is increasing, and it is estimated that by the year 2000 at least 800 million more people will lack a means of making a living. . . .

The United States has already begun to experience the result of excessive Third World population growth and lagging economic development. Today there are an estimated 6 million to 8 million undocumented aliens from Latin America and Mexico in the United States. . . . Many of these immigrants have taken jobs that might be filled by Americans. Many have migrated to our cities, adding to overcrowded housing and welfare rolls. Mexico has one of the highest population growth rates in the world—3.4 percent annually. With 46 percent of the population under 15 years of age, the potential for increased migration to the United States is enormous.

A key to the resolution of the problem of excessive Third World population growth, of course, is family planning, and the key to that is women.

Twenty-five years of accumulated knowledge and experience have told population experts two things:

First, fertility rates begin to decline when a woman is able to nourish her children properly and keep them healthy, thus ensuring that they survive to adulthood. Only then do couples in poor countries begin to understand that they dare limit the number of their children, who traditionally have been perceived as extra labor on the land and support in old age.

And second, fertility rates begin to decline when the educational level of parents rise. The educational level of the father is important. But that of the mother is more so. In almost every country, the more education women have, the fewer children they bear. For example, in a 1972 study from Jordan of women aged 30–34, illiterate women were found to have an average of 6.4 children while those with a primary school education averaged 5.9. For secondary school graduates, the average was 4.0 and for university degree holders, only 2.7 children. In Latin America, studies indicate that women who have completed primary school will average about two children fewer than those who have not.

The message is clear: If population growth rates are to be reduced . . . the education of the women in developing countries is an urgent imperative.

Third World food production is also directly related to U.S. prosperity and security—and to the role of women.

. . . We must face the prospect that by 1985—seven years from now—there will be a global food deficit of 100 million tons in developing countries, directly attributable to population growth outstripping agricultural production. It is most unlikely that the food-producing countries of the West will be able to make up this deficit. Even if they tried, the cost of achieving that additional

Washington Post, June 24, 1978, p. A13. Mr. Gilligan is administrator for the Agency for International Development.

production would be so high that food prices would rise astronomically everywhere.

The only possible solution to this problem is for the less developed countries to increase their own agricultural production to 3 to 5 times their present levels. The people who will have to do this job are the millions of subsistence farmers who scratch out precarious livings on small plots of arid and barren land....

It so happens that those farmers are mostly women. Forty to 70 percent of Third World agricultural labor is female. Depending on the traditions and customs of a particular country, they plant the seed, haul the water, till the soil, harvest the crops, market the produce, tend the animals and strive to keep their families alive by growing the village vegetable gardens.

Today more and more women are being forced into those roles. The lure of the city and cash-producing work is drawing the men away from the farms, leaving the women behind. It is estimated that some 30 percent of rural families in the Third World are now headed by women.... If those women—in their interests and ours— are significantly to increase food production, they must learn the use of new fertilizers, irrigation systems and power machinery. They must have roads to get their produce to market, and they must have transportation on those roads. They must have provision for food processing and storage and understand how to use it, and they must have simple economic structures to provide them with credit.

Women have been handicapped in their efforts to get more from the land they work because of their generally "inferior" social position. They have often been barred from owning or inheriting land, obtaining credit or receiving agricultural inputs from development programs. Even when they have been left behind on the family plot as their men have migrated, they have found their situation difficult because control over economic resources and land was left in the hands of male relatives who have not migrated.

In nearly all developing countries, agricultural training—such as it has been—has been given only to male farmers. Wives, daughters and hired female laborers have been largely ignored. Until very recently, women frequently have not benefitted from projects designed to assist farmers because Western development experts simply assumed that farmers were male....

The conclusion is only too clear: If agricultural production and productivity are to increase, development planning in the Third World must give an equal place to women....

In recent years there has been a growing awareness of a fact that women everywhere have always known: That women play the major role in determining the health of their families in acquiring and preparing food for them.

In some cases, because of the depths of their poverty, there is little they can do to improve their nutrition. But in many cases, malnutrition is the result of ignorance. Without any changes in food supplies, miracles can be wrought with simple changes of diet and food habits if women only had the knowledge to make these changes.

Nutrition specialists in Africa, for example, have found that in most villages women could find the right food for their families, or the right combinations of food, if they knew what to look for. A combination of wild greens, a few beans and an occasional egg, mixed and prepared so it can be spoonfed and fed daily, can save a child's life.

Public health workers in Malaysia noticed that Chinese children were surviving and Malaysian children were dying despite the fact that the same food was available to both. When the situation was investigated it was discovered that Chinese mothers understood the importance of diet—particularly of protein—and the Malaysian women did not.

In respect to health, the story in the Third World is much the same. Knowledgeable women could make an enormous difference to the health of the people, for the single major cause of disease in developing countries is related to the failure to observe elementary household and village sanitation. If a woman lacks that knowledge—if she does not understand how or why disease occurs or how it is transmitted—she has no understanding of the importance of keeping food covered or water clean. If she has no notion of what viruses or bacteria are, she has little incentive to observe even the most elementary sanitation precautions.

The critical word in all the foregoing, of course, is "knowledge," meaning education—and especially education for women. If population growth rates are to be reduced, in the interests of all of us; if food production is to be increased, in the interests of all of us; if the health and nutrition of 87 percent of the world's people is to be improved, in the interests of all of us, the women of developing countries must be educated. The enhancement of their status is critical.

THREE PROBLEMS FOR
AGRICULTURAL MINISTERS

Ministers of Agriculture of OECD countries met on 9th and 10th February for the first time in almost five years. The context was one of agricultural plenty or even surplus in OECD countries. After several years of scarcity, the price of wheat, coarse grains and other feeds have plunged. Farmers in the U.S. have taken to the streets for the first time since the 1950s to press their demands for higher prices. In Europe, the butter mountain has reached an all-time high, and in Australia and New Zealand meat producers have inadequate outlets for their large output. Yet hunger, if not starvation, is a daily fact of life in the poorest countries of the world. This paradox was at the heart of the lively discussion between agricultural ministers, many of them farmers themselves. Some see each other regularly within the European Community, others do not often have the opportunity to discuss their sometimes conflicting interests. Yet all ministers share certain basic problems.

Problem Number One: Instability of Markets

The first concern of OECD's agricultural ministers was how to reduce the unprecedented instability which has plagued agricultural markets over the last five years, causing difficulties not only for farmers themselves but for other sectors as well. The rise in agricultural prices in 1972-1973 took place in boom conditions, creating an atmosphere in which oil prices could quadruple. It also contributed directly to inflation and balance of payments difficulties, not only for OECD countries but equally for the developing world whose purchases are often residual: their needs are met only after others have been satisfied — and they may suffer acutely the effects of price increases.

The story of *cereals* is well known. Stocks had been high and prices depressed for a number of years. A poor harvest in the Soviet Union in 1972 led the Russians to make massive purchases in conditions of secrecy and the rest of the world was suddenly faced with a completely changed stituation. Demand from other countries was also high, particularly from developing countries many of which were badly affected by drought and other adverse weather conditions. Stocks dwindled rapidly and prices rose sharply, thereby stimulating production, at least in countries where farmers' incomes are dependent on market prices. Stocks have been reconstituted (see chart A), but while this gives satisfaction to world leaders, concerned lest there be starvation for the poorest peoples of the world as a result of poor harvests and insufficient reserves, commodity markets respond by moving prices down to such low levels that producers cannot pay their way and have to switch to something else (see chart C).

In the *meat* markets, the synchronisation of increased demand in 1972 and 1973 led cattle producers to increase their herds, and in the short run the amount of meat actually coming onto the market fell as a result; thus prices were given an extra upward impetus and rose to record levels. By the time additional cattle were ready for market in 1974 and 1975, the recession had set in, and demand was dramatically below what producers had expected so that they were badly squeezed by rising costs and falling prices.

Exporting countries suffered from a sharp fall in their outlets in Europe and from the low prices obtained in their sales to North America. Farmers have reacted by cutting back on their herds,

Reprinted from the OECD Observer, March 1978, pp. 3-10.

but the large stocks and recession in the EC, and the still heavy if slowly declining supplies in North America and in exporting countries have delayed the hoped for improvement in world trade, both in terms of volume and of price.

As to *dairy products*, surpluses have been a problem for years and show few signs of improvement: butter stocks are at an all-time high, and skim milk stocks are only slightly lower than their peak (see chart B). The imbalance has been particularly acute in Europe for some time, but more recently the United States has also moved into surplus. Some steps are being taken, however; for example, Canada and Switzerland have introduced production quotas, and the EEC has introduced measures designed to reduce the surpluses. But the situation is difficult because many dairy farmers have no alternative line of production, and the choice is between putting these farmers out of jobs and reducing their incomes to unacceptable levels.

Perhaps the most unstable of the markets is that for *soya beans*. More and more, concentrated high-protein feeds such as fish meal and soya beans are being used in conjunction with feed grains, generally in compound feeds — mainly for dairy cattle, poultry and pigs — prepared by commercial plants which are themselves sensitive to market trends. Soya beans require long days and warm nights and can only be produced in a few areas. At present, production is virtually limited to the United States and Brazil and, in the former, output is concentrated within a single region — the Midwest — so that climatic difficulties are immediately transmitted to importers throughout the world via higher prices. Fishmeal supplies have been reduced by changes in Peruvian fishing conditions. Moreover the distinction between wheat as a food grain and coarse grains as feed is unrealistic: not only is all wheat usable for feed purposes, but some wheat can only be used for feed. Instability in one market contributes to fluctuations in the others, as cereals, feedingstuffs and livestock products are now more closely linked than ever before.

● *Action*

Although the United States has responded to the surplus of grains by introducing programmes to set aside land devoted to wheat and feed grains, the ministers agreed that they must take advantage of the present situation of plenty to build up reserves for the future. "For the bad weather will surely come" as the U.S. Secretary of Agriculture pointed out.

Measures have been taken in the U.S., where two good years "back-to-back" produced the largest carryover of wheat in 13 years. The building of granaries on the farm has been and is being financed by the government and the incentives are now being extended in the hopes of withdrawing from the market 30-35 million tons of wheat, rice and coarse grains, a substantial part of which would be held by farmers. They will contract to hold this grain, at least until prices reach a certain level. Canada too has large stocks which are financed by the farmers themselves but which can be exported only by the Canadian Wheat Board. But ministers were unanimous in thinking that, although Canada and the U.S. provided the world reserves before 1970, national stocks will not suffice now: a system of internationally co-ordinated reserves is necessary. The time, moreover, is right. If this discussion had taken place two years ago, it would have been academic: the cereals with which to build the stocks were simply not available. As expressed in the meeting's official communiqué, ministers agreed on "the need to take rapid action to establish an internationally co-ordinated system of nationally held stocks adequate to provide food security and to introduce a greater measure of stability into the international grains market in the future."

The test of this resolve will come very quickly. Negotiations on an International Wheat Agreement began in the framework of UNCTAD three days after the OECD agricultural ministerial, and parallel talks are being held on other grains. OECD's Secretary General expressed the Organisation's view of the problem in his opening statement. "The burning problem, as I see it, is to achieve, as quickly as possible, an understanding about stocks of cereals. We must act quickly... to prevent an excessive downward adjustment of production."

Agreement in principle on the need for international reserves left many questions open: how the financing should be shared as between producer and consumer countries, where the stocks should be held (some participants in the ministerial favoured holding them in the food deficit countries), which countries should provide what.

International agreements on other agricultural products are also being discussed. "Ministers thought that consultations should continue among interested countries in order to seek together the adjustments necessary to alleviate difficulties in the international markets, in particular those for livestock and dairy products" reads the official communiqué. And both dairy products and meat are on the agenda of the GATT in the Tokyo Round now also underway in Geneva. As to dairy products, the possible extension of existing minimum price agreements to a wider range of products (including whole milk powder, already the subject of a Gentleman's Agreement under the aegis of the OECD) is being discussed. For meat, a less stringent form of agreement appears to be envisaged.

Various proposals have been put forth as to what form international co-operation should take. But the objective is clear — to prevent a single group of countries from bearing the whole burden of the adjustment (generally the exporters in case of surpluses and the importers in case of shortage). The formal agreements are generally made elsewhere; OECD's main contribution to enhancing stability is regular surveillance of sensitive commodity markets and discussion of possible solutions to the difficulties. Since members of the Organisation include both the main producing

and importing countries for the most important agricultural products, such discussions are fruitful the Ministers noted, and they encouraged OECD to intensify these activities so as to provide more — and better — advance warning of possible crises.

Problem Number Two: Food and Development in the Poorest Countries

Ministers' awareness of the close links between agriculture n the OECD countries and the development process in the Third World was implicit in the discussion of both topics. Agricultural exports, for example, are the most important source of foreign exchange earnings for developing countries after petroleum, while grain grown on the farms of OECD countries provides about 10 per cent of the cereals eaten in developing countries.

The complexity of the food problem in the developing world underlines the need on the part of the industrialised nations for a differentiated response but also for more coherent policies in a number of interrelated fields: agricultural production and trade, food aid, food security and development assistance.

For the many developing countries which cannot either produce or import what they need to prevent starvation and meet basic nutritional requirements, the emphasis must be on food aid in the short run and developing agricultural production over a longer period.

Since the World Food Conference, which took place in 1974 at a time when the cereals crisis was causing grave concern about this group of countries, the issues have been clarified and action taken. Assistance for the development of agriculture provided by OECD countries, on both a bilateral and multilateral basis, has expanded. The international Fund for Agricultural Development has been set up with $1 billion in capital provided by OECD countries (56 per cent) and oil producers (44 per cent) and in conjunction with the developing countries who themselves have contributed $19.3 million. Ninety-one countries belong to the Fund which will provide grants and concessional loans for the "food priority countries" (see map) many of which are currently faced with unusually severe food shortages.

As to food aid, a target of 10 million tons a year set by the Conference represents an important switch in itself since it is fixed in the terms that count most — volume. Previous practice, fixing food aid targets in financial terms resulted in a drastic decline — from 12 million tons in the Sixties to less than 5 million tons at the time of the cereals price rise. But the target has proved elusive, in the words of John A. Hannah, Executive Director of the World Food Council, another outgrowth of the World Food Conference: in 1976-1977 only 8.8 million tons were provided and in 1977-1978, with agricultural plenty in the developed countries, it is still estimated that food aid will fall 400,000 tons short of the goal. Food aid is one of the items on the agenda of the UNCTAD discussions on cereals now underway in Geneva since a food aid convention is included in the 1971 International Wheat Agreement currently being negotiated. The grain reserve being discussed in this forum would of course contribute to the food security of the developing countries as well.

The ministers, individually and collectively (in their communique) reaffirmed their intentions both to increase aid to agriculture and to reach the food aid target and, more generally, to enhance food security.

But not all countries in the developing world are food deficit countries. There are also the newly emerging industrial countries which, along with the oil producers, can now afford to import food and have the foreign exchange necessary to do so: countries such as South Korea, Taiwan, Singapore and Nigeria are becoming large purchasers of OECD agricultural products.

But there is still another group of developing countries whose needs must be taken into account — those which can produce food on a competitive basis and for whom agricultural exports are an essential part of development strategy. The important thing for OECD nations vis-à-vis this group is to give greater market access. This is an important part of the structural change which is required in the international economy and which is the object of intensive OECD analysis at the present time. "The developed countries will have to absorb more than they did in the past and take that into account in their policies, even if it creates difficulties for us" OECD's Secretary General pointed out. "But we cannot just stay with the negative consideration that shocks are difficult to absorb; we have to see the positive dimension which has been lacking in our dialogue with the developing countries. We must decide what we really want to do."

Problem Number Three: The Need for a Food Strategy

Concern about the food problem abroad was paralleled by a concern with food policies at home. The contribution of food prices to inflation, the increasing share of food expenditure taken by processors and distributors, growing consumption of "junk" foods — often expensively packed — by consumers in many developed countries, and the diminishing but still important role of food in overall expenditure (see chart E) have led to a search for policies that not only focus on farmers and farm production, but include the rest of the food system, from farm gate to consumer's table.

"It is in the interests of no-one — neither the farmers nor the non-farming community — that agriculture's future be considered and decided on within a narrow horizon as if agricultural policy could be isolated from all other policy areas," OECD's Secretary General noted. "Agricultural policies should increasingly reflect overall social and economic policy objectives."

In some OECD countries, new and imaginative moves are being made in this direction. In Norway, for example, an interministerial co-ordinating group has proposed an "integrated food policy" which would bring many different groups into the policy-making process and include measures having to do with prices and consumer subsidies, industrial processing and imports, marketing, information and education, content and composition of food products as well.

The Canadian minister described the food strategy being evolved in Canada (a green paper has been put forward to stimulate public discussion) as having four major objectives:
• provision of high quality food at reasonable prices;
• a decent return and standard of living for the farmer;
• producing for export those products in which Canada has a competitive advantage;
• providing food aid to countries whose people cannot adequately feed themselves.

Sweden and the United Kingdom have used price subsidies since 1973 to limit price increases on the basic foodstuffs that constitute the staple diet of low-income consumers. The United States has used food stamps and other measures to ensure an adequate diet for low-income consumers since 1964, and many countries promote greater food quality through inspection and the setting of grades and standards with respect to health and hygiene. Measures have also been taken in several countries to improve the efficiency of the food chain

WHO WILL FEED
TOMORROW'S HUNGRY?

by Vernon W. Ruttan

he 1970's have been unkind to the reputations of prophets who tried to plot world food production and scholars who tried to understand agricultural development.

Perspectives have shifted from a sense of impending catastrophe engendered by the world food crisis of the mid-1960's; to the euphoria of the potential of the "Green Revolution"; to the crunch on world grain supplies resulting from poor harvests in 1972-74.

The pessimism that dominates discussions of the prospects for meeting world food demand over the next several decades stems from three sources:
• The rapid growth in demand for food due to population and income growth in the developing countries.
• A series of recent projections that indicate a widening gap between production and demand.
• A belief that the technical changes necessary to meet projected food demand will contribute to a decline in the welfare of the rural population.

Projections prepared by the International Food Policy Research Institute suggest an increase in the staple food deficit of the developing countries from approximately 12 million metric tons in the mid-1970's to 70-85 million metric tons by 1990.

Deficits of this size, if compensated for by commercial imports, will represent a $14-17 billion drain on developing nations' foreign exchange earnings at 1975 price levels. The LDC's would face great difficulty in financing food imports of this magnitude without severely compromising other development objectives. The projected deficits will have to be reduced through some combination of slower growth in

Agenda, September 1978, pp. 5-11. Vernon Ruttan is Professor, Department of Agricultural and Applied Economics, University of Minnesota.

198

demand, greater food aid, and faster growth in domestic production in the LDC's.

During the rest of the 20th century, we must develop and carry out more effective agricultural development strategies than have been available in the past.

Rural institutions in most developing countries do not yet have the ability to increase agricultural productivity to match the growth in demand, or the capability to make effective and equitable use of the new sources of income that improvements in agricultural technology can make available.

The problem of agricultural development is not one of transforming a static agricultural sector into a modern, dynamic sector, but rather one of stepping up the growth of agricultural output and productivity consistent with the growth of other sectors of a modernizing economy.

Historically, there have been six basic models for growth and change in agriculture.

Expansion of the area cultivated or grazed—the Frontier Model—has represented the dominant source of increase in agricultural production. The most dramatic example in Western history was the opening up of the new continents—North and South America and Australia—to European settlement during the 18th and 19th centuries. With the advent of cheap transportation during the latter half of the 19th century, the new continents became important sources of food and raw materials for Western Europe.

Few areas of the world remain where development along the lines of the Frontier Model will represent an efficient source of growth during the last quarter of the 20th century. The 1960's saw the "closing of the frontier" in most areas of Southeast Asia. In Latin America and Africa the opening up of new lands awaits the development of technologies for the control of pests and diseases (such as the Tsetse fly in Africa) and improvement of problem soils.

The 20th century can be viewed

as a transition from a period when most of the increase in world agricultural production sprang from an expansion in area cultivated to a period when most of the increase comes from using a given area of land more efficiently.

The Conservation Model of agricultural development evolved from advances in crop and livestock husbandry—increasingly complex land and labor-intensive cropping systems, the production and use of organic manures, and physical facilities to more effectively utlize land and water.

Within this framework, agricultural production in many areas could increase about 1% a year over long periods. But modern growth in LDC demand typically falls in the 3-5% range.

In the Urban Industrial Impact Model, industrial development stimulates agricultural development by expanding the demand for farm products; by supplying the industrial inputs needed to improve agricultural productivity; and by drawing surplus labor away from agriculture. The importance of a strong non-farm labor market as a stimulus to higher labor productivity in agriculture has been confirmed repeatedly.

The diffusion of better husbandry practices was a major source of growth in agricultural productivity even in early societies. Agricultural development, in this view, is through more effective dissemination of technical knowledge and a narrowing of the productivity differences among farmers and regions. The limitations of the Diffusion Model became increasingly apparent as technical assistance and community development programs failed to generate either rapid modernization of traditional farms and communities or rapid growth in agricultural output.

The inadequacy of policies based on the Conservation, Urban-Industrial Impact, and Diffusion Models led, in the 1960's, to the view that the key to

transforming a traditional agricultural sector into a productive source of economic growth is investment designed to make modern high-payoff inputs available to farmers in poor countries.

Peasants in traditional agricultural systems were viewed as rational, efficient resource allocators. They remained poor because there were limited technical and economic opportunities to which they could respond. The new, high-payoff inputs were classified into three categories: (a) the capacity of public and private research institutions to produce new technical knowledge; (b) the capacity of industry to develop, produce, and market new technical inputs; and (c) the capacity of farmers to acquire new knowledge and use new inputs effectively.

The High-Payoff Input Model remains incomplete as a theory of agricultural development. Typically, education and research are public goods not traded through the market place. The model does not include the mechanism by which resources are allocated among education, research, and other economic activities. It does not explain how economic conditions bring about an efficient set of technologies for a particular society. Nor does it specify how input and product price relationships induce investment in research consistent with a nation's particular resource endowments.

The limitations in the High-Payoff Input Model led to efforts to develop a model in which technical change in agriculture is treated as originating within the development process, rather than as a separate factor operating independently. The Induced Innovation Model was stimulated by historical evidence that different countries had followed alternative paths of technical change in the process of agriculture development.

During the last two decades the institutional capacity to generate technical changes adapted to national and regional resources has been established in many developing countries. More recently these emerging national systems have been buttressed by a new system of international crop and animal research institutes. These have become both important sources of new knowledge and technology and increasingly effective communications links within the developing world.

In the developing countries a fundamental source of the continuing low levels of land and labor productivity in agriculture has been the lag in shifting agriculture from a natural resource base to a scientific base. This lag is also an important source of regional productivity differences in many countries.

The elimination of both the international and domestic differences in agricultural productivity will require reallocations of research resources and development investment in favor of agriculture and rural areas. It was a major step forward when the allocation of research resources in developing countries broke away from the mold established in the developed countries and began to emphasize technologies designed to raise output per unit of land — to release the constraints imposed by an inelastic supply of land.

It is now time to take the next step — to focus attention on the most abundant resource available in most poor countries — human labor.

In spite of the limited land resources in the LDC's, they could achieve levels of output per worker comparable to the European levels of the early 1960's through a combination of investment in human capital; investment in the experiment station and industrial capacity to make modern technical equipment available to their farmers; investment in labor-intensive capital formation characterized by livestock and perennial crops; and by land and water development.

In an agricultural system based on natural resources, few gains are to be realized from education in rural areas. Rural people who have lived for generations with essentially the same resources and the same technology have learned from long experience what their efforts can get out of the available resources. Children acquire worthwhile skills from their parents — formal schooling has little economic value in traditional agriculture.

As soon as new opportunities become available, however, this situation changes. Technical change requires new husbandry skills; additional resources such as new seeds, new chemicals and new equipment from non-traditional sources; new skills in dealing with both natural resources and with factor and product markets; and new and more efficient market institutions linking agriculture with the non-agricultural sector.

In most developing countries the productivity potential remains largely unexploited. High-yield crops are available for few commodities in few areas. Irrigation systems remain underdeveloped and poorly maintained. Fertilizer and other input prices remain high because of biased trade policies, inefficient industries, and costly transportation and marketing. Rural education is only beginning to supply the human capital needed to disseminate, screen and adopt new technical inputs in local farming systems.

The progress of agricultural technology cannot be left to an "invisible hand" — the undirected market forces that will guide technology along an "efficient" pattern determined by "original resource endowments" or relative factor and product prices. New knowledge leading to technical change is the result of institutional development. The public sector agricultural research institute was one of the great institutional innovations of the 19th century.

The problems of agricultural development faced by the developing countries in the immediate future cannot be adequately described in terms of a Malthusian race between food production and population. The developing countries are confronted with very severe trade-offs between meeting the food needs of expanding populations and providing improvements in the quality of life.

They are confronted with demands for institutional innovations that will direct scientific and technical efforts to respond to the stress that is being placed on resource endowments. The development of institutional innovations that can assure both equitable contribution to growth and equitable participation in the fruits of growth will represent a continuing source of stress on relatively fragile political institutions.

INTERNATIONAL STABILITY AND
NORTH-SOUTH RELATIONS

by Lincoln Gordon

ALTERNATIVE LONG-RANGE
DEVELOPMENT STRATEGIES

Strategy signifies a coherent set of means to achieve some explicit or implicit objective. Much of the confusion in discussions of North-South strategies flows from unacknowledged differences concerning the objective—strategy for what? In particular, there are two schools of thought, supposedly from opposite ends of the ideological spectrum, which see North-South relations as a zero-sum game in which any gain for the South is a loss for the North. In that case, the strategic objective from the northern viewpoint is very simple: hold the South down as far and as long as possible. In the Marxist-Leninist framework, which is an important element in the training and outlook of most Third World intellectuals, that is precisely what "capitalist-imperialism" has done and nowadays continues to do under various guises. Most of the prolific *dependencia* literature of recent years reflects that viewpoint. The conservative traditionalist conceptions of international relations, based on great power rivalries and the balance of power, lead to the same kind of conclusion.[6]

For reasons suggested earlier, this author supports the contrary view—that North-South relations already contain large areas of mutual advantage which could be expanded; that the North would benefit from accelerated successful development in the South; that decision-makers in all the significant national units should feel some positive stake in the world order in both its economic and political aspects; and that those wanting and able to become fully incorporated in the First World should have every opportunity and encouragement to do so, recognizing that that status implies responsibilities as well as rights. For others, who do not seek or who lack the potential for diversified economic modernization with a large component of market-oriented enterprise, the posture should be one of broad tolerance, and a search for whatever specific areas of common interest can be found, so long as those nations are not actively hostile to the North.

Developmental success, then, is the core of the strategic objective, but the first set of strategic choices is not on the North-South axis; it is internal to the South. Different national societies have quite different ideas of what they mean by development and how they would like to achieve it. Needless to say, none of those societies is monolithic on these issues, whatever appearances it may present to the outside world. The intense debate over the NIEO has sometimes distracted attention from the criti-

International Stability and North-South Relations, Occasional Paper 17, The Stanley Foundation, Muscatine, Iowa, June 1978, pp. 20-33. Lincoln Gordon is Senior Fellow at Resources for the Future and a Director of the Overseas Development Council.

cal point which cannot be repeated too often: that development depends mainly on policies and actions within the developing countries, and that the external environment can be helpful or harmful but is rarely decisive.

There have been successive waves of conventional wisdom on the "correct" developmental strategy, with the enthusiasts for each new wave decrying their predecessors. The oldest was to base diversification and growth on an export sector composed of mineral or agricultural raw materials in which the country concerned had special natural resource advantages. Most Third World spokesmen would condemn that strategy as a prescription for permanent poverty. The experiences of Canada, Australia, New Zealand, and Denmark suggest that it need not have that result, but it can easily do so if not accompanied by steps to improve productivity in food production and by progressive diversification away from monoculture.[7]

The most widely accepted internal strategies during the 1950s and 1960s focused on industrialization, supposedly following the successive models of Europe, North America, and Japan. The market was to be found partly through replacing imports of manufactured goods ("import substitution") and partly by exporting manufactured goods to the industrial countries. For small countries with limited domestic markets, a regional basis for import substitution was proposed with common markets or free trade areas linking together a group of developing countries. This strategy of industrialization had some apparently spectacular successes: Mexico and Brazil in the 1950s; Korea, Taiwan, and Singapore in the late 1950s and 1960s. As between the two forms of industrialization, the export-oriented focus appeared more efficient than import substitution, because the potential market was much larger and the developing country's enterprises were subjected to the disciplines of international competition. But these kinds of industrialization strategies seemed unable, at least in the Latin American context and in South Asia, to provide enough jobs to keep up with an explosive demography and a huge migration from countryside to towns. Later, they were also criticized for fostering extreme inequalities of income distribution and concentrating resources on consumer durable goods of interest only to a small upper and upper-middle class.

At the same time, countries with rapid population growth found themselves becoming food importers on a dangerously increasing scale, so in the late 1960s a reaction set in favoring agricultural modernization and productivity improvement in parallel with continuing industrialization. There was also some emphasis on smaller rural industries in the hope of stemming the tide toward the cities, for which urban administration was unable to provide even minimal services of water, sanitation, and transport, not to speak of shelter. There were efforts to encourage greater labor-intensity in both public and private investments, getting away from the imitation of technologies and work organization suitable to advanced countries with high labor costs and ample capital supplies.

In the last few years, a more radically reformist kind of challenge has been advanced against all the earlier strategies, placing the main emphasis on more equal income distribution and on development opportunities for marginalized small farmers, landless agricultural laborers, and unskilled in-migrants to the towns. This school also has two branches: one focusing on satisfaction of "basic needs" as the top priority, with overtones of a poverty-line welfare standard, and the other emphasizing opportunities for productive employment for the poorest groups.[8] It should be noted however, that support for these kinds of reformist strategies seems to have come more from the secretariats of international institutions and from groups in European countries with strong social democratic traditions than it has from governments or political leaders within the developing world itself.

Finally, note should be taken of a still more radical challenge which rejects the whole idea of development through capital formation, technological change, increased productivity, and enlarged markets, seeking instead a kind of communitarian socialism close to nature, with voluntary participation in place of "sordid" material motivations. There are echoes here of certain medieval monastic sects, like the Franciscans, of the utopian socialists of the early 19th century, and in some cases of a wistful longing for a single great leap into Karl Marx's ultimate Nirvana without the intermediate phases of either capitalism or the dictatorship of the proletariat. These views are often combined with ecological romanticism and the conviction that resource depletion and environmental pollution are in any case in the course of putting an end to all forms of economic growth.[9]

Except for the last category, which is really a strategy *against* development, all these internal strategies have many elements in common, and they are much less clear-cut alternatives than their advocates assert. They are also usually less novel than is claimed; for example, the current emphasis on social investment and human needs was a major thrust of the Alliance for Progress seventeen years ago, and that program in turn derived from thinking in Latin America dating back to the mid-1950s.

All these strategies require strenuous efforts to encourage saving and to mobilize capital for productive purposes. All require the efficient allocation and use of scarce resources, which in turn calls for some kind of motivation and discipline. All can be destroyed by widespread corruption or by rampant inflation. All are compatible with a wide spectrum of relative emphasis on economic development planning or on market determination of investment directions as well as current resource flows. In the modern world, all require a large degree of governmental effectiveness, since even regimes most unsympathetic to economic planning must act affirmatively to maintain competitive conditions in their restricted markets. That is one reason that what Gunnar Myrdal calls the "soft states" have generally had poor developmental records, whichever strategy they might be trying to pursue.[10]

From the viewpoint of a developing country, North-South strategy should be complementary to its own domestic development strategy. Since the developing countries vary enormously in their degrees of development already achieved, their natural and human resource potentials, their cultural and political traditions, and their priorities for further development, no single North-South strategy can be complementary to all of them. From the northern viewpoint, it is especially important to avoid faddism—the temptation to "discover" some new "key to development" every few years and to make its application the centerpiece and condition of all northern strategies. There is great wisdom in a recent statement by the U.N. Committee for Development Planning, expressing "a certain unease that some of the new ideas—for example, 'basic needs,' 'collective self-reliance'—may already be getting too sloganized."[11]

It follows that a package of strategies is called for, all aimed at the broad objective of accelerating development but complementing the diversity of domestic strategies. Before summarizing the elements of such a package, it is useful to characterize briefly the principal competing strategic ideas currently in circulation.

A. NIEO as a Strategy. In the earlier discussion of NIEO, it was made clear why its moral and political components are inherently unacceptable to the North as a basis for North-South strategy. Its economic program is a package assembled through internal "log-rolling" among the diverse interests represented in the Group of 77. Some of them would be beneficial to all parties and should be incorporated into any comprehensive North-South package, but several, which have been vigorously pressed in U.N. conferences and the CIEC, are either of dubious relevance to effective development or are so directly contrary to northern interests as to be unnegotiable. For example, commodity price indexing would freeze relative prices against changes in supply technology or the structure of demand, encouraging uneconomic substitutions and other market distortions. Generalized rescheduling of indebtedness would impair the credit of "middle-class" developing countries which have gained wide access to private financing institutions. Permanent trade preferences, with guaranteed margins of preference, would hamper the further liberalization of trade among industrial countries and its extension to developing countries on a "most-favored nation" basis. Automatic "resource transfers," unrelated to the quality of domestic developmental strategy and performance, would undermine the influence of the multilateral financing institutions, especially the World Bank and IMF, in improving that performance. Similar doubts apply to the proposals for transfer of technology.

B. The Strategy of Resistance. Selective resistance to ineffectual or otherwise unacceptable proposals is therefore an appropriate part of a Northern strategic package. But that is quite different from a strategy of general resistance, which would be incompatible with the premise that successful development is also in the interest of the North. Some advocates of general resistance profess to favor development but assert that private trade and investment, responding to market forces, is a sufficient northern strategy. But private trade is greatly affected by tariffs, non-tariff barriers, and other governmental actions, while many kinds of investment, especially in human resources and infrastructure, are not effectively promoted through private capital flows.

C. The Strategy of Accommodation. At the other extreme is a strategy of real or professed accommodation to anything requested by the South. In some cases, such as the Tinbergen group report, that tendency reflects basic agreement with the justice of the South's case. In other cases, the prevailing motive may be the "professional deformation" of foreign offices and diplomats—a preference for appeasement and "smoothing things over," especially when it can be argued that concessions will not have substantial practical effects. Such a strategy should be rejected on the ground that North-South relations are too serious to be treated so lightly, and that seemingly "harmless" concessions can accumulate and crystallize into harmful longer-run policies and institutions.

D. The Strategy of Decoupling. Another line of thought, which has won substantial support in the South and some in the North, is to reduce the density of the North-South linkage and accelerate Southern development through "collective self-reliance," with maximum "decoupling" from the North. That is a logical conclusion from those forms of *dependencia* theory which assert that all North-South economic transactions make the North richer and the South poorer. Those theorists squarely reject the conventional belief that the existence of advanced industrialized societies helps the developing countries by providing both capital and markets and spares them the need to reinvent modern technology.[12] Support from the North for a decoupling strategy comes partly from quarters preoccupied with Southern competition at low wage rates in labor-intensive manufacturing.

Although the rationale of *dependencia* theory is highly questionable, the objective of increased trade and investment among developing countries is sound in principle and ultimately necessary to successful global development. Opportunities for adequate growth in the developing countries have in fact been excessively dependent on the boom phase of the industrialized world's business cycles. The probable secular decline in First World growth rates should certainly not have to be matched by a further slowing of Third World development. Common markets and free trade areas among developing countries have not been resisted by the North; their disappointing records are the result of internal tensions. But the needs for goods and services presently supplied by the North are so critical to most Southern development efforts that the "foreign exchange gap," or "capacity to import," is commonly regarded as the controlling quantitative limit on growth. Collective self-reliance may gradually shift some portion of sources of supply and markets to other developing countries, but there is no realistic prospect of successful decoupling from the North in any time frame relevant to current policy-making. Paradoxically, the supposed paradigm of a decoupled development strategy, the People's Republic of China, now appears to be seeking increased trade and technological imports from the North.

E. The Strategy of Planned Restructuring. All the internal development strategies include a substantial shift of the labor force from agriculture and traditional services into industry and modern services, however much they may differ in emphasis on appropriate technologies and in preferences for alternative arrays of manufactured goods. Such changes in structure, extensively analyzed by economic historians, were at the heart of the modernizing transformations in today's industrialized countries; in the spectacular Japanese case, most of that transformation dates only from the post-war recovery. A rapidly growing domestic market usually absorbed the bulk of the industrial output, but some of it spilled over into foreign trade and became part of an ongoing process of redistribution of the international division of labor. Trade in manufactured goods has expanded so enormously in recent decades that it has been able to accommodate a huge growth in the industrial exports of developing countries, which rose from $5 billion in 1955 to $31 billion in 1975, and now account for over 43 percent of their total non-oil exports.[13] Korea, Taiwan, Singapore, Brazil, and Mexico have been major participants in that structural shift.

The question has been raised, however, whether international markets (which means predominantly those of the First World) could absorb correspondingly large portions of the potential manufacturing output of the bigger low-income countries, such as India, Indonesia, and China. At its Lima conference in 1975, the U.N. Industrial Development Organization (UNIDO) adopted a "target" that the developing world's share of global industrial output be 25 percent by the year 2000, compared with 7 percent in 1973. The target was admittedly arbitrary, but it is not completely out of line with relative industrial growth rates of recent years and would still allow for significant expansion of industrial output in the First World, although at a slower pace. In order to increase their industrial production, the developing countries would require large imports of capital goods and raw materials which could be financed only by expanded exports.[14]

The UNIDO and UNCTAD staffs have questioned whether trade liberalization alone would be sufficient to induce such large shifts in structure, although they recognize that it would go a long way in that direction. They also have comprehensible doubts concerning the speed with which industrialized countries may be expected to liberalize their imports from developing countries, especially of labor-intensive products like textiles and shoes. They consequently suggest reinforcing trade liberalization by a more directly planned approach. The Lima Program of Action called for a system of consultations between developed and developing countries concerning industrial restructuring and location, with overtones of some sort of international superboard for controlling and allocating the location of new capacity and even "redeploying" a part of existing capacity. Although it was less explicit as to policy measures, similar targets for structural change in the world distribution of manufacturing and trade emerged from the recent report of Professor Wassily Leontief's team to the United Nations.[15]

In this aspect of North-South relations, any strategy of planned structural change seems chimerical. The institutional obstacles alone are insuperable, since most First World societies would not accept detailed control over industrial expansion by their own national governments, much less by an international board. Moreover, the dynamics of healthy economies can engender extraordinarily large changes in economic structure over a decade or two, including the disappearance of obsolete products and the decline of obsolescent regions. But if those results were to be foreseen and planned for, the political resistance of the interests at stake would be unmanageable, even though the economy as a whole might benefit. In industries of special global significance, such as energy supply, international harmonization of industrial policies is a realistic and desirable goal. In the broad field of general manufacturing, however, including products still to be invented, the most promising strategy is still maximum trade liberalization, coupled with the maintenance of general economic health and provision for more far-reaching adjustment assistance than has yet been forthcoming.

F. The Strategy of Induced Reform. A number of proposed North-South strategies are based on the proposition that the North has a direct interest in the internal development strategies of the South, and that Northern international "concessions" on trade or aid should be bargained against domestic Southern reforms. This proposition is quite distinct from more traditional international bargaining, such as exchanging assurances of raw material markets for assurances of supplies. A few years ago, the proponents were referring mainly to bargaining on so-called "global issues"—the world interest in avoiding over-population or environmental catastrophe. That line of thought, however, seems to have given ground to arguments that the malign effects of over-population are concentrated mainly in the over-populated countries themselves, while the dangers to the global environment (oceans, atmosphere, ozone layer, etc.), as distinct from regional problems like soil erosion or desertification, come mainly from the industrial countries.

From the beginning of systematic bilateral and multilateral aid programs, there has always been some linkage of aid to domestic performance by the recipient—at a minimum to insure that the funds are spent on the agreed purposes. As analysis of developmental strategies has become more sophisticated, and especially in the administration of World Bank programs, these linkages have become steadily broader in scope: from management for a specific project, to policy for an economic sector, to macroeconomic policy for the economy at large, to general socioeconomic and institutional reform. Our own bilateral programs have followed a similar trend, especially during the era of "program loans," but with the addition of special conditions imposed by the Congress, ranging from protection of American private investors and avoidance of competition in farm exports to cessation of gross violations of human rights. We have witnessed a kind of Parkinsonian principle at work in this respect: the smaller the aid program and the fewer the number of countries substantially dependent on continued bilateral aid, the more numerous and complex the legislative conditions!

In current discussions, an especially noteworthy extension of this idea is the proposal by Roger Hansen for bargaining both an increase in aid commitments and other major concessions to the South's NIEO proposals against a concerted shift of Southern development strategies to the "basic human needs" approach.[16] In this case, the Northern interest is essentially humanitarian. Starting with the conviction that the basic needs strategy could eliminate the grossest forms of "absolute poverty" from the entire world within a generation, there is felt to be a moral duty to see that such a strategy is adopted. From Secretary of State Vance's statement of June 23, 1977, which called for a special Organization for Economic Cooperation and Development (OECD) working group to design a program for basic human needs, and from the emphasis on this approach in recent major speeches of World Bank President Robert McNamara, it is evident that this kind of strategy is not of merely academic interest.

The Hansen version, however, should be viewed with great caution. It is one matter to direct a larger share of concessional aid to the poorest countries and to projects related to food production, primary health care, and basic education; those trends have been incorporated into both bilateral and multilateral aid programs for a number of years. It is quite another matter to seek a concerted North-South bargain for explicit internal strategy reforms, with the *quid pro quo* combining concessional aid with only remotely related changes in trade, monetary, food, and oceans policies, and with developing country performance to be monitored by a "neutral" international agency.

The first doubt is whether development technicians in either North or South know as much about effective strategies to eliminate poverty as is assumed. The experience under our own domestic poverty programs should be ample ground for caution. In practice, moreover, as the U.N. Development Planning Committee has stressed, a basic-needs approach cannot be so sharply differentiated from a broader effort toward economic development. The second doubt arises from the somewhat bizarre premise that peoples and governments in the North are more interested in eliminating poverty in the South are than the governments and leaderships of the South itself. For certain groups, that may well be the case, but it does not seem a strong foundation for intergovernmental negotiation. The third doubt concerns the possibility of carrying off such a bargain with the South "as a group," when account is taken of the diversity of developing countries and the jealousy with which each government guards its domestic policies against external intervention. The final doubt concerns the wisdom of linking internal strategy reorientation to "concessions" on other international economic issues. If changes in trade and monetary and other areas cannot stand on their own merits in terms of direct and indirect Northern interests, it is questionable whether they should be incorporated into a bargain simply to secure domestic reforms in the South. _____

ELEMENTS IN A
RECOMMENDED STRATEGY

The preceding review points toward elements of a recommended strategy through its discussion of the various alternatives. Unlike the NIEO itself and several of the other proposals under current discussion, the recommended strategy does not purport to be a revolutionary restructuring of the entire international economic order, a newly discovered panacea, or a novel "grand design" carrying the trade-mark of some catchy slogan. The indicated posture for the North is to emphasize its genuine interest in Southern development as well as in Northern economic welfare; to be neither condescending nor obsequious nor guilt-ridden nor panic-stricken; to maintain the momentum of ongoing policies and institutions which do contribute to developmental success; and to avoid creating expectations of miracles which will not materialize.

Within that framework, there is a great deal to be done. At the macroeconomic level, trade, aid, and monetary policies are all relevant, but the greatest urgency and largest ultimate pay-offs are in trade. Changing trade patterns are both the product and the creator of the long-term changes in economic structure that constitute development and modernization. For the almost half of the developing world which is recognized as "middle-income," and also for countries like India, Pakistan, and Indonesia, trade offers larger and more stable contributions to foreign exchange earning potential than any plausible combination of official aid programs. And for that large group of countries, which account for about three quarters of the developing world population outside of China, enlarging the capacity to import (rather than filling a savings or investment "gap") is the most important contribution that the international economic system can make to their developmental possibilities. Whether those possibilities become prospects depends mainly on the countries themselves.

Within the field of trade, general liberalization on a most-favored-nation basis promises much more important results than do the preferential arrangements which have occupied so much attention since 1964. Real progress at the Geneva Multilateral Tariff Negotiations (MTN), including a sharp reduction in tariff escalation on raw material processing, would be of great benefit to developing countries. If time is needed for adjustments in the industrial countries, safeguards procedures and "orderly marketing arrangements" should be provided, but subject to international rules with phaseout timetables. Commodity market stabilization is also desirable and probably feasible for a few minerals, rubber, and several agricultural products. It should be pursued through producer-consumer negotiations, but its results will be of interest to only a few countries.

Concessional aid remains of the greatest importance to the poorest and least developed countries, and the limited amounts available should be concentrated on their needs. Priority within aid programs should be given measures enhancing the capacity to meet "basic human needs." Encouragement of more broadly-based rural and urban development strategies by the World Bank and bilateral aid donors is certainly in order, but efforts to force such strategies on reluctant governments are not likely to succeed in practice even if they win lip-service.

On the financial and monetary side, far-reaching adjustments in international arrangements have already taken place in recent years, to the considerable benefit of the South. They include major provisions for additional Southern access to IMF resources, moving the *de facto* role of the Fund far in the direction of development assistance and complementing the substantial increases in aid lending from the World Bank group and the regional development banks. The existence of these official resources has facilitated an even larger increase in the volume of private bank lending, mainly to the "middle-class" countries of the Third World. Although some rescheduling of debts has been needed in a few special cases, the widely-feared general crisis in the balance-of-payments position of the oil-importing developing countries has not materialized. In fact, their collective international reserves increased by $10.8 billion in 1976, compared to a loss of $1.8 billion in 1975.

Continued improvements in these financial and monetary mechanisms should certainly be part of the North-South strategy, but they should build on the previous actions rather than constitute a revolutionary change. The indicated improvements include further enlargement of the funds for compensatory financing of shortfalls in foreign exchange earnings for reasons beyond the control of a developing country, with a lengthening and easing of the repayment terms for the poorer countries. As long as the structural balance-of-payments surplus of the low-population OPEC countries persists (and its end is still many years off), there will be an inherent fragility in financing so large a share of it through the private international banks; some form of systematic collaboration is called for between private and official sources of financing. The OPEC members could make a major contribution to exorcising the specter of excessive Third World indebtedness by adopting a "P.L. 480"-type policy of partial grants (or acceptance of local currency) for a major fraction of their oil sales to developing countries, but there are no visible signs of such a policy on the horizon.

In areas of microeconomic and sectoral policy, population control remains of the highest urgency. Selective developmental measures (such as primary health care and education for women) which appear to be highly correlated with fertility reduction should be directed toward that end along with family-planning programs. Expansion of food production in most developing countries, especially in South Asia and Africa, ranks only slightly behind population control. It should be complemented by international systems of food reserves to compensate for harvest fluctuations. The radical change in imported oil costs, and the longer-term prospect for an end to the petroleum era within a few decades, warrants a special international effort to assist developing countries in identifying alternative sources of energy, country by country, and in promoting their timely development. More effective arrangements for discovery and exploitation of other natural resources in the developing countries, especially minerals, would also be beneficial to both South and North. In these and many other fields, including the combat of tropical diseases and the improved usage of tropical raw materials, there is continuing need for internationally organized programs of technical assistance and joint North-South research.

The pursuit of such macro- and microeconomic policies in an integrated fashion, with persistence and cohesion among the countries of the North for their share of the effort, would constitute an important change in the international scene and greatly improve the external environment for southern development efforts. This set of policies would not meet the rhetorical goals of the NIEO, but they could produce substantial results whether or not one chooses to give them the label of a "new order" or "new system."

Beyond these broad categories, the most valid generalization is the impossibility of generalizing. The impulse for development must come from within, and in the varied societies which make up the South it will take many forms. The North cannot and should not try to impose a Procrustean formula for development strategy. As long as developmental efforts are demonstrably carried on in good faith and with at least a modicum of managerial competence, they deserve the tolerance and in most cases the sympathetic support of the North. And the ultimate object of the exercise should never be lost from sight—the gradual abolition of the North-South boundary through the progressive incorporation of the South into a still dynamic and changing industrial or post-industrial world.